"Not to know what happened before we were born is to remain perpetually a child. For what is the worth of a human life unless it is woven into the life of our ancestors by the records of history"

-Cicero (106-43 B.C.E.)

I AM BOUND TO THEM

THOUGH I CANNOT LOOK INTO THEIR EYES

OR

HEAR THEIR VOICES

I HONOR THEIR HISTORY

I CHERISH THEIR LIVES.

I WILL TELL THEIR STORY

BY TRYING TO UNDERSTAND THE PAST

-Author unknown

THE GIRL IMMIGRANT

"History is the ship carrying living memories to the future."

– Sir Stephen Spender, British poet and critic (1909-1995)

Also by Patricia Steele ~

Novels:

Tangled like Music

Callinda Beauvais Mystery Series:

Shoot the Moon, Book One

Wine, Vines and Picasso, Book Two

Thorny Secrets and Pinot Noir, Book Three

Cloisonné, Book Four

Travel Memoirs

A Roundabout Passage to Venice

Mind the Gap in Zip It Socks

Cooking Drunk (and wine tasting 101), a cookbook

Goodbye Balloon, a children's story

Spanish Pearls Series

Book 1: THE GIRL IMMIGRANT

Book 2: SILVÁN LEAVES – Out on a Limb

In Progress: Book 3: RUIZ LEGACIES

"Living with Cystic Fibrosis" in *Your Health Magazine*

THE GIRL IMMIGRANT

Based on the true story of a young girl and her extended family as they agonize over leaving Spain and the watery steps they endured on an immigrant ship to create a life that is now history. Hawaii! Manuela's small Spanish village buzzed with tales of life in a faraway land free of starvation and angst.   And they listened.

Patricia Ruiz Steele

Plumeria Press
Casa Grande, Arizona,
United States

Cover art designed by Patricia Steele
Creatively edited by Joseph Bettencourt (Portland
Computerworks) and Gary Schmalz.

ISBN: 978-0-9890013-0-4

Printed in the United States of America by Plumeria Press

Library of Congress Control Number: 2013912330

To order additional books or to request the privilege to copy
any part of this book, please use contact link at
www.patriciabbsteele.com

Also available at www.amazon.com
And at Barnes and Noble by special order request

Table of Contents

DEDICATION

To my Spanish ancestors and the extended family tree they began so many years ago. Everything starts with the past just as mine started with my abuelita Manuela, my grandmother, and the flower petals she planted along the way.....Of which I am just one among hundreds

I am especially grateful to my daughter, Audrie Abernathy, for acting as my liaison in California. Without her generous and extensive outreach, I would not hold some of the documents I share in this book. Her enthusiasm for this project and pointing out pieces of information I missed from documents was priceless.

Special thanks to my Aunt Manuela "Millie" Ruiz Cortopassi whose interest and eagerness charmed me from the beginning.

To my brothers, Steven, who acted as my translator and travel companion throughout Spain and Richard for his guitar expertise and detailed explanations.

My son, Frank Zaccone, who reads everything I write and tells me he is my biggest fan.

And without my husband, J.D.'s, patience while I lived a hermit's existence in my office nearly five years, this book would probably not have been written for many years.

ACKNOWLEDGEMENTS

My thanks to all the Silván and Ruiz descendants who have lovingly supported me along the way; known family members and those newly-found through the miracle of the Internet. Without their immeasurable trust by sharing documents, pictures and family history.... this book could never be so full of historical information. And I am thrilled to share it with others and their descendants not yet born.

My immeasurable gratitude to Joseph Bettencourt at Portland Computerworks for recovering my Word document when it became corrupted and saving my sanity with his computer wizardry.

For their stories and guidance, I thank my grandmother, Manuela Silván Trascasas, my biological father Michael Silván Ruiz and my mother, Neyda Bettencourt. My cousins: Jeff Cortopassi, Robert Ruiz, Vicki Souza Gersey, Alicia Gonzales, LuCinda, Kathy and Christina Silván, their mother, Mary Louise Hutchinson Silván. Lynda Medeiros Ely, Julie Elliott, Cheryl Souza Edwards, Linda & John Hyatt, Theresa Gonzales Sackett, Victorina Gonzales Weber, Rose Marie Dugger, Virginia Gonzales, Bobbie Gonzales Fortunati, John Gonzales, Anna Gonzales Manley, Jenifer Arney, Jerilyn Riorden, Julie Borges-Stuber, Patte Gonzales Kronlund, Linda Gonzales Rhoades, Felix Huckaby. Ángela Ruiz Fernandez, Kelly Ruiz, Janet Martin McCooey, Joe Silvan, Jr. and Jeri Vance Kurtz.

I was fortunate to find volunteers and privileged to have had Steven Alonzo assist me in the difficult task of translating Spanish documents and consistently believe in my vision along the journey.

I want to thank Cristóbal Navas Pérez whose knowledge of Spanish villages helped me and Steven Alonzo transcribe the SS Orteric's manifest more accurately. Fernando Hidalgo Lerdo de Tejada, a genealogist in Sevilla guided me to a Spanish author, Nicolas Salas who in turn helped me find the boat from Sevilla to Sanlúcar and explained coins in that time period. José Carlos de Lera Maillo from the Diocese of Zamora found family documents!

Thanks to Robert Rodriguez for editing my Spanish. And Rick Pinheiro, a stranger and genealogist found Felisa Silván for me under her American name of Alice. Thanks to Frances Alva Pugliese and her daughter, Judy Pugliese Aguilar whose family was also in Fuentesaúco. Their friendship connection gave me family stories and one of my Silvan cousins! The Juzgado clerk in *Toro*, Spain sent documents for the Trascasas family to me at his own expense. Mercedes Trascasas found me on www.mundia.com (whose ancestors make us cousins) and she gave me information for another three generations from Toro, Spain.

Thanks to the authors of *Angel Island*, Erika Lee at University of Minnesota and Judy Yung, at University of CA, Santa Cruz; as well as their contact, Marisa Louie, the Archivist at the National Archives at San Francisco in San Bruno, California, whose quick response and investigations gave me answers I never would have found without them.

If you don't see your name on this list, please be assured you certainly have my immeasurable gratitude.

With roots in the Middle Ages, Spanish surnames have been around since the 12th century. Children are commonly given two surnames, one from each parent. The middle name (1st surname) is the father's name (apellido paterno), and the last name (2nd surname) is the mother's maiden name (apellidos materno).

Celestino Pedro **Silván** Dovales ~ Agustína **Hernández** Martin
Felipe Silván Hernández   - Unknown
Agapita Silván Hernández   1864 - Unknown
Matías Silván Hernández 1867 - Unknown

Victorino Luciano Silván Hernández   1868 – 1925
Married: Santa María del Castillo Church, *Fuentesaúco*   30 May 1896
Romana (Ramona) Martin Lorenzo 1877 - 1955
Teodora Silván Martin 1899-1991
Felisa Silván Martin 1904-1991
Jacinto Silván Martin 1906-1911
Celestino Silván Martin1906-1983

Edmundo Silván Hernández – 1870 – Unknown

Ángel Silván Hernández – 1873 - Unknown
Juan Francisco Silván Hernández   1875 – 1945
Married: Iglesia de Santa María del Castillo, *Fuentesaúco*   11 May, 1900

Eustoquia Rita Trascasas Marzo 1880 - 1953
Manuela Silván Trascasas 1901-2001
Augustin Silván Marzo 1908-1994
José Silván Marzo 1910-1979
María Silván Trascasas 1914-1997
Juanita Silván Trascasas 1918-1981
Celestino Silván Fernández[1] 1919-1973
Ramona Silván Trascasas 1922-1922

---

[1] Celestino is the only child without the Marzo or Trascasas surname; My theory is Grandpa John Silván pronounced his full name as Juan Francisco Silván Hernandez to the court recorder and the name sounded like "Fernandez", so that was the name Celestino carried all his life. It is unknown why Augustin and José had the Marzo name.

Geronimo Silván Hernández   30 Sep 1877 – Unknown
Married: Iglesia de Santa María del Castillo, *Fuentesaúco*
Joaquina Bragado Vicente   1876 –

Lorenzo Silván Hernández 1880 - Unknown

Crescéncia Silván Hernández   1884 - 1946
Married: Iglesia de Santa María del Castillo, *Fuentesaúco*   6 May, 1906
Felix Gonzales Hernandez 1881-1963
Alejandro Gonzales Silván   1909-1975
Juan Gonzales Silván 1910-1961
María Gregoria Gonzales Silván 1912-2004
Christina Barceliza Gonzales Silván 1915-2003
Augustina Gonzales Silván 1916-2005
Victorina Gonzales Silván 1917-
Acension Alfredo Gonzales Silván[2]   1919-1999
Theresa Gonzales Silván 1921-
Eusebio Felix Gonzales Silván 1923-2004

Agustín Silván Hernández   1887 – Unknown

---

[2] Acension Alfred Gonzales / Alfred Geronimo "Jerry" Gonzales

PREFACE

History is the human experience.   It's about people, not facts and figures. This book is about a journey, a family and finding a better future.   During my research, I felt like a mountain goat picking its way gingerly over the rocks and pebbles trying to retain its footing, intent on keeping her feet on the right track.   I thought about all the everyday people who came to America who were my ancestors.   And there were lots of children! Who were they?   I asked myself what was so terrible to leave Spain and sail two months on a filthy, disease-riddled ship to go someplace else?

Just when this passion to follow in my grandmother's footsteps began, I am unable to say; but when my children were young, I was too busy. And I did not question my abuelita[3] or my father[4] while they were alive, but I took note of their many stories. Now I can imagine her journey; my wandering steps, genealogy courses and many inquiries have embraced something of everything.

Dreams of faraway Spain have meandered through my mind since junior high school but it was not until nearly half a century later that my longing came to fruition.   Wanting to learn Castilian Spanish, I asked my brother, Steven, and our cousin, Ramona, for help.   I knew I had accumulated so little practicable Spanish that my first moments in Spain would exhaust my store. Ramona (a

---

[3]   Abuelita will refer to Manuela Silvan Trascasas throughout story
[4]   Michael Silvan Ruiz

Spanish teacher) suggested flash cards and Spanish movies.

Steven lisps his *c's* and *z's* when he might have hissed them in Spanglish.   Our father tutored him and I surely would have profited by his instruction.   Now he is gone.

As I began *The Girl Immigrant*, I ached to know the world they came from and follow their lives toward a surreal existence beyond anything they'd known before going to a place described on a broadsheet flyer.   What began as a family-history essay has evolved into a story of mammoth proportions.   I wandered through many pages of Spanish history intent on pinpointing the 1911's culture that propelled them to emigrate from their homeland.

While searching and investigating these historical truths, I also relied on Spanish friends and family to gather a preponderance of evidence to flesh out my ancestor's lives. As it came into focus, what began as a simple family history wasn't simple at all.   With scrupulous even-handedness, I examined Spain's culture in 1911-1912; noting areas of angst and bliss, music and food, agreements, awareness and familial relationships.

Through abuelita's eyes, her story will unfold as I open the window into their lives.   It is my hope that descendants feel enriched reading the living story of their pursuits for a better life. Even though I can't truly know the child my abuelita was except by walking backwards through time based on the precocious woman I remember, I can mirror her moods and thoughts about leaving the only home she had ever known; in my young life, Oregon was a place on the other side of the world.   Leaving California when I was also nine, I'd memorized every corner of my house on Northwood Drive in Woodland, California and promised myself I would someday return!   I did not want to leave my friends and family and my heart cried... as I was sure she did when they fled Spain to a mysterious future when fears raced against promises.

I wanted people to think about the history that our ancestors touched and breathed. Armed with my historical facts, I walked in Manuela Silván Trascasas' footsteps.   This is her story for the petals she produced (her children) and the dazzling flowers (grandchildren) she nurtured.   She produced a massive family tree that I am proud to be part of; this loving tribute contains kisses between its pages for her and those who shared in this venture.

The Girl Immigrant is a synopsis of Manuela's petals not yet born based on proven and documented facts but embroidered with imagination through research into time, place and their villages

A glance at the early migrant waves, according to "*The Peopling of Hawaii*" by Eleanor Nordyke and immigration records at the Hawaii State Archives:.

SPAIN, the Homeland

The Planters Society, predecessor to the Hawaii Sugar Planters Association, secured workers from Madeira and the Azores. Unlike the single men from China that were imported in the late eighteenth century by Hawaiian landowners, the later Portuguese laborers' contracts included wives and families, which provided more stability. A second wave was recruited in 1906-1913. When Hawaii became a territory, U.S. laws which banned Asians from becoming citizens caused Hawaii to look to Portugal and Spain. Enhanced deals included land, a house and better working conditions. The Portuguese became the *lunas* -- plantation foremen -- and settled there, while many Spaniards generally later moved on to California.

As novelist, Jeronimo Becker stated, "the dawning of the 19th century was a sad day for Spain." During the early 1900s in America, changes were occurring daily while Spain sat back and watched. In America, social and cultural changes included the first landing of an aircraft on a ship when Eugene Ely brought his biplane in for a safe landing on the deck of the USS Pennsylvania in San Francisco Harbor; the year before at a White House dinner hosted by President Taft, Baroness Rosen, the wife of the Russian ambassador, caused a stir by requesting and smoking a cigarette, the first time a woman had smoked openly during a public function in the executive mansion;

As it was simultaneously the case in other American countries, the immigration to Hawaii was subsidized. Until 1908 the fares, promotion, and recruiting were funded in equal parts by the island government and the cane and pineapple plantation

20

owners. From that date, they were paid with special funds from the general taxes of the Hawaiian Territory. In total, ten million dollars were spent from 1885 through 1914 to bring immigrants to the far away Mid Pacific. The trip from Spain would take more than two months and its cost, per person, was $69 in 1911.

With Gibraltar as the main center of operations, the recruiting agency J. Lucas Imossi & Sons was commissioned by the Board of Immigration of Hawaii to perform a wide propaganda and enticement campaign from 1906, with the never-failing lure of offering free of charge the long trip and the promise of work on arrival at the islands. "Recruiting", as G. Rueda aptly states, "was exclusively directed towards low laborers and field hands given the nature of work to do in Hawaii."

The emigration operation in Spain by the Hawaiian authorities and plantation owners was intense from 1907 to 1913, with Andalusia its almost-exclusive field of recruitment. In total they were able to embark 7,702 Andalusians, first from Malaga, later from Gibraltar in six successive sailings.

Year of Departure	Port of Departure	Number of Passengers	Name of Ship
1907	Málaga	2,246	Heliopolis
1911	Gibraltar	1,494	Orteric
1911	Gibraltar	1,300	Willesden
1912	Gibraltar	890	Harpalion
1913	Gibraltar	1,090	Willesden
1913	Gibraltar	1,312	Ascot

The almost eight thousand Spaniards that reached Hawaii between 1907 and 1913 came mainly from eastern Andalusia (Almeria, Granada, Jaen and Malaga). Most of them were adult males (62.4%) although complete families emigrated as well.

Their main employment destinations were the sugar plantations of Kauai, Niihau, Oahu, Molokai, Hawaii, Lanai and Kahoolawe. Very few remained in Honolulu. Labor conditions varied from the beginning of immigration to later entrants with ten hour work days. Plant work consisted of digging, fertilizing and irrigating the land; cane cutting, defoliation of dried leaves; construction of ditches, wells, dams, etc. The salaries were from $24 to $30 per month with 26 days' work; the house, wood, water, medical assistance and school were provided. In any case, a middle size family of four needed $30-$40 monthly. The information reports from the Spanish consul speak of, as early as 1917, of a "rapid impoverishment" and "astonishing premature aging" caused by excessive work in a tropical climate.

Coupled with the almost insurmountable language obstacle, it was no surprise that the majority immigrated to California where the salaries were higher and the cultural environment more favorable. This was an unstoppable "drift" that would take to the North American Pacific coast, between 1908 and 1920, 5,747 Spaniards that had originally gone to Hawaii.

THE BEGINNING

A BRIEF HISTORY OF SPAIN

I am the descendent of Iberians.·

I launch myself into the center of history and point in both directions.

Life was hard in Spain before and during 1911 where Spanish political life was sparked by the menace of revolution.   Food was scarce and civil unrest dominated conversations.   Many peasants were destitute, eking out an existence with back-breaking work and persistence to create a life for themselves. Many were farmers, growing fruit trees lovingly, thrilled at the first tiny green leaves in spring.   Olive orchards were grown for their oil and sustenance to help keep them clothed.   The men reaffirmed their strength in familial gathering at the end of the day, often too tired to enjoy the blessings they worked so hard to attain.   Everyone worked as they all had very specific jobs.   Work was second nature and they wore pride like a coat of varnish and a defied adversity.

Late December 1874, when Juan Francisco Silván Hernández was four months old, General Arsenio Martinez Campos issued a pronounciamiento in the Mediterranean town of *Sagunto* against the presidency of General Francisco Serrano, putting Spain's future in the hands of the military and civilian monarchists who later orchestrated the return of the Bourbons to the throne, Alfonso XII.

Spanish society changed greatly between 1875 and 1914. By the time my great grandmother (bisabuelita) Eustoquia Rita Trascasas Marzo, was five years old, this new regime was christened, the *Restoration*. The Restoration provided the country with stability which allowed for sustained, though uneven, industrial development and economic growth. The country still remained largely agricultural.

Early in 1902, before my (grandmother) *abuelita*, Manuela Silván Trascasas, had her first birthday, the crowning of a sixteen-year old teenage king generated more anxiety. This young man chose to intervene actively in politics, becoming entangled in party disputes; hope faltered for the poor and middle class. King Alfonso XIII (Alfonso León Fernando María Jaime Isidro Pasqual Antonio de Borbón y Austria-Lorena) was proclaimed King at his birth, but his mother, Queen María Crescéncia, was appointed regent during his minority. Now the boy controlled Spain. As early as the summer of 1909, a rebellion of locals reached the walls of *Melilla* and the government went down in flames during the *Tragic Week*, a bloody anti-conscription uprising in *Barcelona*, triggered by a call up of troops to fight in Spain's last important holding, the *Protectorate of Morocco*. Mob violence resulted in the burning of churches on a scale not seen in the city since 1835. Only after the horrors of the *Tragic Week* were Liberals able to resolve their differences. The new *Canalejas* government recaptured the democracy by abolishing the hated *consumos* tax (excise or municipal tax) and decreed obligatory military service. A growing blood-bath quota was paid exclusively by those too poor to buy their way out of the military service and it was one of the main reasons for growing discontent.

But Spain was isolated from the European mainstream and the country was sluggish and long-established. Spain knew education was the most important avenue of opportunity to better their station in life, but public systems were under-funded and under-staffed. In *Fuentesaúco,* the school was housed in the church with irregular classes and did not offer the education that larger cities fought so hard to achieve. Spain's rulers had not established schools or paid any attention to the intellectual development of the nation.

The Spanish monarchy had but one serious preoccupation ~ to flatter the Army. Once the rulers succeeded in getting the fighting forces of the country under control, they felt their worrying was over; all they had to do to stop protests was to turn on their guns.

The Bourbons preferred silence from the people and punished anyone with the audacity to speak or act against them. Every time the workers in Spain expressed their wants, they received a hail of bullets. The Spanish workmen could not hope to fight soldiers equipped with all the tools of death so he was tormented with the choice of violence. As a result, the class war assumed the characteristics of the most savage warfare.

At this time, while intrigue seethed through Spain, the Silván Hernández brothers and their sister, Crescéncia, and her husband (Felix Gonzales Hernandez) often discussed their vulnerable situation with other family members and their village friends. They feared the hurried changeover to King Alfonso XIII. After the turn of the century, nation-building in Spain was being called regeneration, a national revival of what the liberal revolution had left undone. It hoped to bring Spain into the modern world, refuting all who claimed that the Spanish race was beyond all recovery; there was some dispute as to whether the rebirth would come to the agricultural communities like *Fuentesaúco*.

By the early twentieth century a majority of the population worked in agriculture and lived in rural settings like our families. Although the Spanish countryside had been historically compliant, revolts swirled around them. The long process of opposition forced new owners to invest in and improve their land. While it resulted in increased productivity by landowners, it also had the effect of worsening the condition for the poorest sector of the farming population, the landless laborers, or *braceros*, who had always eked out a marginal existence.

Consumer protests arose from lack of access to affordable basics such as bread, meat and fuel for cooking and heating. One such period was the turn-of-the-century, when a series of bad harvests sent agricultural prices spiraling and sparked a series of riots across the country.

Bits and pieces of history between 1900 and 1910 led to our ancestor's exodus to Hawaii; the great strife they feared came to pass; anarchists threw bombs at the wedding of Alfonso and Ena, the farm workers strike, the government bringing in Spanish troops to break it up.

There was enormous upheaval and unions grew in strength. When the socialist government finally grew strong enough, civil war ensued. By then, our ancestors had already fled and this is their story.

Thus, outside interests found a vulnerable and needy group of people waiting for the opportunities they could offer them. Hawaii's *Act for the Government of Masters and Servants* in 1850 stated laborers could come into Hawaii as five-year plantation apprentices. The *1876 Reciprocity Treaty*, which allowed Hawaii sugar to be imported duty-free to the United States, was one of the main factors that led Hawaii's territorial government to bring in immigrant laborers en masse and increased the demand for sugar, however, so went immigration. The determination of Hawaii's new land barons to grow sugar into the new isle economy and the need for overseas field laborers to supplement the native Hawaiians dying from foreign diseases generated a flyer that painted a rosy picture, devoid of any malcontent or pessimism. Of course, it was a marketing tool, was it not?

EMIGRACION CON PASAJE GRATUITO AL ESTADO
DE HAWAI,
(ESTADOS-UNIDOS DE AMÉRICA)
Descripción de las Islas Haway, según el célebre viajero M. C. de Variony

...Es punto menos que imposible hacer comprender, á quien no los ha disfrutado, los incomparables atractivos del clima de las Islas de Hawai. Una temperatura constantemente igual, que todo lo una varia diez grados, y que casi siempre está á 30° centígrados; un cielo purísimo, apenas velado de vez en cuando por frescas nubecillas y lluvias oportunas; una naturaleza alegre y lozana, admirablemente iluminada por un sol radiante, constituyen el atractivo mas poderoso para atraer al extranjero y obligarle á prolongar su permanencia en aquellas Islas. Las tempestades son muy raras allí, tan raras como los huracanes, que suelen ser el azote de los países intertropicales; las noches, sobre todo, son sumamente apacibles, y cuando brilla la luna, envolviendo los campiñas en los suaves y misteriosos efluvios de sus rayos, cualquiera se creería víctima de una ilusión encantadora. Es tan pura y despejada la atmósfera que á media noche se puede leer á la claridad combinada de la luz y las estrellas. En ninguna parte se extiende la vía láctea con tanto explendor y majestad como allí: las constelaciones inviables en Europa, iluminan el espacio y brillan como deslumbradoras perlas: el mar despliega en la costa sus oleadas fosforescentes y mece sus plácidos ensueños con lento y monótono movimiento ....

Los emigrantes Españoles que quieran acoerse á las concesiones y beneficios que ofrecen as Leyes de Inmigración y Colonización del Estado de HAWAI, obtienen passage gratuito desde Málaga para dicho Estado, en magníficos Vapores de marcha rápida, de más te 12.000 toneladas, con comida, durante el viaje, á la Española, condimentada por cocineros mbarcados expresamente para ello.

El Gobierno de dicho Estado, bajo cuya garantía se efectúa la emigración, ofrece, á los SEÑORES AGRICULTORES un porvenir halagüeño, cuyas ventajas son las siguientes:

Los varones cabeza de familia

20 duros americanos oro, al mes, durante el primer año de trabajo.

21 duros americanos oro, al mes, durante el segundo año.

22 duros americanos oro, al mes, durante el tercer año.

las mujeres, sus esposas 12 duros oro al mes.

Los demás individuos de su familia que sean mayores de 15 años, 15 duros mensuales, si son varones y 10 duros si son hembras.

Desde que desembarquen, se les facilita una magnífica casa-vivienda (que vale más de 500 pesos oro) agua y lumbre y escuela gratuita, donde reciben educación los hijos menores, para los que es obligatorio asistir á ella.

Y á los tres años de trabajo, con buena conducta y en los que hayan demostrado que son buenos Labradores (y especialmente para el cultivo de la caña de azúcar), se les cede gratuitamente y en propiedad absoluta y sin gravámen alguno, la casa donde estén viviendo y además una fanega de tierra.

Condiciones que deben reunir los emigrantes

Es condición indispensable que los emigrantes sean agricultores que gozen de buena salud, no padezcan de la vista, que no tengan defectos físicos y ue formen precisamente familias cuya constitución puede ser, como sigue:
1.º   Marido y mujer sin hijos, no teniendo el marido más de 45 años, ni la mujer más de 40.
2.º   Marido y mujer con hijos, no pudiendo los jefes tener más de 45 años, con tal que haya en la familia un hombre útil de 17 á 45 años.
3.º   Viudo ó viuda con hijos, teniendo siempre un hombre útil mayor de 17 años y menor de 45 años.
4.º   Hombre casado no llevando la mujer, pero si llevando hijos con tal que haya siempre un hombre útil de 17 á 45 años.
5.º   Mujer casada no llevando su marido, pero si llevando hijos con tal que haya uno útil de 17 á 45 años.
Podrán ir como agregados á las familias antes expresadas, todos los parientes, carnales y políticos, menores de 40 años.
Las personas mayores de 45 años no gozan de pasaje gratuito: estas tienen que pagarse el pasaje que cuesta Pesetas 400.

Documentos que necesitan presentar las familias que deseen emigrar

1.º   Cédula personal para todos los mayores de 14 años.
2.º   Los varones y mujeres solteras, hasta la edad de 23 años, una autorización de sus padres ó tutores, otorgada ante Notario ó ante el Alcalde del pueblo de su vecindad. Este documento no es necesario cuando vayan en compañía de sus padres, pero en todo caso las mujeres solteras han de presentar un certificado que acredite su estado de soltería.
3.º   Partida de bautismo para los varones y mujeres solteros.
4.º   Los varones de 15 á 20 años no pueden embarcar sin presentar un certificado que acredite haber consignado en la Caja de Depósito la suma de 500 pesetas á las resultas de la quinta, según previene la ley.
5.º   Los varones de 20 á 40 años han de presentar la licencia absoluta si son licenciados definitivos. Los que pertenezcan á la reserva ó á la clase de reclutas disponibles han de presentar un permiso del Capitán General del distrito respectivo, autorizándoles para efectuar su embarque ó ausentarse de la Península. Este documento no puede tener más de 4 meses á contarse desde la fecha de su expedición.
6.º   Las mujeres casadas que no vayan acompañadas de sus maridos han de presentar un permiso de éste, visado por la Alcaldía del pueblo de su residencia ó por Notario, siendo en la Capital.
7.º   Partida de casamiento para los matrimonios.
8.º   Partida de viudedad para las viudas.
9.º   Certificado de buena conducta expedido por la Alcaldía de su residencia con las señas personales, para todos los individuos mayores de 14 años.
10   Certificado de no estar procesado, expedido por el Juzgado del pueblo donde residan, para todos los mayores de 14 años, ó de la Audiencia siendo en la Capital.

DESCONFIAR DE LOS INTERMEDIARIOS
Para mayores detalles y presentación de documentos:
DON CARLOS CROVETTO, Encargado del Departamento de Revisión
CALLE DE RIOS ROSAS (antes Cañón) núm. 3.--Málaga

7

What was the push factor?   Why did they leave?

I had so many questions!   And Aunt Millie Ruiz Cortopassi delivered the goods!   She pulled out a Spanish poster (broadsheet) from her mother's box of mementos along with a treasure trove of various documents that aided in the germination of this book; documented copies are included within these pages.

TRANSLATION: EMIGRATION WITH FREE PASSAGE
TO THE STATE OF HAWAII
(UNITED STATES OF AMERICA,)
Description of the Hawaiian Islands from the famous traveler,
M.C.Variony

".... It is less than impossible to understand, for those who have not seen the unique attractions of the Hawaiian Island's climate. A constant temperature, which varies at most ten degrees, and regularly about 30 degrees Celsius; a pure sky, only occasionally veiled by mist and rain to freshen the air; A cheerful nature, admirably illuminated by a bright sun, are the most powerful attractions to foreigners that force him to want to extend his stay in the islands. The storms are very rare there, as rare as hurricanes, which are often the scourge of the inter-tropical countries; Nights, especially, are extremely quiet, and when the moon shines, wrapping one in a soft and mysterious ray, anybody would think they were a victim of an enchanted illusion. The atmosphere is so pure and clear that you can read clearly at midnight from the combination of light and stars. The Milky Way is splendor and majesty: the constellations visible here in Europe, illuminate space and shine, dazzlingly, like pearls. Displays along the seacoast with its phosphorescent waves rock dreams with their monotonous slow motion.

The Spanish emigrants that want to enjoy the benefits that are offered by the Law of Immigration and Colonization of the State of Hawaii will obtain free passage from Malaga for said State, in a magnificent, a quick moving ship, with food during the trip, flavored by cooks embarked explicitly for it. See various seaports for embarkation at Gibraltar.

The government of that State, under whose guarantee is made for your emigration, offers the farmers a REAL bright future, whose advantages include:

Men - heads of households
$20 American gold per month, during the first year of work
$21 American gold per month, during the second year
$22 American gold, a month during the third year

The men's wives: $12 hard gold per month
Other individuals in your family who are over 15:

$15 American hard gold per month, if they are males and
$10 American hard gold for females

After arriving in Hawaii, you will be provided with a magnificent dwelling-house, (worth over 500 gold pesos) water, wood and free school, where children receive the education. They are required to attend.

And after three years of work, good conduct and those which have demonstrated they are good laborers (and especially for the cultivation of sugarcane), they give gratuity and absolute ownership, without any charge, the house where they are living and also a parcel of soil.

Conditions for the emigrants
It is essential that all migrants are farmers who are in good health, not weak of sight, having no obvious physical defects and their families whose constitution may be, as follows:

1. Husband and wife without children, the husband having no more than 45 years, or women over 40.

2. Husband and wife without children, the heads may not be over 45 years, or women over 40.
3. Widow or widower with children, must be useful to a man older than 17 years and under 45 years.
4. Men bringing a woman, who is unmarried, with children with such a man, must be useful 17 to 45 years.

5. Married women without a husband can have children as long as they are useful 17 to 45 years.

Eligible people may be added to the families above: all relatives, carnal and political, less than 40 years. People over 45 do not have free passage: these have to pay for the ticket which costs 400 pesetas.

Documents you need to present for the families that wish to migrate:

- Personal paperwork for all those of 14 years.

- Men and unmarried women up to age 23 years, a parent or guardian authorization granted before a notary or before the Mayor of the people of his neighborhood. This document is not necessary when they are accompanied by their parents, but in any case, unmarried women have to submit a certificate attesting to their unmarried status.

- Baptismal record for all single men and women.

- Men 15 to 20 years of age cannot be present without having a certificate placed in the Deposit Fund in the sum of 1,500 pesetas.

- Those men of 20 to 40 years must present their graduation license. Those who belong in the reserve class of recruits must present a permit from the Captain General of the respective district, authorizing you to leave the Peninsula. This document cannot be over 4 months from the date of issue.

- Married women not accompanied by their husbands must submit a valid permit, endorsed by the mayor of your town or neighborhood in front of a notary in the Capital.

- Certificate of Marriage license

- Certificate proving widowhood.

- Certificate of good conduct issued by the mayor's residence with his personal details, for all individuals older than 14 years.

- A Certificate cannot be processed for children over age 14 if not issued by the court of the people where they live, unless they have an audience in the Capital.

Be wary of middlemen

For more details, present your documents to: Don Carlos Crovetto, Head of the Department of Revision
Rios Rosas Street (formerly Canon) num. 3, Malaga

THE GIRL IMMIGRANT

THE SILVÁN FAMILY

From humble beginnings in a small farming village in northern Spain called *Fuentesaúco* in the *Province of Zamora*, Manuela Silván Trascasas and her family lived a simple life.   Bernardo Ruiz Romero, who would later become her husband and my abuelo (grandfather), lived on the southern coast of Spain in a tiny village near *Campanillas* in the *Province of Malaga*. I have pieced together their tale in a garden of remembrance with the help of many family members, photographs, family history and my steadfast research. This is the story from whence they came.......

Agustína Hernández Martin and Celestino Pedro Silván Dovales' children numbered twelve; ten sons and two daughters, all born in *Fuentesaúco, Zamora, Spain.*   Juan Francisco Silván Hernández was my great grandfather, born on 16 August 1875.   At 5′ 6″ tall, hair the color of cocoa and eyes as blue as the sky he never missed what was important.   He was a typical Spaniard; hard working, loyal, responsible and friendly.   His mustache was dark and luxuriant which he would often twist to encourage the ends to twirl properly.

By the turn of the century, he was often playing his faithful *el bombo*, a large floor drum, in a musical band called *John's Song and Drums.*   His music became a kind of flying carpet by which he could travel to an entirely different place --- a private world of his own.   Several men made up the group of musicians, entertaining the people of *Fuentesaúco* and surrounding villages.   Their buoyant

34

music encouraged their listeners to dance or simply tap their feet during fiestas or at the many large family gatherings that were so popular in that time period and in that place.

Often at these gatherings or village festivals, Spanish ladies wore long skirts and fringe edged shawls to enjoy the music and dance. However, these young women were not allowed to attend alone, but accompanied by a matron to assure their chastity and reputation.

When the music swelled, ladies would leap up to dance *la Sevillanas* or *la Jota*, which were Spanish dances typically filled with passion and spontaneity. They'd click shiny castanets and tap their feet in staccato fashion as their music thrilled to a crescendo and filled the night air.

Juan and his group always enjoyed watching these vibrant dancers and winked to one another when an especially pretty girl danced solo among their friends and family. Agustína smiled when she listened to them.

Music throbbed through Juan's veins like a love affair. He was a simple farmer, but also earned extra money at the bull fights. His job was a messy one; when the bull was killed in the bullring and spectators screamed, he launched his horse into the ring to drag the bull out to wagons where butchers waited. The butchers would bleed it out, cut it up and sell the meat; some portions were given to the poor.

Bullfighting season started in March and ended in October with the *toro de lidia,* the fighting bull, entertained in the *plaza de toros,* the bullring. The bullfight consisted of three matadors alternately fighting two bulls each. Each matador had a *cuadrilla,* or team of men consisting of two *picadors* and three *banderilleros,* assistants who help prepare the bull for the kill. It was a series of taunting, thrusting, and dancing in the dust, waving the cape, running for the fence and the final kill. Usually the bull lost the battle. That was when Juan's job would begin.

Sometimes, whether he was dirty from farming or dragging a dead bull, he put aside his weariness, cleaned himself up and grabbed his drum.

If he could have supported himself as a musician he would have been a happy man. Farming, on the other hand, was a necessity of life and working beside his family was the way it would be. But for those starry nights when *el bombo* was beneath his hands and the music filled his soul, he could forget the day job and enjoy a rush of contentment.

His older brother, Victorino, stood 5' 5" tall. His swarthy skin was clear but for a small mole on the left side of his neck. He had married Romana Martinez Lorenzo some years before and his daughter, Teodora, toddled around generating many adoring smiles. And she always had a big smile for her tio Juan (uncle), who could not imagine a sweeter child nor visualize a child of his own anytime soon.

Juan's mind wandered, thinking about the child, his family and his own life. He was thirty years old and couldn't read or write. He reminded himself he was just a farmer so who cared? He did not resent his older brothers education for that was tradition. Juan had his music. What else did he really need?

In Spain at that time young men gathered in groups or shared an evening with ladies in pairs[5]. Young women were always accompanied by others and required proper introductions.

---

[5] Story from Manuela Silvan Trascasas

And Juan had not met a woman worth breaking the strict rules for. He worked hard in the orchards with olives, figs, grapes, almonds, wheat and apricot trees which kept him busy, his fingers callused and hands dirty.   He toiled hard by day but put aside his weariness for music.

He was a quiet man whom others regarded as warm-hearted, serious and fun loving.   He respected his elders, had loved his father and adored his mother and Crescéncia, his young sister. His parents had always moved with the flow, adapting to life in Spain. Their children like others in the younger generation, questioned Spanish authority and their life as they moved into the twentieth century.   The old ways were paved with sadness, economic strife and rules that were difficult to accept but held family camaraderie, age-old history, spiritual guidance, good plain food, and parents who did their best in a stark homeland.

By the spring of 1900, Juan longed for more; the swan song of his music became the balm to stoke it down.   Often, when his band struck up their first notes at dusk, he smiled in the glow of applause and his discontent and restlessness was soon lost in the dark.

One extraordinary evening in the Spring of 1900, not long after his recent mind chatter, he was spruced up and ready for the night; his drum taut.   Juan sang with the band and his band mates ad-libbed with him when he added extra beats to *Alla en el Rancho Grande*.

That particular night local villagers and friends from the mountain village of *Toro* were gathered in anticipation.   Dark red wine flowed and dancing feet tapped.   Suddenly, through the smoky haze, a young woman wearing a bright red skirt with a black lace shawl tossed over her slight shoulders caught his attention.

Her rich dark hair was lush and wavy; a red rose pinned to one side. The musical segment began. His drumbeat slipped in and around the room, echoing through him while he watched her.

The young woman chose that moment to stand, swirl her long full skirt, raise her arms and snap brown castanets while she danced *la Jota*. Juan saw others move aside allowing her room to spin and dance. He had never seen such a graceful woman; watching her through half lowered lids, he sang openly to her. The woman lowered her lashes but not before he saw her bright eyes mirror his interest when his music was greeted with loud applause.

Eustoquia Rita Trascasas Marzo recognized Juan. It seemed that Agustína's son was known as far away as *Toro* for his musical talent. In fact, that was why she was there at the gathering. She wanted to see him again. Trained as a seamstress, she sewed costumes for matadors, called *suits of lights*[6]. She also worked as a servant to earn money for her family, cleaning houses. During a recent religious fair in *Toro*, she'd joined others at her employer's window to peek through wooden slats at the musicians parading by. The young women loved music Rita's eyes tracked Juan and followed him until he was just a speck down her village's street. She couldn't stop smiling. Her friends teased her unmercifully when they returned to their chores. And she didn't forget him.

After watching the dancer, Juan lowered his drum, telling his band mates she was his and they should play the next song without him. He wanted to meet her and reminded them he saw her first. Hearing them snort with laughter, he walked over to the young woman who sat fanning herself rapidly with a small black lace fan.

---

[6] Story: Rose Marie Dugger, daughter of Mary Silván Cuellar

He respectfully bowed to the older men and other women sharing her table. One woman swayed with the music; she had only one leg. The other woman tapped her toes. The men watched him silently. Each nodded in response to his attention. They knew why he'd come to their table. The older man nodded at the one-legged woman. Her voice was soft as she formally introduced the dark-haired young woman to him.

"Quiero presentarle a mi hija, Eustoquia Rita Trascasas Marzo." I want to present my daughter, Eustoquia Rita...... The matron's dark eyes moved over Juan as her mouth twitched, before sliding a peek toward her daughter, Rita, who was not yet twenty years old.

Manuela Marzo Garcia gave her brothers, José and Jacinto, a devious look. Jacinto, Rita's godfather, kept careful watch over her even though his sister, Manuela, kept her own counsel. Both men wanted Rita settled and out of the house. Their sister's husband was a frightening stepfather who became increasingly aggravated with life every day.

They knew Manuela would not be able to protect Rita from him much longer and shuddered as they remembered the dagger. He'd tossed the blade across the room a few days earlier, slamming it harshly into the dining table, barely missing Rita's arm[7].

Gripping her handkerchief fiercely, Manuela Marzo inhaled deeply. Rita must be safe! She still grieved for her daughter, Jacinta Modesta, who died just eight years old in 1891; losing her remaining child would be too daunting to imagine.   If only Manuel Trascasas had been younger when they married --- had

---

[7]Source: Rose Marie Dugger, daughter of Mary Silván Cuellar

lived to see Rita to adulthood… But Manuela admitted no amount of wishing could change the life she was forced to lead. Diabetes had eaten away at her. Only forty-six years old in weakened health, she'd already lost a leg; as a widow she'd needed a husband to support her and now she had one.

"Me llamo Juan Francisco Silván Hernández, señorita. Con mucho gusto..." My name is Juan Francisco……..Miss. It is with much pleasure…. Juan wiped his damp palms on his pants surreptitiously. He couldn't remember when he'd been so nervous.

They shared shy and silly smiles.

Rita clenched her hands. She tried to appear nonchalant. No laughing. Sit up straight. Breathe normally, count to ten. Her eyes cut to the women sharing her table. She knew they shared her pleasure because she'd not stopped talking or thinking about him.

Juan was delighted to be invited to join their table. He extended his hand to the uncles and her mother; dark eyes studied him. His heartbeat seemed louder than the flamenco music. He knew this tiny feisty woman, who stood only five feet and one inch tall, was very special. And he wanted her family's approval.

Rita shyly glanced at him again. He had eyes the color of periwinkle.

Fuentesaúco was a Catholic town with several churches and in each church there was a bell tower. Bells told the hour, summoned the faithful to Mass, and reminded them when it was time to say their prayers, announced births and deaths, called citizens to fight fires and to announce a wedding.

AND THE BELLS RANG. The wedding vows took place on

a perfect spring day at 8 o'clock in the morning at the Iglesia de Santa María de Castillo Catholic Church.   The sun was brilliant, but the air didn't have the touch of fire that made the summer months so hot.   As that bell tower spread the news in *Fuentesaúco* on the 23rd day of April in 1900, Eustoquia Rita Marzo Trascasas from the neighboring village of *Toro*, in the Province of Zamora, Spain, became the wife of Juan Silván Hernández.

Their long life began in *Fuentesaúco* as Rita learned to love his mother, Agustína Hernández, and his siblings as her own.   Their first child, Manuela Silván Trascasas was born thirteen months and fourteen days after their wedding day on June 25, 1901.   She was fair skinned; brown eyed and had a wisp of light-colored hair.   Rita couldn't stop staring into her tiny face and continually reminded herself the tiny girl was her own daughter.   Juan was smitten and in love with both of them.

I can only assume Rita may have birthed one or several children, who died young, because it was seven years before their son, Agustín Silván Marzo, was born in 1908.   He was named after his Uncle Agustín Silván Hernández and his abuela, Agustína Hernández Martin.   His birth was followed two years later by a second son, José Silván Marzo, named after his great Uncle José Marzo Garcia.

Most of the houses in *Fuentesaúco* were two-rooms built shoulder to shoulder and painted a soft color; some whitewashed, some left plain stone.   The  Silvan house was stone built, square-walled and huddled close against its neighbors on 6 Calle San Salvador. Windows opened front and back.   It stood near the middle of the village. Juan's mother, Agustína, birthed and raised their children there with her now-deceased husband, Celestino.   And it was still a close family.

Behind the family's house was a small garden that included herbs, sugar beets, potatoes, onions, garlic, herbs and garbanzo beans.   There was a pump outside the kitchen door for water, an outhouse at the far end of the yard adjacent to the pig pen.

More pigs and goats roamed the lanes than people.   Beside the small house ran a narrow road.   Most houses had small rooms attached to hold their pigs and other small animals.   Since bartering was important for life in the village, they often traded garbanzo beans, olives, and root vegetables, depending on the season, to a neighboring farmer.   In return, the farmer arrived early in the mornings to pick up everyone's pigs, which would follow him down the road just like dogs.   He would take them away each day, feed them, and at the end of the day, he would walk down the street, and the pigs would return to their respective homes. Apparently those pigs were very smart.[8]

Their history was in the soil; olive trees and grapevines grew spindly and sparse waiting for spring and a promise of fresh green buds. It had been a long year, the garden dry, less fertile and slow to grow but they were persistent.

---

[8] Source: Cheryl Souza Edwards, great granddaughter to Victorino and Ramona Silván

FUENTESAÚCO, 1910

SOME YEARS AFTER JUAN AND RITA'S MARRIAGE, our ancestors felt the growing social unrest and the weak economy. Incessant talk surrounded a poster being circulated in their village again, just as it had in 1907. It appeared at a time when conversations spilt with dissatisfaction and disheartening worries. Little did they know the boy-king would destroy Spain's constitution and the military would spawn a civil war years later in 1936.

Now, they wondered if their only salvation was to uproot themselves from the land they loved. Crawling through their minds was the fear that Spain was neglecting them. Was it self-indulgence to remain in Spain? Could a better future lie across the ocean? The poster dispersed throughout Spain and Portugal advertised that a place called *Hawaii* needed farm workers. While only a fleeting interest in the emigration in 1907, now the poster spawned serious consideration inviting some dissention among them. Could they make this change and fail, dragging themselves back to voices that said "I told you so?" Could they drag their family through miles of unknown land to reach Gibraltar in the south? Could the children make it? Their women?

Hawaii was courting transplants. The recruiters were sent by sugar agencies named Castle and Cooke and also H. Hackfeld and Company, to describe Hawaii as a paradise, a place where poor men could find work and a better life. Hawaiian plantations needed farm workers and our men qualified since they'd felt soil roll through their fingers all their lives. They were told they could inhale fresh island air and feel pride in their accomplishments. But Hawaii was forever away from Spain…a hazy *someplace* across the sea.

The agent from the plantations stayed with a family nearby and pled his case in their home and anywhere he found a group talking, especially in the Plaza Mayor.

The women sighed, hard to convince, when their men brought their discussions home after these meetings. Their mother, Agustína Hernández, now lost without her husband's moral support and strength, listened and prayed it would remain that: only discussions.

Telesforo Alejano Alva, a good family friend, had also seen the poster and was frequently part of the familial discussion, arguing in earnest to keep his friends in *Fuentesaúco*. Juan, Victorino and Felix's[9] exhaustive justifications left them limp as rags.   While sipping short glasses of Anisette, an opaque, tongue-numbing, brain-warming liquid smelling of anise[10], they asked themselves, "When will our life get better?"   "And how?"   "How can we turn from the possibility of earning twenty or thirty American dollars each month compared to their meager pesetas?"

Small groups of villagers often drew together, some sitting on the ground to discuss the fate of the world in Spain and Hawaii, others circled around the Plaza's large stone water fountain in the village square.   Small children blissfully ran around one another or sat on the ground under a large tree idly scratching in the loose rocks blithely unaware that their futures lay in the discussions around them.

Homesteading conversations about Hawaii had more allure each day.   They promised themselves they could someday return to their family and homeland....surely so.

Our impoverished ancestors clutched those dog-eared flyers, feeling disloyal to *Fuentesaúco* and *Toro*, both Provinces of Zamora. Ernest Hemingway said that a Spaniard was only really loyal to his village in the end; first Spain, then his province, then his village, his family and finally his trade.   Our ancestors felt the same but some looked beyond their national pride, many agreeing that too much pride could diminish everything they'd ever known before.

With that mindset, they were infected with emigration fever and by early January of 1911, the women knew the stalemate was over.   How could they turn down daily rations, lodging, a garden

---

[9]   Felix Gonzales Hernandez was married to Crescéncia Silván   Hernandez, their sister
[10]   This description of Anisette, excerpt from For Whom the Bell Tolls by Ernest Hemingway

plot, medical care, free schools, transportation to the islands and wages?   And their restlessness grew.

When Telesforo Alva began to weaken against all arguments, he and his wife, Marcelina Zamorano Velasco, knew the time had come.   They met with the alcalde.   Their daughter, Gala Alva Zamorano was two years old.   They would sail on the S.S. Willesden in October after the Silváns sailed in February.

And then Marcelina's brother, Eusebio Zamorano Velasco and his wife, Paula Entizne Este and their daughter Eulalia who was six years old followed.

Paula's younger sister, María Asunción Entizne Este, begged her not to go.   Her baby was only eight months old and losing her sister was an unacceptable blow; she turned to her husband beseeching him to talk to Eusebio.   Instead, Jesús Boiza Corral chose to follow the clan and the papers were drawn up at the alcalde's office.

The mass exits of groups of families astounded the village who chose to remain and the tally grew each day.

The Silvan women listened cautiously to the impassioned discussion in the outer room, where the men congregated beside the arched doorway.   While preparing *Tortilla Española*[11] for their children's meal, *la merienda*, the humble thick, flat egg and potato omelets were filled with dried peas and chopped onions and served onto crockery.   Typically this was cooked for second breakfast but they often served it later in the day; they had plenty of eggs and potatoes -- often not much else.   Cooking aromas invited the children to scoot into their places.   The air was filled with intense whispering and tension was thick as morning fog.   Silently eating

---

[11] Tortilla Española: Spanish version of an egg and potato omelet -- no flour or corn tortillas

their meal, young eyes darted between their mother's faces and their *abuelita* Agustína's stiff countenance.

Rita and Ramona[12] placed tin cups filled with red wine, balancing thick bread slices topped with cheese [13] near their husband's chairs. The men, deep in conversation, barely nodded their acknowledgement as they automatically reached for the wine, lifted the tapas and sipped.

The adult meals would be prepared later, *la cena*, a simple meal about 8:30 or 9:00 p.m. Their similar fare would include *vino común*, an everyday table wine. In better years, a good amount of stored food was kept in the outbuilding. The cooler root cellar stored the carrots, onions, garlic and potatoes. There were also dried apples and wild yams. But no cloth-wrapped roasting meat sat inside their larder. There would be chicken for the following day's *cocido*, a rich peasant stew. Hens were never expensive to keep, and the logic was if you fed the hen, it would feed you. Dried fruit was used to cook and eat on its own, but even that was running low; it was January and the winter had been an exceedingly long one.

Rita pushed aside the eight bread loaves she and her mother-in-law had baked that day in the conical brick oven behind the house. The farm-house ovens, called *el horno*, were typical of the villages and traditionally used to spit-roast meat over burning vine clippings, *hornos de asar*. The golden loaves lent a pleasing scent

---

[12] Various documents show Romana. For our story, I use Ramona for consistency

[13] Precursor to tapas, defined as a lid or cover. Tapas got their name from the days when a slice of bread covered with jamon (ham) or queso (cheese) was placed on top of a wine or sherry glass to keep flies out while serving weary travelers. The price of simple tapas was once included in cost of drinks, but that tradition, sadly, has all but died out.

throughout the small house.

She secretly thought theirs were as light as the famous bread[14] from *Astorga*. She patted the end loaf on the wooden countertop thoughtfully and watched bits of flour flake and fly from beneath her fingers. She blinked quickly and swallowed the lump in her throat. Raising her eyes to the other women's faces, she saw her fears mirrored there. And separation anxiety; they could be leaving Agustína, their own relations; a second or fourth or twelfth cousin…..

Hawaii seemed as far away as the moon, looming tantalizingly for the men. Despite leaving the land of their birth at their impossible choice, their hands shook as practicality fought with racing hearts. They wrestled with the flyer's promises and the possible lifeline that awaited their decision. What was really being offered and why? They were, as the Spanish refer to a stubborn person, very *iberos*. But they were also intelligent and thoughtful and knew changes could be imperative to their survival. Since Victorino could read, unlike his brothers or Felix, he'd read the flyer aloud; each part discussed in minute detail.

It seems reasonable to imagine that they stood poised for change but utterly frozen in debate. The Silváns all agreed the Spanish monarchy had bewildered the Spanish mind and clouded judgment. They'd watched the peseta steadily lose value and it would not be the first time men had shed the burden of bravery, reason, civilization and laws to kneel down to practicality and

---

[14] Castilla is also known for its wonderful bread and the history of baking is a very long one. In ancient times the Celtic people who inhabited what is now Spain were already making something similar to modern day bread. Later, Iberian people used beer to leaven their bread. The tradition of the communal oven, where all members of the community were allowed to bake bread, lived on into the 20th century

fearful confusion. They also worried about leaving their mother, which left them indecisive and disheartened.

Juan was 36, Victorino 42, and Crescéncia 26 years old; their other brothers all in between but Agustín, the youngest. They watched the rapidly changing panorama of their country with sad eyes and Agustina watched them.

Juan Francisco Silván Hernández and Victorino Silván Hernández felt their eyes grow misty. Both knew their futures could also be rocky in Hawaii if they left Spain behind. But did they really have a choice? They loved the village and the pleasures derived from their daily routines although some houses had no running water and some roofs were on the verge of falling in. It was still their home, dirt floors and all.

Fuentesaúco, the village of poppies, chickpeas and unseen gardens, turned overnight into a place demanding final decisions. Their narrow streets, with their houses close together which had previously brought them comfort, now made them shiver with apprehension. They would miss the house's cold clear smell, with its nuances of old plaster and aging wood. And above all, they'd miss their mother, who was clearly heartbroken.

They'd miss their ancient 16th century church, Santa María del Castillo, where they'd worshiped, been baptized, married and baptized their children. And building houses for friends and family where adobe was created from sand, dirt, water, small pebbles and dried grass for binding it all together. The mixture was poured into frames about six inches at a time around the walls. When it was dry, new layers would be added until it was tall enough for the red tiled roof. The walls were about eighteen inches deep which served as insulation both summer and winter. There was no electricity. Instead, light came from hurricane lamps and water from rain barrels and the plaza's fountain.

They were torn between love of Spain, their struggling life and a quest for their head-of-household dignity. With rocks lodged in their throats, raspy words conveyed their decision to walk away from their incomprehensible poverty. They were poor, yes, but they should not be without food or the wherewithal to grow orchards of fruits and olives. They'd listen more intently to the beguiling beckoning from Hawaii.

PAINFUL DECISIONS

They wouldn't be the first Spanish immigrants to leave *Fuentesaúco* for Hawaii.   In 1907, Hawaiian posters had lured several families away on the S.S. Heliopolis.   At that time, the thought of the Silván family leaving was only a distant seed for thought, although Juan asked the mayor to give him a character letter that was dated May 11, 1907.   Family heartaches held them back but he kept it because he thought one day...maybe they would go.

Afterward, many of their friends received letters from Hawaii and the seed began to find fertile ground again in the winter of 1910.   The islands sounded like paradise, though work was undoubtedly hard.   Their friends wrote about a house of their own, schooling for their children, animals and gardens to grow.   They earned nearly thirty American dollars each month....

Their decision was agonizing.   They talked, talked, and talked some more.   Times were desperate and they certainly couldn't just laze around under umbrellas and smell wine corks[15]. And finally it was decided.   They would go.

"*Hoy mismo, no mañana.*" Today, not tomorrow.   They

---

[15] *For Whom the Bell Tolls* by Ernest Hemingway

would leave Spain in its death-like sleep. Their country might unite and come alive one day but probably not in their lifetime. They would accept the indentured status and three-year commitment for themselves and their families to work in the sugar cane fields of Hawaii in exchange for the promise of food and shelter, but only as a stopover for their ultimate dream of living in America or returning to a richer Spain one day.

Deep sighs echoed through their women's minds as they whispered through tear-choked throats.   There were nine children among them, ranging in age from Eustoquia Rita's small baby José to Ramona's 12-year old daughter, Teodora.

Discussions had gone on for weeks in the village square after church and during the Paseo in *Fuentesaúco*.   Many friends and some relatives would also go.   They would not be alone.

SS ORTERIC SHIP MANIFEST

IMMIGRANTS-FUENTESAUCO, ZAMORA, SPAIN

Surnames	Given Name			Status
Madroñal Caballero	Andres	25	M	Single
Arevalo Rodriguez	Ramon	27	M	Married
Tejada Sanchez	Segunda	28	F	Married
Arevalo Tejada	Santiago	2	M	Single
Blanco Martín	Silverio Eusebio	24	M	Married
Saez Galache	Alejandra[1]	22	F	Married
Boiza Corral	Jesús	26	M	Married
Entizne Este	MaríaAsunción	23	F	Married
Boiza Entizne	Eustoquia[2]	8mo	F	Single
Cano Martín	José	36	M	Married
Hernandez Hernández	Lucila	33	F	Married
Cano Hernández	Isabel	9	F	Single
Cano Hernández	Eustasio	6	M	Single
Cano Hernández	Trinidad	3	M	Single
Corrales González	Eugenio	26	M	Married
Gonzales Vallejo	Dominica	24	F	Married
Corrales González	María Magdalena[3]	7mo	F	Single
Gonzáles Hernández	Félix (b. 1881)	30	M	Married
Silván Hernández	Crescéncia	26	F	Married
Gonzáles Silván	Alejandro	3	M	Single
Gonzáles Silván	Juan	2	M	Single
González Fernandez	Casimino	30	M	Single
Garcia Valdunciel	Serafin	26	M	Married
(Garcia Valdunciel)	Dionicia	24	F	Married
Hernández de la Iglesia	Martín	27	M	Single
Hernández de la Iglesia	Segundo Agapito	19	M	Single
Hernández de la Iglesia Vasquez	Claudio	27	M	Married
Vicente Hidalgo	Dolores	26	F	Married

		6m		
Hernández Vicente	Anita	0	F	Single
Vicente Hidalgo	Leoncio	17	M	Single
Hidalgo Grande	Ignacio	47	M	Married
Arevalo Hernández	Tomasa	47	F	Married
Hidalgo Arevalo	Brigida	5	F	Single
Hidalgo Arevalo	Socorro	2	F	Single
Hidalgo Arevalo	Bernarda	11	F	Single
Lopez del Rio	Celestino	36	M	Married
Lopez Martín	Domingo	2	M	Single
Martín Vadunciel	Carmen	36	F	Married
Lopez Martín	José[4]	1m 0	M	Single
*[5]Lamas Zamorano	Brigida	46	F	Widow
*Lamas	Casto	10	M	Single
*Lamas	Teodora	14	F	Single
*Lamas	Pedro	19	M	Single
Miguel Juarez	Crispulo	33	M	Married
Santos del Rio	Francisca	21	F	Married
Miguel Santos	Adelia	7	F	Single
Mella	Gabino	20	M	Single
Morales Pereña	Fidel	28	M	Married
Magdalena Caballero	Juana	26	F	Married
Martín González	Enrique	39	M	Married
Sesmilo Alejo	Felipa[6]	37	F	Married
Martín Sesmilo	Antonia	10	F	Single
Martín Sesmilo	Juliana	7	F	Single
Martín Sesmilo	María	5	F	Single
Martín Sesmilo	Simon[7]	2	F	Single
Martín Galache	Genaro	30	M	Married
Prada	Eusebia	28	F	Married
Puerta Entizne	Severiano	28	M	Married
Texeira Santos	Juana	24	F	Married
Ramozal Delval	Alonso	33	M	Married

Corrales Jimenez	Paulina	28	F	Married
Ramozal Corrales	Eusebia	8	F	Single
Ramozal Corrales	Juliana	5	F	Single
Ramozal Corrales	Balbina[8]	1	F	Single
Corrales Roque	Jacinto	45	M	Married
Corrales Morales	Juliana	5	F	Single
Corrales Morales	Vicente	10	M	Single
Morales Pereña	Evarista	35	F	Married
Corrales Morales	Félix	15	M	Single
Silván Hernández	Juan Francisco	31	M	Married
Trascasas Marzo	Eustoquia Rita	30	F	Married
Silván Trascasas	Manuela	9	F	Single
Silván Trascasas	Agustin	3	M	Single
Silván Trascasas	José	10 m	M	Single
Silván Hernández	Victorino L	42	M	Married
Martínez Lorenzo	Ramona	32	F	Married
Silván Martínez	Teodora	12	F	Single
Silván Martínez	Felisa	7	F	Single
Silván Martínez	Celestino	5	M	Single
Silván Martínez	Jacinto[9]	5	M	Single
Valle Hernández	Segundo	34	M	Married
Arias Blanco	Matea	32	F	Married
Valle Blanco	Félix	8	M	Single
Arias (____?)	Domingo	62	M	Single
Zamorano Velasco	Eusebio	34	M	Married
Entizne Este	Paula[10]	30	F	Married
Zamorano Entizne	Eulalia	6	F	Single
Valdunciel Martín	Gregorio	36	M	Married
Martín Miguel	Ignacia	22	F	Married

- Alejandra was pregnant at embarkation but baby died in shipboard accident
- Eustoquia Boiza Entizne died at sea
- María Magdalena Corrales Gonzales died at sea
- Jose Lopez Martin was born at sea

- The Lamas Zamorano family did not embark, but sailed later in year
- The Martin Family were Silvan cousins
- Simon Martin died at sea
- Balbina Ramozal Corrales died at sea
- Jacinto Silvan Martin died at sea
- They left your Tomas in Spain, but he arrived later

Now that the decision was made, there were days of lingering embraces, tears and prayers. Their Catholic faith gave them strength in the past and would again. With winter's frosty chill in the air, they contemplated the trip with misgivings and not just a little excitement and began fervent planning after receiving their acceptance notification.

Two ports of embarkation were involved with the transportation of Spaniards to Hawaii. The mode of travel depended on the remoteness of their homes from the major centers of transportation. The first leg of the journey was to get to the water and would be the most difficult. Their final embarkation would

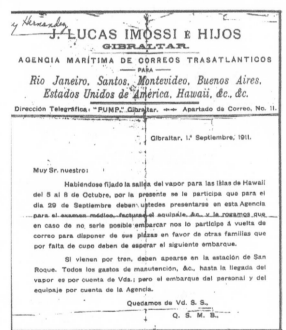

be at the *Rock of Gibraltar.* Carefully, they counted their money; our three families would ride the train over the mountains to *Sevilla.* From there, they'd sail on the *Guadalquivir River* to the mouth of the sea and then walk and camp at night following railroad tracks the rest of the way to La Línea, the Spanish side of the border between Spain and Gibraltar.

Many would ride on mules, some in burro-drawn carts; others would ride the train from the Salamanca train station all the way to the San Roque Station at *La Línea* beyond *Cadiz* and then another seventy miles to wait for the ship in Gibraltar. Many, like the Silváns and Gonzales families, would not be so lucky, their traveling plans quite different.

Agustína Hernández' entire life had revolved around her children, watching their childish curiosity grow, change to adulthood and later, to become parents. They were a closely-knit family and since her husband, Celestino Pedro Silván Dovales, had died she'd relied on her sons a great deal. Family loyalty and responsibility had clashed with the needs of the whole. Their growing frustrations and fears did not go unnoticed and her belly clenched with the unknown because *Fuentesaúco* and the surrounding village boundaries were the sum of her existence.

She sometimes stared at the far horizon wishing she were younger, stronger and richer. These were the times she missed her Celestino the most – those hours before sunset as she listened to her sons discuss a future she could not share. She would not leave the soil of her parents and their parents nor the parents before.

And she wouldn't leave Celestino. She visited his grave often; although it was marked only with a small cross… she knew his spirit was close. She always whispered prayers among the *composteria*, the cemetery, and in the church where she became his wife more than fifty years earlier. Now, she felt the sun setting on her soul. How would God ever ease her pain when watching two sons, her only living daughter, their spouses and her nine grandchildren go down the road away from *Fuentesaúco?* Her throat filled, her lips quivered. Her heart was breaking as she squeezed her eyes closed against the aching tears that fought their way through her thick lashes. She was taught to corral emotions but that day she threw that to the winds.

Agustín and Geronimo would stake their future on Spain; they would remain to care for the home place and their mother. Lorenzo was torn with indecision. Agustína never once entertained the idea of joining the exodus. She knew the boys were torn, wanting to follow their brothers and sister. But did they only pretend it was foolhardy to disagree with Victorino and Juan's leaving based on the promises of strangers? She knew her children. They were like bulls raring at the red capes. Maybe they drew the short straws? Maybe they lost the lottery between the brothers, who would stay and who would go? Maybe the angel of Celestino peeked through their windows and spoke to them? She cared not the reason. She would keep her remaining sons close. She was old. They'd have their chance to leave if they chose to do so after she joined her Celestino. One never knew what God had planned. But oh! She sagged against the window and gripped her thin arms. She looked upwards toward the winter moon as tears slid down her cheeks and dripped on the sill below.

While struggling with the heavy sadness of leaving their mother and siblings, the brother's smiles were wide and slow when the distant promise of a better future lured their baby sister, Crescéncia. She'd finally agreed with her husband, Felix Gonzales Hernández. Breathless with nervous anticipation, Crescéncia's heart had hammered when he'd outlined the life-changing move ahead of them. Clutching their two young boys, she'd begged her other brothers to go with them, thinking it might change her mother's mind to be part of the new life. But, they didn't budge.

Crescéncia looked out the window to the small garden plot, already missing her mother and the gardens she would leave behind. It was an ongoing storm of concern but she forced her thoughts to believe leaving was the best choice and pushed hopeful feelings into a deceptive lull. The rain had begun by then. It was not but a drizzle, yet the patter on the leaves was like listening to music. Her mind started to drift…

Felix touched her shoulder and saw the look in her blue eyes set below a mane of red-blond hair struggling for peace and whispered, "*Lo siento mucho, querida. Sé fuerte.*" I am so sorry, dear one. Have strength.

It took her a moment to bring her thoughts back, but her voice sounded normal when she answered. "*No hay otra opción ahora.*" There is no other option now.

Felix turned his wife into his arms, his actions speaking louder than words and held her there as a shroud of loneliness enveloped her.

« Febrero 1911 »

Lunes	Martes	Miércoles	Jueves	Viernes	Sábado	Domingo
		1	2	3	4	5
6	7	8	9	10	11	12
13	14	15	16	17	18	19
20	21	22	23	24	25	26
27	28					

The days sped by while the villagers packed their basic needs for a massive change in their lives and walked in droves to the alcalde's office with supporting documents. Sometimes it took several trips, some missing certain items, some forgetting a doctor's note was required, and others had to get military conscription paperwork. February was looming and they must be gone.

EMIGRATION PREPARATIONS

Despite their mind chatter, there was much to do. The Hawaiian government wanted proof that they had no outstanding debts and those of age had served their time in the armed forces for Spain. They needed birth and marriage certificates, a letter from the village alcalde (mayor) stating they were persons of good standing, a formal certificate stating their children were legitimate offspring and a statement from their doctor showing all were in good health to become good farm workers. Juan and Victorino met Don Emilio Ladron de Cegama, the Attorney and Deputy Municipal Justice for *Fuentesaúco* district and administrator of the Municipal Civil Registry on January 27, 1911. Afterward, they each held the required documents in their hands, signed by the secretary, Julio Corrales.

As the ink dried on our ancestor's document, many of their friends met with the alcalde, securing their documentation, preparing to pack up their families. They were related through Ramona Martinez Lorenzo to Enrique Martin Gonzalez and Felipa

Sesmilo Alejo, whose family included Antonia, Juliana, María and Simon.   Enrique was often a part of those long discussions that ran into the night.   The documentation Enrique needed was also stored safely away for the day they would climb on the boat they'd been told would be waiting to leave the third week of February.

And then Lorenzo caved.   Despite loving his mother as much as his brothers and sister, his brain hummed.   The plantations accepted only healthy men and he hoped a limp would go unnoticed.   He folded the signed document amid the scramble of packing just inside the door and stared at his mother's trembling lips.

Edmundo Silván Hernández, (Mundo) had listened gravely to all the conversation, watched his brothers and Felix gather the required paperwork, studied the logic after long discussions with the Martin and Alva families as well --- and when he spoke of South America instead of Hawaii, conversation stopped; everyone looked at him blankly.

But why South America?   Some single men had ventured south for work either in the fields or the ranches... Five years younger than Juan, Mundo felt adventure scrambling his loyalties just like his brothers.   Somehow the lure of gauchos and bolos was more inviting than sugar cane.

As he saw their personal belongings packed into the wagon, his dream wavered looking at his mother's face.   He knew his brother was right; it was the destination he focused on.   He would come back after earning money but would his reasoning smooth the worry lines off of Agustína's face or the scowls from those who heard his plan.

B. 7.821.474

Don Emilio Castor de Cegama, Abogado, Juez Municipal Suplente en funciones del Distrito de ésta villa de Fuentesaúco y encargado del Registro Civil de la misma.

Certifico: Que según aparece de los antecedentes suministrados por las dependencias de la administración municipal y de los Libros del Registro Civil de mi cargo ====

Juan Francisco Silban Hernández, natural y domiciliado en esta villa, hijo legítimo de Celestino Silban y Faustina Hernández, contrajo matrimonio en la Iglesia parroquial de Santa María de ésta villa, con Custodia Rita Trascasas Marzo, natural de Cañó hija legítima de Manuel Trascasas y de Manuela Marzo, á las ocho de la mañana del día veinte y tres de Abril de mil novecientos; según aparece en el tomo 9º de matrimonios, al folio 14 º puesto, señalado con el número 12 ====

Que Manuela Silban Trascasas, hija legítima de Juan Silban Hernández, natural y domiciliado en esta villa y de Custodia Rita Trascasas Marzo, natural de Cañó, nieta por línea paterna de Celestino Silban y de Faustina Hernández y nieta por línea materna de Manuel Trascasas y Manuela Marzo, nació en esta villa á las veinte y tres y media del día veinte y uno de Junio de mil novecientos uno; inscripción número 23 folio 316, del Libro 1º de nacimientos. ====

Para los efectos que concernían á Juan Francisco Silban Hernández, para los efectos de emigrar, expido la presente sella...

6/25/1901

63

Translation of Document B. 7.821.474[16]

Don Emilio Ladron de Cegama, Attorney and Deputy Municipal Justice for the district of this village of *Fuentesaúco* and administrator of the Municipal Civil Registry of said district certifies to the following:

Certificate: That according to the entries recorded in the archives of the Civil Registry.

Juan Francisco Silban Hernández, native and resident of this village, natural son of **Celestino Silban** and **Agustína Hernández,** married **Eustoquia Rita Trascasas Marzo** a native and resident of the village of *Toro*, natural daughter of **Manuel Trascasas** and of **Manuela Marzo**. The marriage ceremony took place at the parochial church of *Santa María* in the same village on 23 of April in 1900 at 8:00 a.m. as recorded in the matrimonial volume 7, page 149, column 12 of the Registry.

That **Manuela Silban Trascasas** natural daughter of **Juan Francisco Silban Hernández,** a native and resident of this village and **Eustoquia Rita Trascasas Marzo**, a native and resident of the village of *Toro*, and paternal granddaughter of **Celestino Silban** and **Agustína Hernández,** maternal granddaughter of **Manuel Trascasas** and **Manuela Marzo**, was born in this village at 3:20 p.m. on 25 June 1901 as recorded in the birth volume 93, page 346, column 15.

I grant this statement at the request of **Juan Francisco Silban Hernández** for immigration purposes. The Municipal Justice of *Fuentesaúco* has affixed his Seal of Office on this 27th day of January, 1911.

Signed: Julio Corrales

The Secretary

---

[16] See certificate for Victorino Silban Hernandez and Romana Martin Lorenzo

As the Silván children watched their parents pivot between happiness and sadness and back again, they rejoiced in the fact they would have many of their cousins and friends with them. Among them were Felisa Silván and Juliana Martin, cousins and best friends. Even though Manuela was nearly two years older than Antonia Martin, they often sat together, murmuring and watching those around them along with her older cousin, Teodora Silván. During the voyage to Hawaii these children would cement their friendship further with shared losses.

The amount of baggage would be severely limited on board the ship. Which of their prized possessions should they take? Fear stalled excitement; clothing, cooking utensils, pots along with garbanzo beans, grapevine starts and flower seeds. As they packed their meager belongings, they included a few mementos, pictures and their small cache of jewelry early in February, 1911. Rita pushed aside the cook pot and stuffed a beautiful long skirt into the folds of the bag, her mother's wedding dress. It was a softened pale gold with a bustle that was nearly gone with age. It was silk with strips of beautiful embroidery from the tiny tucked waistband to the hem.

Everything was packed with great care; all bundled as tightly and thriftily as possible along with Juan's drum inside a case to ward off the weather. It would be readily available deep into the evenings on their trek from *Sanlúcar*. Singing and playing *el bombo* was a way of life he would forever hold dear; his family couldn't imagine life without it; there was no question of leaving it behind and it fit into their trunk snugly.

Victorino's and Crescéncia's families packed similar items and the five-year old twins, Jacinto and Celestino, helped drag the filled bags for their sisters, Teodora and Felisa. They were small boys but determined to be part of the preparations. Their parents fought smiles as the boys pushed and puffed, pulling the load in front for a while and then huffing and trying to push the packages from behind. Everyone helped each other and the children made a game of it, laughing and playing. They would not realize the distance and possibility of never returning until much later. For now, it was an unparalleled adventure.

The families were ready and several goodbye visits lay ahead. Juan and Rita bundled up their children in the horse and buggy that would carry them southeast about six miles to *Villaescusa*. From this village, came Ángel Silván  Martin (who married María Dovales Alejo, the father of Celestino Pedro Silván Dovales, Juan's paternal grandfather) and Margarita Martin Rodriguez, his maternal grandmother (mother of Agustína Hernández Martin). It was a farming community where each small house fit together like playing blocks; a church at its center and the cemetery behind.

They entered the village, with its tightly-clustered whitewashed houses and its twisting streets so narrow the pedestrians hugged the wall to let the horse and buggy pass. The entrance road was sparsely lined with a few separate houses but when they entered into the old part of the village, everything changed. Slowing a bit, they found a few old gentlemen sitting in their tiny Plaza Mayor just before the ayuntamiento. Dogs barked while a woman in a flowered dress hung laundry above them where she stood on a beautiful balcony nearby. Sniffing the air appreciatively and watching the play of light on the fields around them, Juan felt the friendly silence follow the family as the buggy lurched forward.

The ancient church stood in its own little corner, with white houses abutting the crux of avenues that intersected before them. The church was graceful, built with stone bricks in the front and cemented smaller stones at the back end. Arched, worn-wood doors hung below a tall pointed pinnacle with a massive cigüeña nest securely sharing the bell tower.

Juan made a clicking sound with his mouth and the wagon clip-clopped past the church and slipped behind it to follow the solitary road that ran into farmland. And there it was. Juan Francisco Silván embraced it all.

Several generations from the Silván family started there and some ended. The setting was pastoral and quiet. Juan drove silently through the gate and the family walked up the slight inclining road toward the gated cemetery. It was a peaceful place.

Standing headstones stretched in loosely-structured rows though some were old and weathered, spotted white with lichen; some leaned and some had fallen altogether with their age. There were graves marked beside hard stones, bricks, while steel railings bordered others.   Rita held José while Manuela pulled Agustín along beside her. Juan led them the length and breadth of the small cemetery toward the resting places for Silván, Martin, Alejo, Dovales and Rodriguez.   There were crosses marking their spots; no stones, but they felt touched and loved as they poked through the narrow openings.   He knew they were all there and he would probably never be able to say a prayer over them again.

Leaving quietly after jamming the lopsided gate's bar back into place, he felt his family's aura embrace them as they stepped away.   Back in the wagon, they followed the small, twisting streets while its cluster of houses appeared like a mirage; one could almost imagine the wavering edges, blurry and hidden as they nosed the horse through its strangely laid grid of streets.

And then they were suddenly on the road toward *Villamor de los Escuderos* beyond *Fuentesaúco* for the second of their three goodbye trips.

Agustína Hernández Martin was born in Villamor, as was her father and those before him.   The road was longer and the land lay flatter as the road curved away from *Fuentesaúco* toward the northwest about four miles beyond the bullring at the edge of town. The village was only slightly larger than *Villaescusa*, friendly and welcoming.   The church steeple could be seen from the main road as Juan guided the horse toward the spire and an old stone church rose above them.   There was only one church and cemetery in the village.

The stones were ochre; golden yellow with a touch of umber in every direction.   Close behind the church sat the cemetery…and a locked gate.   Shaking it a bit, Juan rattled it open and the family slipped through.

Juan walked toward his grandfather's gravestone. Miguel Hernández Hernández was the father to the Silván family's mother, Agustína Hernández Martin, also born in *Villamor*. Although Celestino Silván took her to *Fuentesaúco* after their marriage to live and raise their children, Agustína's  roots would always whisper home in this place.

The cemetery held many ancestors in the soil around them and walking through the graveyard gave them a prickle within its old stone walls.   Too poor for etched stones, they knew where his people were buried.   Manuela nudged Agustín's head down as her family shared a few spiritual moments, took some photos in their minds and returned to *Fuentesaúco*, melancholy and quiet.   Those spiritual goodbyes would follow them always.

Their last goodbye would take place the next day in *Toro*, the village of Rita's family; that would be harder since there were living relatives there and leaving them would slap them with the reality of their decision.   Tomorrow would be soon enough as it was farther to *Toro* and they would spend the day and night there.

THE ROAD TO *TORO* was awash with mud but the family braved the weather to be part of the family gathering.   *Toro* was twenty four miles northwest from her house in *Fuentesaúco* and it was a very long ride in the wagon.   It was chilly that early morning when they climbed into the wagon but blankets and boxes surrounded them to keep the cool breeze off their faces.

Agustín grinned; another adventure.   Manuela held a squirming José while her own excitement mounted. She loved going to *Toro* where the cobblestone streets led beneath arches into the village that sat high on the mountain top. The town of *Toro* is built in the shape of a fan, in whose center stands the Collegiate Church of Santa María la Mayor during the 12th century. People from *Toro* are called *toresanos*. Its wines were the first to be taken to America by Christopher Columbus in the ship, Pinta, which was

half filled with the *Toro* wine.

Always, as they came closer and the massive church came

into view, she would begin to sing, "*Veo la casa de la abuela. Veo la casa de la abuela. Veo la casa de la abuela.*" I see grandmother's house... Her mother always laughed and Agustín would climb higher so he could see also. But that day her mother didn't laugh. Instead, she swung her head to look at Manuela with wet eyes and squeezed her daughter's shoulder.

The bell was ringing loudly in the tower when the horse pulled the buggy beneath its archway heading toward the *Calle Doctor de Olivares* near the *Iglesia de Santo Tomas*. When they arrived, she saw her cousin jump wildly when they pulled up in front of the home.

A special treat waited and made her mother smile: a photographer was coming!

But first they would eat.

Rita Silván's tio (uncle) José Marzo and his daughter, Manuela, ushered the visitors into the room where his widowed sister, Manuela Marzo Garcia, waited. She was fifty six years old and diabetes had withered her health. To honor her, Jose and Rita both named their daughters Manuela. It made for a rousing household when anyone wanted their attention, especially since Jose's Manuela also named her daughter Manuela....... Manuela! Four heads swiveled.

That day was somber but the food, as always, covered the table and brought camaraderie to the group, as it is most Spanish families' answer to every occasion. Eggs, fresh-baked bread, milk from their goats, bacon and potatoes waited. And the sweets were covered on a sideboard for later with their afternoon coffee.

Juan gripped José Marzo's hand. José didn't agree with his nephew's decision to leave, just as he hadn't agreed back in 1907 when the conversations first began zipping through the family.   He would miss his niece, Rita, and the men stared at one another hard before José nodded in defeat.

The adult cousins, Rita and Manuela held their hands to their hearts, misty eyed and quiet. Both young Manuela cousins held one another tightly as tears seeped out of their tightly-closed eyelids. They were best friends and neither could imagine life without the other. Hawaii was far, far from their homes and the distance seemed insurmountable, unimaginable. Another world. It could have been the moon.

After their meal, the photographer's knock lightened the mood and everyone chattered while he brought the camera and black box into the house. Agustín, José and the girls stood shyly but they stretched to stare; they didn't want to miss seeing the strange items he lifted from his bag.

Within minutes, a black drape covered the man's head and his camera. The girls stood together, hands entwined like grapevines. The man kept repeating, *"No se muevan!"* Do not move. And he frightened them into statues. That photo would one day become a memorable piece of history but that is for another story.

Our Manuela listened as the adults talked far into the night. She heard her mother and grandmother cry and the men and her aunt whispering in between. Her chest hurt and she covered her ears to stop the sadness from sliding into her mind; there were so many goodbyes!

The next morning, her grandmother pulled Manuela near her chair to place a ball of yarn, a crochet needle and a small doily square into her hands.   She held her granddaughter's hand tightly with a trembling fist.

"Always keep your hands busy, Manuela.   Crochet just a little on this doily every day and you will learn to create beautiful things.   It is all I can give to you to remember me and I will crochet here and think of you doing this across the ocean.   Do not ever stop crocheting and I will smile at my memory of you and this day to stop the tears."

Manuela's heart lurched as she promised her grandmother, hugged her aunt, uncle and pressed her cousin tightly to her before joining her family in the wagon for the leaving.   In her pocket, she held a well-worn family photograph to keep safe and remember from her Tia Manuela.

Juan's horse pulled them to the cemetery where they once again said their prayers over the gravestones of their ancestors.   Rita shook her head to dispel the agony of visiting her family's graves for the last time.   Her father,   Manuel   Trascasas Alonso, was buried near her Godfather, tio Jacinto.   And then her sister's grave on the other side.

Manuela looked at the many rocks covering the dirt where her grandfather   and   uncles   were buried.   The Madonna statue stood over   Manuel   Trascasas'   grave

73

where Rita had placed it so long ago. She had trouble walking away until Juan nudged her with a hand to her shoulder. Rita turned to Manuela and pointed to another, smaller grave near the fence.

"Tu tia, your aunt, Jacinta Modesta," Rita whispered. "It *is* important to remember."

The family walked to the fence, the mud caked onto their shoes but they hardly noticed. They said their goodbye to the Trascasas and Marzo family ghosts that day; Rita especially remembered her little sister, a wonderful child who died just shy of her ninth birthday.

The gravestone for Rita's grandfather was etched with barely discernible letters. Santiago Diogracias Trascasas Conejo. Beside him lay her grandmother, María Alonso de la Vega. She could not make her mind believe she was leaving all the graves, all the family.

Our Manuela glanced around and bent quickly to pick up two rocks; the first from the area where her grandfather, Manuel Trascasas, was buried, the second near an aunt she'd never known. She would keep them with the photograph her Tia Manuela promised to send to faraway Hawaii when it was printed. She stopped to stare at the rocks in the palm of her hand. She would have only two rocks and one photograph. Gripping her skirts with her closed fist, she followed her family where the horse stood impatiently. She would not cry, she promised. She would not cry.

The families would write letters. Someone would help her send a letter. She could not lose complete touch with her family.

Tomás Toribio Trascasas Alonso was the last stop. Her uncle was her father's youngest brother and the aunts and cousins had given up begging Juan to remain in Spain. Rita felt their perplexed anger over the decision to leave but Juan had continued to stand firm and the families ached through their goodbye visit. More food, more hugs, more tears.

Before finally leaving the *Toro*, Rita wanted to say a prayer in the place that was her spiritual home since she was born, *Church of St. Thomas Cantuariense*. By unspoken agreement, Juan drove the short distance to the church where she and her sister were baptized. Rita led the way and clasped her son's hand, little José in his father's arms, Manuela shuffling in behind.

THE LEAVING

The day had finally arrived --- Agustína's living nightmare. There were three women, four men and nine children, the youngest still in diapers, the eldest on the brink of womanhood; eighty nine total from their pueblo in Fuentesaúco.

She squeezed the bridge of her nose and heaved a deep breath.   She felt hollow, numb to her core and drenched in sorrow. She memorized the dear sweet face of her baby girl, Crescéncia, as her daughter quietly surveyed the home she grew up in before walking into her mother's open arms.

"*Madre*," she whispered achingly, devastated. Would she ever see her mother again?   Caressing her mother's back, she kissed her neck and rocked, wracked with guilt.

Agustína held her daughter's quaking body tightly to her own and squeezed her until she feared broken bones.   Their throats burned, their chests ached as if a stone was lodged within.   "*Si, mi hija.   Yo te amo,*" Agustína cried, broken. Yes, my daughter.   I love you.

Next, Agustína's son stood tall before her, his black felt hat squeezed firmly between his callused fingers.   Victorino's eyes glistened as he tossed it and wrapped his arms tightly around his mother and prayed to God he would, indeed, see her again.   He'd given up asking her to go. They both knew she could never make the hard trip ahead of them and the Hawaiian government would not pay the 400 pesetas[17] for a boat ticket since she was over forty five. His heart jerked. She patted his back and kissed each of his weathered cheeks. She looked upward and stared into his deep brown eyes and nodded. He'd made the right decision and she respected his commitment to attain a successful life. She must allow him to believe it, so she smiled when he responded to her message of understanding by nodding solemnly in return.

Victorino picked up his hat and blindly made room for Juan and Lorenzo, who went through similar heart-wrenching goodbyes and then the women took turns hugging their goodbyes. Rita and Ramona talked quietly to their mother-in-law until there were no free moments left. They'd already had a tear-jerking leaving of their own families and they were unsure if their hearts could hold the grief. Then the children swarmed around their abuela and uncles to be caught up in fierce hugs. Promises were made to never forget those they left behind.

Those staying in Spain were forced to accept their loss; some were angry, others unsure as they watched the entourage gather with small trunks and packs wrapped in heavy fabric. Gripping tightly to trunk handles, the brothers led their wives, Eustoquia Rita Trascasas Marzo and Ramona Martinez Lorenzo, and their children to the appointed wagon. The children were aged 12, 9, 7, 5-year

---

[17]In 1911, 400 pesetas equaled about $80. The peseta was introduced in 1869 after Spain joined the Latin Monetary Union in 1868. The Spanish Law of June 26, 1864 decreed that in preparation for joining the Latin Monetary Union (set up in 1865), the peseta became a subdivision of the peso. 1 peso duro = 5 pesetas. The peseta replaced the escudo= 5 pesetas = 1 peso duro = 2 escudos. The peseta was equal to 4.5 grams of silver or 0.290322 grams of gold, the standard used by all the currencies of the Latin Monetary Union. From 1873, only the gold standard applied.

old twin boys, a 3-year old and a 10-month old baby.   Felix and Crescéncia followed closely with their two children, Alejandro, age 3 and Juanito, age 2; their bags tied together and luggage handles also gripped in white-knuckled fists.   Lorenzo brought up the rear with his single bedraggled piece of baggage, his heavy coat swirling around him.

Their brothers were somber.   Geronimo helped load the women and children and Agustín drove the wagon as the neighbor's donkey strained to pull the weight in the quiet glow of the morning street.   They would buy a cart for the last leg toward La Línea when they got off the boat in Sanlúcar.   Their brother, friends and cousins waved sadly; crying could be heard among the crowd as they turned inward and returned to their own homes.

"*Vayan con Dios,*" Agustína murmured and exhaled deeply. Go with God.   As she watched, eyes that had blinked against countless tears squinted narrowly down the street at the edge of town and the horizon beyond.   "*Madre de Dios......*" She trailed off drawing herself in.   She'd kept trying to turn the clock back to the time before the talk of Hawaii had ripped their lives apart.   Yet reality kept imposing itself.   She dreaded the prospect of the quiet house without these children, the sharing of stories and the sight of her sons coming in from the gardens.   What was home without Victorino, Juan, Lorenzo and Crescéncia?   Would Mundo really leave her too?   Would her life feel empty again as when her husband, Celestino, died?

She hunkered down into the rocker in front of her door on Calle San Salvador.   She would survive again she told herself as she gripped the arms and began to rock back and forth, back and forth, her legs dangling over the edge of the chair.   Somehow she would put one foot in front of the other and would struggle through the weeks and years ahead. She rubbed her throbbing eyes and thought back to a time when she didn't feel so helpless.

She flicked through the pages of their childhood in her mind like a thirsty one at the fountain. She had been so blessed! She saw a sixteen-year old Victorino hanging upside-down in the olive tree behind the house with nine-year old Juan asking for a lift up. Victorino was laughing, refusing to help his younger brother, wanting to be king of the mountain. Juan had run to the tree's trunk and proceeded to climb upward, only to fall, scraping his shins and his neck to bleeding but he hadn't given up. He carried the scar on the back of his neck still. Up he climbed again and that time he made it, gratified to see Victorino's scowl. Geronimo, two years younger than Juan, laughed at his elder brother's discomfort.

Lorenzo, then four years old, had followed Juan, angry when he couldn't join his brothers, kicking the tree and crying. His face was dirty with tears and it was Juan who jumped down to wipe his face and tickled him into laughter. Ángel just stood and watched his little sister enjoy it all. Crescéncia, just learning to walk, had clapped her hands, entertained by the scene and walked unevenly around the olive tree and along the garden edges looking like a wine-soaked drunk.

She smiled at the recollection, their long-ago words musical in her mind and tried to hold the moment before turning to memories of her daughter and the waif she had been as a small child. She learned how to make *rosquetas* and *mantecados* (cookies) before she was six, could slop the pigs alongside her brothers before she was seven and stitched perfect seams alongside adults. She loved to cook, could make a stew of garbanzo beans, greens and vegetables and made it taste like heaven... She was such a good girl.   After losing her first daughter, Agapita, she ached with yearning to see Crescéncia grow older...

When she turned her memories to her grandchildren, her breath caught and she swallowed hastily.   She pressed her hand to her chest, leaned back against the chair's headboard, closed her eyes and resumed rocking.

She was more than worried for her children.   She'd lied to herself for weeks before admitting the merits of leaving outweighed the fruitlessness of staying.   For her grandchildren, she knew they would have a better life, one without deprivation or the whispered fears that lingered in Spain and the sons she would still hold close.   Thank God Agustín, Mundo (Edmundo) and Geronimo would remain behind.   At least for now.

Her eyes burned.   She went inside and listened to the quiet, watched dust motes stream in the window on a ray of sunshine and heard the pigs rooting out back.   Standing in the doorway, she looked at the long street imagining dots on the horizon that were her children.   Turning from the aching visualization, she covered her face with both hands to stifle sobs but could not stop the torrent that followed.

RIDING THE RAILS TO *SEVILLA*

It was February, a month of hope as it pushes away the dark days of winter, bringing more sunlight.   Each year when February arrived, they knew spring was waiting in the wings, the worst must be over.   The sun would get warmer and flowers would awaken and push their green tips up through the cool earth.

During the past week, nearly eighty members of *Fuentesaúco* along with meager belongings left sporadically.

Now it was the Silvan's turn.   Their adventure began as the sun broke over the horizon; a light dust of rime coated the ground. The air was sparked with tension and excitement.

Just outside *Fuentesaúco* lie the *Sierra de Gredos*, a montage of mountainous peaks, thundering waterfalls, verdant plains, fragrant fruit orchards and glacial lagoons. The *Pico Almanzor* is the highest mountain peak in central Spain, 8,504 feet high, made of granite.   They offer a glorious mix of Alpine and Mediterranean scenery: olive groves, jagged mountains, fragrant lemon trees and abundant bird life.

The main road out of *Fuentesaúco* was dusty and narrow. The siblings decided to ride a train through those treacherous mountains; they agreed walking would be impossible for themselves and their family. Pooling their money, they'd saved enough for their thrifty travel, food along the way and the boat tickets from *Sevilla* that would take them as far as Sanlúcar to the south.

After stashing their train tickets at the Salamanca train station, the brothers hugged one another goodbye. Leaving their mother had been difficult, but their hope was to see these brothers also leave Spain to join them eventually.

Agustín talked about leaving one day but Geronimo was silent, watching his family walk across the train station's platform away from him. And remembering Edmundo's talk about going to South America didn't bode well for them.

The men were anxious to return to their mother. She would need them now more than before. The two brothers turned the wagon, markedly subdued and silent all the way home, shaking their heads and sighing loudly at their sibling's daunting odds.

It would be the Silván s first experience in a Spanish railroad car. In Spain the railroad gauge is five feet, six inches and very spacious and clean. It was hard to get into, with steep narrow footholds worse than flights of steps; and no ample racks. They were given an allowance of a hundred and thirty-two pounds free and their excess baggage in two medium trunks cost approximately 14 pesetas.

The train was immense, noisy, loud and fascinating. At first, Manuela thought her stomach would tumble her breakfast as she bounced and stared out the window, mesmerized and excited.

As the train took its time mounting the countryside toward *Sevilla* that early February morning, the air that rushed through the slightly-open window breathed as if from a spring morning and warm soothing sunlight streamed through the windows.

She thought of a village she would leave forever behind her, a village where so great a part of her life had passed. And in that magical air the butterflies in her belly blended in a fascinated blur. Her youth dwelled on her loss for some moments and linked into the enchanted flicker from the past which had given her shelter. And then something caught her eye and her melancholy mood vanished.

In that dignified and deliberate Spanish train, the families of Celestino Silván and Agustína Hernandez crossed the last sweet hills of their past and flew on their unguided way as if through some Spanish story. From its car window, they saw olive groves and white cottages of Spanish peasants and meadows stretching to the woods that walled drowsing villages. As the morning deepened, the train slipped slowly from the hills.

They felt the bondage of love for Spain and ached with the fear of leaving it. Not for an instant could they have imagined that their journey would be researched and written down nearly a hundred years later by their descendants.

Manuela ignored Agustín and José's chattering as her world sped by. She could not pretend her heart was completely in the trip as the train began to slope rather more rapidly toward the valley as it found its way over the hills. But when she saw castles and stone churches her interest mounted. Suddenly, she felt in harmony with the family as they made their Spanish journey together, while dreaming of tomorrow. But would her life ever be calm again?   Would she ever see Manuela Marzo or *Toro* again? Her abuelitas?   Her uncles, aunts and other cousins?

The train was called a *rapido* in Spain; and though they were devouring miles at twenty five miles per hour, Manuela did not miss a detail of the scenery.   In the first few hours, they ran through valleys that embraced gentle hills with groves of chestnut trees. There were no vineyards, but orchards aplenty.   The houses were gathered in villages around a tall church below bell-towers.   From time to time a mountain stream crawled from under a bridge and then spread a quiet tide for women to kneel beside it and wash the clothes and spread to dry on bushes along the banks.

It had taken their train nearly an hour to get by the pretty hamlets. But that was fast for a Spanish train, which does not run but walks with dignity as it made long stops at stations, to rest and let the locomotive roll at idle

MANUELA SILVÁN TRASCASAS

85

Nine-year old Manuela was brown-eyed with a small sun-drenched face. She hadn't had time to be a child. Her little brothers needed her to do any number of chores for them. Despite her age, she helped with their breakfast, learned how to cook and mix and knead bread. She'd milked goats, chased pigs, emptied buckets of kitchen garbage and learned to wash laundry and crochet pretties without a pattern.

In spite of the work load, she would still find bits of time for music and dancing. Her mother, Rita, and her aunts, Ramona and Crescéncia, were her best teachers. Pulling her skirts to her shins and swaying to the beat of her father's drum, she'd learned to dance beside the women and the memories of those sweet days lingered. Tia Ramona danced at every opportunity so where there was music, she knew there would be dancing. And Ramona's younger daughter, Felisa, was right there beside them, watching, smiling and dancing. She left her sister, Teodora in the dust, who seemed disinclined to lose herself in music.

The dancing and music couldn't change! Manuela's mind rattled the words as she gazed sideways at the women quietly gripping bags and nudging children.

Excitement assaulted the child's senses as she propped up her youngest brother, José, in the coziest corner of the car and tried to keep him still, but he would not keep silent. In fact, everyone babbled above the luncheon basket her Tia Ramona opened after springing up a table-leaf by the window. They watched her spread out pieces of *chorizo, olivas* (olives) and tempting dried fruit: *cerezas* (cherries) and *higos* (figs). As she brought out these victuals, together with a Bota[18] of *vino* (wine) and a bottle of milk, she offered it to her husband, Victorino. When it was duly refused, she made the children eat and drink, especially the milk.

Eating a meal among chickens and a goat tied nearby was an experience that made them laugh, every one.

AS MANUELA RODE the train, she munched on her food and studied the beautiful scenery. She saw grassy valleys with white cattle grazing, fields of Indian corn and apple orchards. The hillsides were often terraced; cork-trees, groves by the green boundaries of mountain brooks and vineyards reddening up to the doors of distant farmhouses.

Afterward, everyone asked how long their train ride would last. When must they get off and their walk begin? The men created a good deal of pleasant excitement by making a game of it. When the conductor yelled the village name at each station stop, the children's heads swung to their father's faces. Now? Now?

With the business of packing their meager belongings, the many goodbyes and trying to imagine the train and then actually riding on one, Manuela hadn't had time to be afraid. The boat, the ocean and Hawaii? That was another story. She could visualize a train but she'd never seen the ocean. Listening to the villagers and her family discussing the broadsheet about had Hawaii sounded like a different world; one she could not fathom.

During one of the stops, Manuela saw a girl who looked like young Manuela Marzo. Her heart skipped a beat and she leaned

---

[18] Bota wine bag is iconic of Spain. Historically, hand-stitched goat skins created wine botas. They were used to carry and drink wine for thousands of years. The traditional bota is sealed with pine pitch, and with proper care will last a lifetime

her face nearer the window. She tapped on the glass to attract her attention but when the girl turned toward the noise, Manuela shrank back into her seat. A stranger peered up into the train and her throat clogged. She suddenly ached with loneliness. What was abuelita doing? Was she still crying and pretending the tears didn't slide from her eyes? Was she still rocking? Were tio Geronimo, tio Mundo and tio Agustín helping her to feel better? And abuelita in *Toro*… was she still crocheting and thinking of her too? She ached.

She tried not to think about her cousin, Manuela. It was too sad. She would miss her too much. The old family photo crinkled inside her pocket. Huddling on the train bench, her forehead wrinkled with the memory of the day it was taken when everyone had laughed so much together.

Listlessly, she watched buildings and trees drift by. They crossed a bridge over sparkling water. Where were they going? Papa didn't know exactly. Nobody knew exactly. And she sensed they were all a little afraid. Sitting on the edge of her seat, she pressed her nose against the window as the train sped south. And her small forehead gently bumped the glass while unplanned moments waited.

She glanced under the bench across from her seat and studied the box holding her father's drum, *el bombo*. She'd learned to dance to the beat of his drum as soon as she could toddle across the floor. She laughed to herself when she remembered the first time she'd surprised him by creating her own tunes using a spoon beating against the table. At times, her mother clucked about her daughter's insatiable desire to sing and dance but then remembered that's what charmed her so long ago: Juan Silván and the music.

One day Manuela had burst out yodeling. She remembered stunned faces and other memories juggled through her brain. Manuela chuckled.

Agustín looked at her, clearly startled.

She adored both her brothers. Agustín followed her around like a shadow and turned to his big sister for meals, to soothe his hurts and entertainment. José was only ten months old when their world was turned upside down, but she carried the babe on her slim hip as her mother had gathered, packed and generally readied her family for the move into the unknown.

Rita expected much from Manuela and her little daughter tried to do as she was told. But there were times when Manuela wanted to stomp her foot and run down the road with her arms swinging to the sky. It was a rare moment when time was hers to do with as she chose. Maybe Hawaii would be different. Her father told her there may be a little garden where she could grow flowers. And maybe she could get another pig. She'd missed the one they had to trade away for food, fuel and dinero for the train. A pig and a garden! Yes. She tried to focus away from her abuela rocking back and forth on the rocking chair with wet eyes and her mouth moving funny when she thought nobody was watching.

Suddenly, her twin cousins, Jacinto and Celestino squealed, "*Vacas!*" Cows lazed beneath trees and the boys jumped and pointed. Victorino's arm kept them from falling off the bench when the train jerked and pulled Agustín, Alejandro and Juanito up beside them. Manuela grimaced as she stopped José from crawling over her lap and up the twins back for a look of his own.

She gripped the bundle wrapped in the square of table cloth

that she, like other Spanish girls and women, carried on their heads when they walked to leave their hands free. It was filled with crochet thread, clean undergarments, handkerchiefs, wash cloths and a towel with soap she'd inserted inside a crocheted pocket shaped like a frog. It was one of the first detailed crocheted projects she'd actually finished.

After José settled, she rummaged inside her bag. They were still there; a hard slate and book. Even though she couldn't read, she looked at the pictures or drew on her slate. Teodora often guided her hands to write and she recognized letters. She lovingly smoothed her fingers over the cover.

Teodora and Felisa shared with cousin, Juliana Martin, but if a smaller child reached for them, the girls held them safely beyond their reach and shook their heads, no!

THE TRAIN JOURNEY

The train stations began to blur. The plateau changed dramatically and hundreds of puffy-round trees covered the area for miles. These were carob trees[19] she'd been told and the seeds fed many starving Spaniards through history.

She wondered if they would eat them on that long walk she kept hearing about...

Wind suddenly buffeted the train car and her stomach

---

[19] Locust bean gum (also known as carob gum, carob bean gum) is a vegetable gum extracted from the seeds of the carob tree, mostly found in the Mediterranean region. The long pods that grow on the tree are used to make this gum. The pods are kibbled to separate the seed from the pulp. A seed is then split and gently milled, to produce the final locust bean gum powder. Locust bean gum occurs as a white to yellow-white powder. The bean, when made into powder, is sweet—with a flavor similar to chocolate—and is used to sweeten foods and as a chocolate substitute. It is soluble in hot water.

wobbled.   The chickens squawked and the goat stood his ground. Hands gripped benches and children and then relaxed as the train rode smoothly once again.

Just before *Béjar* the hills became mountains again.   In, out, over and around the mountains… There were so many --- too many to count.   As the train rumbled through one of the villages, she saw two gigantic birds gracefully swoop over the roof nesting atop a stone face jutting from a church bell tower.

The old man gripped the bench across from her, saw her watching them intently and explained that the cigüeña migrates all the way from Scandinavia to Spain every year with its lifelong mate--2500 kilometers with no rest[20]. He said it made a clicking noise but she could not hear it for the train.

Then she saw the rocks.   Millions of flat rocks piled into miles of stacked walls.   The rocks were embedded into mountainsides, dry stacked in ridged fences at angles beside and away from the train as if they were drawn with a child's pencil. The stones began to change, growing larger, rounder and piled higher.

Manuela and Felisa edged closer to each other and shared a view without blinking.   The country so far from home was amazing and they didn't want to miss anything.   The girls were not the only family members with their faces pressed to the windows; the adults juggled children and baggage as scenery slipped by.

By the time *Béjar* finally came into view, pine trees clotted the mountainsides; the train belched and noisily trudged south again among terraced hills.   They held their breath just before *Plasencia*

---

[20] Source: Under the Clock by Rafaela Molina, P. 32 – Cigüeña = Stork

where miles of panorama took them into *Tras la Sierra Mountain* range near the Rio Jerte.

The train swayed into the plains before *Canaveral* moving closer to *Plasencia.* The Sierra de Los Ángeles Mountain range rose above them by then and the train was stuffy with the overwhelming smells of so many beings crushed together. The girls wished they could open the window again but were told the brisk air would be bad for José, who was not feeling well, didn't like being held tightly and sometimes whimpered with discomfort.

They levered themselves upward on the baggage to retain their view of the passing world around them. Adults craned their necks to view the mountains, rivers, orchards and especially the stations as they stopped to disgorge travelers and let others on.

Photo: 1900s Train replica in museum at Plaza de España in Sevilla

A fellow traveler pointed in the direction of the Plaza Mayor in Plasencia where a market had been held continuously since the 12th century. The children were fascinated when a giant elf in a clock tower struck the bell to mark the half hour as the train jerked away again.

Soon afterward, *Caceres* and *Mérida* stations loaded more travelers. Manuela stared them from the bench seat, her small hands gripping the smudged window sill. Noise filled the rail car. The land flattened.

Olive trees. Almond trees. Grapevines. Orchards across the mountainsides, a large hacienda wedged at its center. The girls stared and swiveled toward their parents. Had they noticed? Yes, of course, everyone stared; none of those poor farmers had ever seen the like.

Las Santos de Maimona near *Zafra* was a small village reminding Manuela of home. Her throat clogged and she squeezed her eyes closed. When she opened them, her mother gave her a look that said she understood; she'd also lost the life left behind. Manuela swallowed.

The trees disappeared along with the grapevines. The landscape became dryer, less lush; mountains still surrounded the train as it wove its way toward *Sevilla* but the hills were colored; more yellow. Suddenly, a canopy of forested trees popped up as they drifted below the mountains into a valley called *Arroyo de Culebrin*.

As the station came into view, the train chugged to a noisy stop at *Santiponce*, just north of *Sevilla*. Inside the train car, the air was thick with smoke, tired and crying children, twitching passengers, sore butts and anticipation.

And then they saw it. An ancient castle stood above the village of white houses with tall Roman columns, some broken with time, some reaching toward the sky. People chattered around them. Chickens squawked and ruffled their feathers. Tall, slender trees and clusters of bushes circled the area and despite their perches inside the train, their view was stunning. It was called Itálica, with underground tunnels, courtyards and multiple stone buildings plus the impressive *Monasterio de San Isidoro del Campo*. The wonders never ceased to amaze.

Then they were moving again. The air swooshed as the train departed with a clang, a man's loud voice rang out, *"Pasajeros, al tren!"*

Clearly startled, the tired and sleepy children jumped before slumping onto the benches again. The clock's hand had already made its circle from early morning to evening; they were swamped from exhaustion.

Lights twinkled against the dark night when her father's face and body language alerted Manuela. Her back ached from holding José bundled against her chest, sleeping and sweating.

Juan stood as the train approached the platform at the foot of the mountains. And everyone moved. Their ticket ended here. The train belched the family out with their baggage and strength of character.

Manuela smiled curiously at the ladies at the station in their long dresses and white gloves. She laughed in her mind. White gloves? She and Teodora had never seen anything like it. And someone said the first woman named Blanche Scott, recently flew an airplane into the sky somewhere called Indiana in America. An airplane?

The thoughts raised goose bumps on her arms and she rubbed them smooth.

Agustín reached for her hand.

They were almost to *Sevilla*.   She knew they would soon take a ride on a large boat near the *Torre del Oro* on a street called Paseo Cristóbal Colón.   It was difficult keeping all the names of places and cities in her head so she pushed them aside and squeezed her brother's hand and hugged him closely.

SEVILLA AND A RIVER TRIP

With the highest mountains behind them, they lugged their belongings off the train and onto the station platform. They knew they must get to the *Rio Guadalquivir* in *Sevilla*.

During the train ride, the men talked of finding odd jobs in villages to earn money for food. They'd talked of camping over open fires or finding friendly spaces along their way to sleep. The train had already brought them south past the mountains and through the villages of *Plasencia, Caceres, Mérida, Almendralejo, Zafra* and *Santiponce*. Now they anticipated *Sevilla* and a boat ride toward a bigger boat and their future.

Juan Francisco fought his misgivings once they passed through a customs inspection employed by a disagreeable gentleman. But the friendly porter read their papers and then helped the struggling families pull the trunks off the platform.

The family soon threaded themselves through the peculiarly narrow exit and the train breezed away from the station quickly.

Manuela grinned after her train ride and would always carry the memory with her to analyze time and again. Things can't be all bad with such adventures she thought as she raised her head and gazed with blinking astonishment. However, she wished they

97

were still aboard because the walking and camping lying ahead didn't sound easy. The men's fierce timetable sounded fearful. And she could not imagine walking so far.

Lugging the trunks and bundles wasn't easy either but the *camión* driver helped load everything into his large wagon. The children sat between everything and the women bounced on hard bench side seats. The footholds numbered just enough for the four men to stand and they were moving. Skirting the area around the train station, the driver cut through town and picked up the road to *Sevilla*.

They entered the City more than a little exhausted and not just a little afraid and stupefied with wonder. They saw countryside thickly clad with oak trees and marveled at the imposing religious architecture. They had been riding the train rails for fourteen hours and the boat would sail toward the ocean soon.

The Silván brothers had been told *Sevilla* was the artistic, cultural, and financial capital of southern Spain, the capital of *Andalusia* and the province of *Sevilla*. The city was situated on the plain of the *Rio Guadalquivir*[21], set in the heart of a fertile river valley while many of the settlements were scattered around the gently rolling *Guadalquivir* river plain, known as *la Campiña*, planted with wheat and olive groves. But they'd had no idea what to expect.

With the time restriction rattling through their apprehensive

---

[21] River Guadalquivir at an elevation of 23 feet above sea level, the second longest river in Spain, the longest in Andalusia and the only great navigable river in Spain. It begins at Cañada de las Fuentes and flows into the Gulf of Cadiz in the Atlantic Ocean.

minds, Felix and the brothers pointed toward the massive river that dominated the skyline, feeling unquestionably sad to be rushing through the sights surrounding them. Coming from the small village of *Fuentesaúco, Sevilla* was a sight to behold, with cathedrals and ancient Moorish architecture within touching distance. Good God! The sights knocked them in the gut. The Gothic splendor of the still-used cathedral, spiking high into the blue sky…….. But they were not on a holiday Juan reminded himself and they didn't want to literally *miss the boat.*

The driver got lost several times before a man pointed out the avenue that led to the pier beside the tall tower called *Torre del Oro* and unloaded the bulk of his wagon close to the river's edge. It was agreed Lorenzo would stay with the baggage, women and children near the cobblestone steps while his brothers purchased the tickets. Everyone stared at the steamboat that would carry them down the *Guadalquivir* toward *La Línea, Spain* on the southern coast of the *Port of Gibraltar.*

The boat would take them only as far as Sanlúcar at the mouth of the ocean. The building entrance was clotted with travelers where reality and panic set in and their overwhelming decision whipped at them.

Juan and Victorino gripped their spouse's hands and stared at Lorenzo and their baggage. The women mirrored their emotions, responding with equal pressure and their eyes snapped.

Although Spaniards rarely showed emotion in public at that time, this occasion was atypical and so were our ancestors. The children stood dazed, their parents dumbstruck.

Crescéncia, her nose and cheekbones sprinkled with freckles, looked steadily at Felix as he lifted little Juan to his broad shoulders and she reached for red-headed Alejandro's upraised hand. It was very crowded. Her smaller son arched toward her with outstretched arms, whimpering when the crowd surged around them.

"Estamos aquí." We are here.

The *Torre del Oro* sapped their breath as it slumbered beside the ship. The stones were perfectly aligned and the top had a golden glint that Manuela couldn't define. Her brain was in overdrive, her heart thudded.

The boat sat in the smooth water a stone's throw in front of them. She looked at Teodora to gauge her reaction. They'd never seen a ship and the water made them nervous.

Felisa stood close to the older girls with a fist full of Teodora's skirt held fast between her fingers. Holding hands, they reassured each other that they were not afraid. But when their eyes met, Manuela felt a spark of excitement tamping down the apprehension from the adults above her.

The city sounds kept the girls animated as their large dark eyes tried to capture the scenery within their minds. They would indelibly etch the foreign-city sounds, the smells of the avenue and the brisk movement of the big boat among the strange people into their brains and think about it for years afterward.

After they arrived, they sat for hours on the edge of the short stone wall at the side of the tower by the river's bridge. It wasn't the kind of pier Juan thought it would be, after all the stories they'd heard the past few months.

Crescéncia wandered near, Juanito squeezed in her arms, nodding for Alejandro to follow. She chose a spot near her nieces and her eyes strayed toward the water, the boat moored there.

Manuela grinned, barely able to swallow her spit. Agustín yanked on her long skirt; he wanted up so he could see the big boat. She was already holding baby José and laughed as her father, Juan, whisked him up on his shoulders for a better view in the slight breeze by the river.

After purchasing tickets at the kiosk, the embarkation experience was slow. The men strained their way down a long wooden quay. The women and children were weighted down as they joined other travelers. A uniformed man pointed to long benches to wait and despite hard seats, they wearily slumped down with relief.

The clerk was an elderly man, but he came on board as nimbly as a boy and landed with a soft thump. He carried a register book in a sling across his chest and a lead pencil stuck in the corner of his mouth like a pipe. And he quickly sorted through the passengers, writing furiously.

RIO GRADALQUIVIR AND BEYOND

The immigrants looked around with glazed eyes, wondering what would happen next. Staying close together, they saw acquaintances from their villages that were also aboard. Their presence lent a normalcy to the strangeness as they rested on the benches, pulling their belongings closer, waiting. José was passed between the girls and women as Juanito Gonzales was held in Felix's arms. The twin boys, Jacinto and Celestino, stared with eyes big as walnuts; they had never seen so many people at once and often turned questioning eyes toward their father. Victorino smiled tiredly and then patted Jacinto before pulling his boys forward to rest.

The next few hours were spent waiting before major activity brought them up; several men prepared to unloose huge chains that held the boat fast by heavy steel cleats attached to the stone pier. Their ears rang when the foghorn blasted. Alejendro's small body jumped at the sound and his eyes filled with tears, so Crescéncia pulled him onto her lap and patted him quiet.

The boat was ready to roll down the large river and so were the Silváns. They held tightly to their loads while others stood at the railing to watch *Sevilla* disappear from view.

Felix Gonzales stood next to his nieces, his hands clasped

firmly around the rail and when the wind was slashing across their faces, he soothed them with soft words.

For the rest of the afternoon Manuela stood at the rail with Lorenzo, looking back at the *Sevilla* skyline. There was nothing to see at the wharves but farmers' carts and farmland and forested hills beyond. This was where the Atlantic Ocean washed the coastline. Now and then they caught a glimpse of a country house through the trees but soon there was no sign of a city at all.

With her uncle on one side and strangers on the other, Manuela could find no words for what she was feeling, not so much fright or even confusion but the simple knowledge that she was losing something very important and goose bumps prickled her arms.

Her head was throbbing. She made herself breathe deeply, once and then again, and when she opened her eyes she noticed the wind had blown her mother's scarf from around her head to lodge in the crook of a tall scaffold too far to reach.

A chill wind blew off the bow as the families stood tightly woven together. Swiveling their heads to watch the somewhat monotonous landscape relieved by the occasional whitewashed town or village, they stared across the water. It descended toward the southern coast of Spain and entered the marshy wetlands at the river's end, known as *Las Marismas*. They were quiet. They were tired. And they were still a little frightened.

Food was simple but substantial. Sleeping was difficult but manageable. They sailed all day, all night and another day before the boat slowed, pulled up to a pier and stopped. A foghorn whistle announced embarkation and the crowd gathered. It was the end of the line: Sanlúcar de Barrameda.

Counting heads and holding everyone together was a chore. Avoiding the mad dash of those around them, they eventually reassembled beside the quay, glad to be on soil again. And it was just the beginning.

The women pulled children along, clutched babies and followed their men from the noisy crowd. Victorino studied the well-worn map he had worried thin from handling since they left home. The four men looked at each other with lifted brows and sighed deeply. Now the trek overland would begin where the family would learn to endure it, a long ribbon of patience between them.

They needed a burro and large wooden cart for the trunks and babies. Coins[22] jingled in their pockets and they hated the thought of spending them, but it was impossible to imagine carrying the trunks and the children so far. First they must find a protected spot. It was a slow-moving straggling procession overwhelmed with fatigue.

---

[22] In 1869-1870, coins were 1, 2, 5, 10 & 50 céntimos, 1, 2 and 5 pesetas. The lowest 4 denominations were copper (replaced by bronze from 1877), with 50 céntimos. Gold 25 peseta coins in 1876 were followed by 20 pesetas in 1878. In 1889, 20 pesetas coins were introduced and 25 pesetas ceased. In 1897, a single issue of gold 100 pesetas was made. Production of gold coins ceased in 1904, followed by that of silver coins in 1910.

SANLÚCAR & ATLANTIC OCEAN

Sanlúcar in 1911...

This is a city in the northwest of Cadiz in southern Spain. Sanlúcar is located on the left bank at the mouth of the Guadalquivir River on the Atlantic coast, 32 miles from Cádiz and 74 miles from *Sevilla*.

Although a seaside town, Sanlúcar de Barrameda is the home to the oldest horse races in Spain. The races take place just before sunset along the beach at the mouth of the river Guadalquivir every August.... but the Silván family would miss the festival and the races.

Following the pier master's directions, the men found the women and children a sheltered area and left them to find a cart to carry the trunks and bundles toward their destination. The town was old and felt lived in. The men's pants, jackets and shirts needed washing badly but they had no choice but to ignore that for the moment and dodged the crowded landing once they found the street sign pointing to the *mercado*, market.

The women soothed the children, their aching shoulders, arms, backs and feet. And the walking had not yet begun. They looked like a large dark mound huddled together, certainly not a group ready to hike across miles of unknown terrain.

It didn't take the men long to locate what they needed: cart, fruit, bread; sausages could be smelled along the streets coming and going. The aromas reminded the men how hungry they were and gathered up all they felt they could afford. Though coins lay in their pockets, *dinero* had been disappearing with each mile.

The air was cool but quite comfortable. Loosening their coats and removing the scarves that covered their heads, the women settled themselves among the baggage and children to wait. Activity kept the children's mind occupied as the people along the waterfront yelled at one another, boats were pulled in, fish thrown onto canvas tarps.

Shacks of sail menders and rope makers kept watch in the shadows like sagging old soldiers. Someone had nailed a piece of paper to the door and it flapped weakly in the breeze. Barrels and buckets and a cold fire pit, all the smells that added up to docks; rusting metal, fish and all the things Manuela could not name.

Suddenly, the sound of rolling carts cut across the cobblestones nearby and the children jumped up expectantly, untwining their scarves and scrambling to meet their fathers. But it wasn't their men, but a stranger that led his donkey and cart toward the market, the bed filled with boxes and bottles that shook noisily. He tossed a gruff "hola!" and swift nod of his head as he trundled by.

Everyone slumped down again and waited some more.

Within a short time the men returned from their canvassing of the seaside area with carts enough to undertake the next stage in the journey. The group smelled food. The sound of cart wheels along the path and a burro! The wooden cart rocked and jolted before coming to a stop and the animal brayed hello. The cart had wooden sides, four wheels and round, post-like gripping handles along the inside framing; the men positioned the wheels firmly against a boulder and tied the animal to a wooden railing beside them set into the ground for that purpose.

The women and children stared into the big brown eyes framed with long curly lashes and grinned at the animal.

However, they didn't get too close to the burro other than a pat here and a low voice there because his nostrils steamed and feet danced as he contemplated his new family.

A large pile of straw rose above the cart and Rita immediately imagined José burrowed down, sleeping in it.

Short conversations and some moments later, the burro was moving; the wagon's bed was filled with trunks, boxes and the two smallest children.   It was still unclear how they would manage and they'd encountered several groups of Spanish families while on the river voyage, each talking of their plans to reach the ship at Gibraltar.

There were several pregnant women, many small children, some barely able to walk on their own.   It was as if their countrymen had a plan but did not know anything further than to get to Gibraltar.

They'd listened to the words on the broadsheet explaining what they could expect on the ship but they were unsure if they could believe it.   How would they manage the trip when they struggled to find their way to the pier?   How had they managed so far, the train, the boat, and the expectations?

They saw families with their wives riding donkeys and children being carried on men's shoulders.   There were single men with one small bag that must have contained just a change of clothing? Their papers? Their hearts seized as they contemplated the exodus they joined. Sometimes in the quiet times, they'd think, God, what have I done? It would be a question they asked themselves many times during the long trip and sometimes after they arrived. For now, they moved forward. Always forward.

THE LONG WALK

HEADACHES, HILLS AND EXHAUSTION

They pointed themselves west as the men led the way to find a spot to gather and eat.   Victorino and Juan gave Felix a look when they spotted dry outcroppings near a small bridge, still in the town.   They were all hungry and would need the sustenance to walk the miles they still couldn't imagine until the drumbeat of their feet hit the soil.

Settling themselves and pulling scarves from their heads and around themselves, they all agreed the breezes off the coast route were much warmer compared to home but it was still cool in the early morning.   The bottles were filled at the nearby fountain in the center of the plaza and the hot meat pies were quickly consumed.

Victorino pulled newsprint from his jacket, handed to him by a vendor in the plaza while he munched on his apple.   He read the flyer aloud, telling them that the origins of the city center were from Arabic times and to expect narrow streets, zigzagging towards the river and the sea. The town had a mild climate and they agreed the breeze was warmer there.   He pointed out the 15th century castle of Santiago, the palace of the *Infantes of Orleans* and *Borbón,* and the church of *Nuestra Señora de la O* and the 16th century convent of *Santo Domingo.*

Then their conversation switched to the walking journey

ahead.   They had their plan and knew it would be comprised of toil and hurry.

Noticeably hampered by the heavily-laden wooden cart, they also knew the trip would be arduous and slow --- so they chose to follow the railroad tracks as closely as possible to avoid the ruts and rocks across the valleys and hillsides.   The coast route would guide them and they could avoid the hills and mountains they knew stood between them and Gibraltar --- 90 miles.

Carefully studying the calendar, they formulated their plan; they must arrive at the pier three or four days before the ship sailed on February 24th.   The men on the boat from *Sevilla* explained that the paperwork and health exams had to be completed before anyone boarded the ship and they should expect hundreds of immigrants when they arrived.   It was unfathomable.

Then the long walk began.

Victorino stashed his map.   It was still early morning and the sun shone on the Atlantic between gray clouds.   Their layered clothing protected them from the ocean's early-morning breeze. The older children helped steer the younger ones after their parents, sometimes lifting a child onto their young hips, other times --- pulling them along by hand.   They told the smaller brothers, sisters and cousins they would soon see train tracks but they couldn't get on the train.   Puzzled, they shrugged and crept close to their parents. They would follow the railroad tracks to stay safe and avoid getting lost.

The day was long.   Day turned to dusk and they had to go farther before stopping.

It had been an endless, dusty walk from the waterway.

Manuela's feet ached. Her head ached. Where were they going now? What was going to happen to them? How far away was *Fuentesaúco?* A train ride away, that's how far. Would she ever get back home? It made her feel sick to think about it. Where were they? They skirted *Chipiona* and managed to push themselves nearly three miles past the town. It lay in a very flat valley so the walking was much easier than the low mountains lying ahead. They'd marveled at the tall lighthouse, immense against the sandy skyline.

Hunger and exhaustion finally pulled them to a stop. And it was getting dark. They would need a fire. And their thoughts were on the olives, cheese, bread and drinking water in jugs they'd stashed inside the cart. With a nod from the men, the women gladly put down their burdens; bundles carried on their heads or children in their arms.

Little José fell asleep on his mother's lap quickly. Rita picked up the little boy's hand and traced the delicate bones of the forearm as he slept. The small belly showed signs of bloat from malnutrition and his collar bones were sharp as hack blades. She nodded to her husband who was also very worried when his son lay listless. Everyone needed more food.

Crescéncia brought out a package from her bag, placed it on the cloth-covered makeshift serving table and smiled at her brothers and sisters-in-law before unwrapping it slowly and deliberately to increase their anticipation. She chuckled at their faces. *Iberico* Ham. It was small but succulent from the medieval mountain village of *la Alberca,* cured in the cool, dry air filtered through their family bodega[23].   The two-year curing process gave it a deep maroon color and intense flavor, marbled with flavorful fat, rarely served in the Silván household.

Crescéncia had used her own coins to purchase it from money she'd earned selling her herbs; that day, that moment it was a meal beyond compare. The resulting oohs and aahs made every coin she'd paid worth it and her chest expanded with pride when her husband nodded his approval though he momentarily wished she'd put the coins into their money bag instead. He also wondered how she'd kept the ham hidden so long.

Soon after the meal was completed, it was Ramona's turn to get everyone's mind off the long walk ahead of them. From the basket she'd filled for the train and boat's earlier meals, she pulled a bundle out that the children had missed. Eyebrows lifted and grins spread across their small faces when she offered the lard cookies, called *Mantecados*[24]. They were a bit crumbly from the trip but sweet, with a smooth consistency flavored with *almendra* (almonds.)

Afterward, Manuela wiped her hands on her skirt and heard the comforting crackle of paper. She fingered the photograph she'd pushed inside her pocket. It was too dark to see it but she saw it in her mind.   Could she ever find *Toro* again? She sighed deeply and replaced the photograph, making sure it was safely in the deep pocket. She was very anxious to see the new one the photographer had taken…and then she rose to pick up the traces of their meal.

The air was cooler at night. The sweaters, coats, scarves and

---

[23] Bodega = a small Spanish shop selling wine and groceries

[24] Mantecado recipe in back of book

shawls were wrapped around their bodies; their stockings itched. Victorino built up the fire and the family gathered close together for warmth to sleep, drowsily wondering how they could possibly walk a hundred miles.   The youngest, José and Juanito whimpered a bit before falling asleep among the bundles but the other children remained awake, trying to make sense of their day.   Manuela, Teodora and Felisa tried to get comfortable among the bedding while straining to hear the low conversation around the fire.

Manuela's eyes shone in the dark.   She should be going to sleep.   She needed it and the ground's unevenness didn't help her insomnia.   She was tired but she laid awake a long time.

THE NEXT DAY she stood on the edge of the clearing a moment, breathing the cold bright air of the early morning.   The sun had already drifted into the trees beyond their campsite; the curve of its glowing disk visible in shadow through leaves just beginning to bud.   And she was hungry again.

The sun was barely above the horizon when the family ate pieces of chorizo and bread.   The air was brisk and not just a little windy.   A quilt of open vistas stretched before them as they plodded along.   One day ran into the next.   The children began to tire and baby José was a heavy load, not yet walking so the wagon carried him often putting him to sleep.   Sometimes Manuela and Teodora took turns carrying him when he twisted and turned in the adult's aching arms.   Felisa was too small to carry him, but she kept the children entertained.   The turf was uneven, the roads dusty, and the lower mountainous terrain was rugged on their feet.   They rested sporadically, but the men's strict regimen kept them focused on their deadline.

The children played tag along the way now and then, when they weren't whimpering from tiredness or hunger. Everyone took turns carrying bundles and some had boxes tied with heavy string. Alejandro's bright red head could be seen above the small bag he carried but it was usually from the shoulders of his father, Felix. The twins, Jacinto and Celestino, gripped their bundles tightly, wanting to share the load since they were the oldest boys in the family.

Daily, the ragtag band of Spanish immigrants looked eagerly toward each city, anxious to see the spires that climbed into the air and village streets fanning out from their plazas. With pioneering spirits, they stared at the stunning views and ancient buildings they'd never seen before. The people they met were friendly and often shared water and sometimes their outbuildings for the night's comfort. The men were overwhelmed with gratitude as their Spanish countrymen reached out to their homelessness, cautiously interested in their story of Hawaii and a new life.

They arose each morning, ate *el Desayuno*, a quick breakfast that sometimes consisted of fruit and bread. And walked toward the southwest, while praising God for the railroad tracks to use as their guide. And they smiled at the good weather. No rain yet.

As they moved along, Manuela's throat clogged with tears. She vowed to remember every inch, every corner and every memory inside her house. Someday she would return, she promised. She looked at her parents through wet eyes, shrugged onward while clutching her heavy bag and followed the group again....

One day, they saw a farmer near a village who offered them cool water and bits of home-made cheese and crusty bread.

The man eyed them carefully before asking them what brought them his way.   The conversation bounced around as each brother told of the journey, the reason and the way they'd come.

Thoughtful, the farmer turned toward his wagon and hauled out a small bag and raised his eyebrows to the Silvan brothers.

"¿Manzanas, señores?" Apples?

The men smiled their thanks and offered the farmer a copper which he took in exchange for the burlap bag of winter apples.

"Gracias, amigo."

The farmer shook hands and pocketed the coin.

The family moved on.

"Manuela."   She turned toward her mother. She would carry the apples instead of José for a while.   She smiled and hugged the apples close, inhaling the fruit's welcome fragrance as the itchy yute saco[25] tickled her nose.

Muscles ached, feet burned and their spirits sank with each long mile.   The journey was working on everyone's nerves; patience became as thin as the shoe soles under their throbbing feet.

Lorenzo's limp was more noticeable by dusk but he kept on, unwilling to slow down the family.   Gripping his bag and digging his fingers into his right hip, he remained stoic and refused to stop until his brothers were ready.   He would not allow his bum leg to hold him back and practiced walking straight and stiff whenever possible.

Manuela smiled gratefully when her father and tio Lorenzo touched her shoulder for a rest stop.   Would they ever get there?

---

[25]   Yute saco = burlap sack

117

They'd walked so far already.

As they gathered around, the apples were distributed while Victorino pointed with his finger... Another village and maybe a place to sleep under cover? Slurping juice from their apples, they soon lifted their burdens again.....as packages and children were lifted and carried in tired arms that cried for rest.

EXPLORING ROTA - A CATHOLIC MASS

The town of *Rota* was a welcomed site.   The narrow, crooked lanes in the old village lifted their spirits in the presence of its oldness.   The children played tag and the older girls saw the charm of adventure. Sometimes in those glistening cobblestone streets, they encountered amusement, temporarily forgetting their adversities.

The tangle of streets around the cathedral led to a beautiful public garden, with statues and fountains densely shaded. Manuela watched small boys play at bull-fighting in the streets below and in the public garden.   They flapped a colored old shawl in the face of the bull to avoid his furious charges, and doubtless to deal him his death-wound, though to that end she closed her eyes.

A minute's walk up a sloping stony street brought them into the beautiful and revered presence of a cathedral, *Nuestra Señora de la O del Castillo*.   The Silváns pushed open the doors and in another moment stood, safe and hidden in the thick smell of immemorial incense.   Inhaling its familiarity, they felt emotionally drenched in the scent amid its cool stones.

They simply wandered in the vast twilight spaces; and craned their necks near to breaking while trying to pierce the gathered gloom in the vaulted ceiling overhead. A sacristan set red candlesticks about a bier. He willingly paused in his task and explained that he was preparing for the funeral of a church dignitary to take place the next day at noon; and at that hour they should hear some beautiful music. The men hoped to be several miles away by noon the next day but seeing their wives' faces, stoically agreed to remain for early mass.

Outside they lingered a moment to feel the solemn joy of the chapel. Manuela bent her pretty head shyly and stared at a group of monks pointing to the *patio,* a roofless colonnaded court. The spaces between many of the columns had long been bricked in, but there was fine carving on the front and its staircase that climbed upward. So many feet had trodden its steps that they were worn hollow in the middle, and to keep from falling one must go up next to the wall.

Wine-skins, distended with wine, clogged the narrow street. Piled high on a vintner's wagon, they reminded our family of wine-skins hung from the many trees in *Fuentesaúco* waiting to tap and drink its contents. For Manuela and Teodora, the sight of them was magic and their eyes grew wide in astonished wonder.

They found a covered portico that had plenty of room for their belongings and the burro the children called *Pepino.* After asking for permission from the adjoining chapel to sleep there, the men heaved sighs of relief even though they wanted to be on their way....

The next morning, the nuns came beautifully dressed for mass in the chapel adjoining the church. The pews were cool but the family hardly noticed. Catholicism was ingrained in their way of life and several of their cousins were nuns[26]. Carrying their belongings into mass was not an option, so Felix offered to wait

---

[26] Source: Michael RUIZ Silván

with Pepino and their pile of luggage, boxes and baskets that littered the far corner near the doors. Pepino stopped and stared around him, snickering and braying for attention.

They'd missed their Ash Wednesday mass.

The church smelled of candle wax and incense. After dipping the tips of their fingers into the holy water font near the immense front doors, Rita, Crescéncia and Ramona led their children into the sacred area. The pews, worn smooth by the sliding and shifting of a multitude of congregants before them were nearly full for the service. A statue of a blue-robed Jesús looked down upon them, hand raised in benediction. A pleasant, religious light came through the stained-glass windows shining over them. The alter, draped with its cloth and flanked by candles, offered a spiritual invitation as they heartened to the priest's words as he led *la misa*, the mass.

Crescéncia held little Juan close to her chest and shushed him when he whimpered. José sat on his father's lap next to Alejendro. The three girls kneeled with reverence and bowed their heads over folded hands after first kneeling in prayer as they'd been taught at Santa María. The twin boys and Agustín wiggled on the pew until Ramona shook her head at them. The women's heads were covered with small squares of silken lace, called *mantillas*. They'd exchanged their head scarves to these and felt the tiny bit of lace transform them into ladies for the moment.

Lord have mercy. Christ have mercy. The Lord be with you. And with your spirit. And then the Liturgy. The congregation stood for the Creed.

Later, at the smooth wooden communion rail, Manuela spied the shiny chalice as the priest lifted it to the lips of the few congregants kneeling beside her. It was 6 ½ inches tall, with a square base sculpted with wheat chaff and grapes in relief made of delicate hammered silver that added reverence amid the smoky smell of incense. The wine clung to her tongue and dripped down her throat along with the softened blessed wafer. She crossed herself after whispering *"Alabado sea Dios* [27]*"* and touched her forehead, the lower middle of her chest, her left shoulder and then her right shoulder as she said each of the words, *"In nomine Patris et Filii et Espiritus Sancti. Amen.*[28]*"* Then she stood and followed her mother back to the pew in silence along with the others, their heads bowed and hands clasped near their hearts.

After the final prayer and while music from the beautiful organ echoed around them, they quietly filed out behind Juan and Victorino. They felt enriched with spirituality and their clothes carried the scent of incense amidst the travel smells that dogged them daily.

The women directed the children to lift their loads before joining the men ahead and near the open portal of a leafy patio everyone picked up their baggage and Victorino led *Pepino* with the cart. They'd been given directions to the road eastward but to reach this they had to pass through another square, which they found full of ox-carts and mule-teams.   They stood around with shuffling feet waiting for the way to clear.

Through an open archway, Manuela spotted postal cards for sale.   Lingering beside them, she stared at the pictures.   She sighed, wondering again how far beyond the village lay Gibraltar?

Much later, while he munched his bread and sausage, Juan

---

[27] "Praise be to God" a dutiful response after receiving communion in Catholic Church.
[28] In the name of the Father, and of the Son, and of the Holy Spirit.   Amen

looked at a newspaper, as if he could read the print. He'd found it withering on the bench near the train station; pictures displayed on its front page fascinated him. He was amazed with a Spain he'd not seen before and would remember always. He had not gone to school as long as Victorino, so he had not looked through many picture books of Spain or the outside world. As a younger son, it was understood his schooling would be basic; the eldest would learn to read and write. But he hoped he might learn one day. A new life held many promises. Maybe reading and writing was one of them. For now, he enjoyed the world around him, the beauty and the good weather guiding them south and eastward. And the paper was a bonus.

The railroad tracks ran past stretches of vineyard where vintners with donkeys and carts walked between rows of newly budded grapevines in the paling light of the afternoon. They walked through Roman ruins on a dusty road that wound around the town to the major plaza. That day they purchased potatoes, garbanzo beans, bread and smoked pork. And more barley straw as it is high in fiber and low in sugar, and closely resembles what a donkey would eat in the wild. Oat straw was better for Pepino but the last farmer shook his head, offered what he had. Pepino loved carrots and apples chopped small so he wouldn't choke. The children fought to feed him; many arguments were stopped with a look from the men.

The air was cool on Manuela's skin and it felt good. The smell of rain was in the air, along with a faint tinge of fish that settled on her tongue, a taste as sweet as candy. She was hungry. She could not stop the jumble of questions her mind produced. She hoped there would be some kind of shelter --- a barn, a shed ---

any place with a roof and walls to cut out the breeze.

Ramona and Rita took turns holding José while Crescéncia kept Juanito wedged against her in a large serape twisted around her neck and beneath her arms. It balanced the child and allowed her to freely carry the basket and small bits of personal clothing.

Teodora and Manuela walked ramrod straight with small wrapped bundles on top of their heads. It was an age-old traditional way of carrying items and they'd learned as very young children. They laughed when Felisa's bundle kept slipping and the poor girl spent more time lifting it off the ground than she did taking one step in front of the other.

Felisa scowled at the bundle and then at the older girls but watched them from the corner of her eye to learn the way of it.

The wagon was heavy but the little burro pulled his burden and walked where he was guided. He knew there would be straw and apples at the end of the day. But sometimes, he'd bray loudly, stop and look over his shoulder, getting grumpy too. Sometimes the men had to push and prod to get him moving, bribe and cajole. They refused to let a burro rule the journey. Sometimes Pepino listened. Sometimes he did not.

They walked for a long time.

They saw farmers taking their milk cows home below fluffy white clouds. They saw streams of water gurgling beneath narrow wooden bridges. They saw larger rivers of water cascading over rocks beneath sturdy rock bridges where sometimes they caught sight of women washing clothes, children beside them.

WALKING INTO FOREVER

Manuela looked down at her shoes, dusty and dull. They were falling apart. Yet they had been her best pair; the pair for special occasions like church, festivals, and visiting abuelita and the families in the other villages, *Toro, Villaescusa* and *Villamor de los Escuderos*. It seemed like so long ago. Like another life. Her dress looked like it had been tossed off the mountainside and she wondered when she would feel clean again. Teodora and Felisa nodded toward her as they lifted their hems to compare with hers.

The next afternoon, well before sunset, they arrived in *La Puerto de Santa María*. They were filled with sweat and treading on sore feet. They halted near a public fountain, where already the mothers and daughters of the neighborhood were gathered with earthen jars for the night's supply of water. The jars were not so large as to overburden any of them when, after a short delay for exchange of gossip, the girls put them on their heads and marched erectly away with them, each beautifully picturesque irrespective of her age or looks. Our family also filled their water jugs and rested.

The air was soft and warm; something almost southern. It made emotions flood among them. The place was arcaded and bordered with little shops, where young people walked up and down in groups and talked and talked. They were in the standard proportion of two girls to one young man; they mostly wore skirts and hats and filled the avenue from side to side on *el Paseo*.

The happy laughter and low replies that rose with the chirp and whisper of their feet cheered the night as our family sat and listened from the open plaza near the fountain. Manuela was mesmerized but Teodora more so. Their mothers smiled slightly and shared a look, remembering their own youth as they enjoyed the music playing nearby. Their feet tapped in tandem, each recalling their love of dancing, especially *la Jota*. Felisa tapped her feet beside Manuela and moved her shoulders in time with the music, itching to jump up and dance around.

La Jota is the national folk dance of *Aragon* in Spain and sometimes known as the Christmas dance. It has a fast-moving tempo. In Aragon, it is said that a pretty girl dancing *la Jota* will send an arrow through the heart with each and every movement. Manuela would later tell this story about her parents. Juan played his favorite drum, *el Bombo*, and Rita danced. Abuelita Manuela said they were married soon afterward. So, the story must be true...

The weather warmed as their progress marked off the miles. Near the square, the men saw a bath house; they counted their *dinero*. They were in sore need but they were also hungry. After quiet conversation, they motioned for the women to sit and wait and they wandered toward the open, arched doorway. Several minutes later, they returned; Juan twisted the end of his mustache before turning to the sad, tired group and his bright blue eyes smiled.

"*Vamos a trabajar y tendremos comida suficiente. Nos dan duchas gratis para todos.*" We will work and food will be enough for us.

126

And everyone has bathwater.

Rita pressed her hand to her chest and her sherry-colored eyes blinked; with a liquid smile, she pulled her dark cardigan sweater tightly around her and looked into her husband's eyes, nodding vigorously. They had, indeed, been blessed.

"Gracias, sí." She gathered little José to her and motioned for Manuela to get Agustín. All the women and children followed. It would be a good day and she knew feeling dirt-free for a change would give everyone an emotional lift.

Two hours later, the children were squeaky clean and into almost-fresh clothes. Manuela felt her stockings itch but otherwise felt renewed, just as her mother had hoped. Everyone chattered and waited for Victorino, Lorenzo and Juan to finish in the kitchens. They were famished.

The whole house was brilliantly lighted with electricity. Sausage spit in the pan. Floured tomatoes sizzled beside them; eggs and bread and orange juice and coffee that smelled sharp and rich and heavenly. It was delicious, and the table was of an abundance typically available for about two dollars a day for bed and board, wine included. After earning their food and wine that day, pride accompanied each bite as they watched their families get their fill.

Only the rich could afford hotels that included meals and a bed. That luxury was not for the Silváns. It would be another night of camping but their bellies were full as they settled near the city plaza.

Felix and Alejandro were not with the burro as she'd suspected. Crescéncia tried to stay calm but the days and nights did not much allow calmness. Pepino munched straw close by and tossed his head anxiously.

Her brothers and sisters gathered children and blankets. She held Juanito and glanced around again, clearly anxious. Suddenly she drew in a short sharp breath when Felix came out of the shadows. He was carrying a lantern that swung in rhythm with his step with Alejandro following him. Quick tears surfaced and she brought a hand to her chest. She wondered when their lives would be normal again. Would it ever be so?

Victorino held the map he'd nearly fingered into tatters and promised only a few miles to go. Despite their early February start, they'd enjoyed crisp clear days, only a bit of rain. That day they'd seen long intervals of sunshine.

It was 8 o'clock and full dark when the *Paseo* began. The villagers greeted one another, laughed, the children played and the Silván family missed home.

Manuela had started the day as she did many: with a lecture to herself. It would get easier. She would stop thinking all day long about home. She would be attentive to her family who had taken her away from a poor life and…. She still woke mornings fully expecting to see the walls of her room on Calle San Salvador but the disappointment that followed didn't last through the day as it once had.

Street cars groaned through the night.

They woke to find the sun barely peaking over the horizon and the promenade astir with life; a newsboy seated under an arcade was crying his papers and soldiers clicked their boots in tandem by the archway near women in lace *mantillas*.

The women sighed at the normality of the scene. The men

just wanted to get moving again.

Hunger and wet and dirty diapers slowed them down and the men learned there were some things you just could not hurry along.

As the sun rose higher in the sky, they munched on bits of food and drank water from the central fountain near their night's lodging. It made for a good start to the day with the fresh water but the food could have been better. They longed for a good meal that would fill them up but pushed the wayward thoughts deep inside their minds to concentrate again on getting to Gibraltar.

They'd been walking about ten miles per day, sometimes farther, sometimes not so far. Every one of them was worn down to a nub.

After leaving *Rota*, it was a never-ending trudging affair. Centuries-old gray stone walls dotted the landscape, up one hillside and down the next amid the ruins of castles that loomed out of nowhere. Flocks of sheep taking their time crossing narrow, curvy roads forced them, quite happily, to stop. As little villages spotted the horizon, they pushed on, resting periodically and to eat.

Puerto Real eventually came into view beyond the San Pedro River. Strolling through the narrow streets, they were too tired to enjoy it and on the outskirts they were careful to watch their step. Wetlands, composed of lagoons as well as salt marshes, were filled with huge flocks of migratory birds en route to their new seasonal homes. Also, on the outskirts of *Puerto Real*, there were pine forests, among them, Las Canteras (the Forest of Quarries) and La Algaida (Mare's Meadow Forest).

The next few days took them through *San Fernando*, then *Chiclana de la Frontera* and finally into *Barrio Nuevo* before the view of *Vejer de la Frontera* stopped them in their tracks...

Vejer de la Frontera is a Spanish hilltop town in the province of Cadiz, Andalusia, on the right bank of the Rio *Barbate*. The town occupies a low hill overlooking the Straits of Gibraltar surrounded by orchards and orange groves. Several ancient churches and a cluster of white houses in the Moorish design dotted the hill before them. Incongruously, the orchards butted up next to a very large bull pen.

A flock of geese was coming toward them on the lane, waddling with purpose, propelled by a young girl with a stick and a very serious expression. She glanced at them shyly but did not linger near the group of strangers.

The village had a former convent that offered sleeping arrangements for a small fee. The women's eyes implored the men and Manuela nearly jumped for joy when they nodded their assent. The old town had an impressive concentration of medieval stonemasonry. However, the Silváns could not think beyond a bed regardless of the stones or its history.

Early the next morning, some locals recommended they walk over to the western wall, pass through one of the old gates and down the steps to the Plaza Major. The women sighed with relief when, after just a small hesitation, the men agreed to spend an extra hour before putting their feet to the road and the grueling walk that still waited.

They stood in the plaza where several interesting streets fanned off into the lower city. The men paused to feel the ancients breathe near them, but their timetable squelched a longer exploration. Crescéncia grumbled. She could usually sweet talk her brothers into anything but their timetable won and Felix shook his head at her.

The next part of the journey would be nearly fifty miles.

They tried not to talk about food because they had little; food was as short as their patience.

"Those toadstools are beginning to look good..." Felisa pulled one out of the ground, ate one and pushed the other into Teodora's hand.

"Who in her right mind would eat toadstools?" Teodora hissed, wiping her hand on her skirt with a slight shudder.

"Well, we don't have any more chorizo."

"Why did you have to mention chorizo?" Teodora whispered to Felisa.

"Because I want some!" she replied, huffy and tired and beyond caring if her sister was angry.

Victorino raised his eyebrows at the girls. He knew they were all hungry and their supplies were low. The men agreed all walk and little food would not get them to Gibraltar.

Later in the day, the men found work with a local farmer who was taking his olives to market. He agreed to carry the older children in his wagon and pay them a small wage in exchange for their muscled help unloading the containers in the market. The men gladly approved and they earned enough money to feed their families and Pepino for the next two days, the length of time it took the family to walk to *Facinas*.

After leaving the farmer and getting close enough to view the town, they stood staring. It looked like *Fuentesaúco*. Farmland, orchards, dirt roads, small houses hooked together as one. The major difference was the rocky outcrops along one side where the Straits of Gibraltar waited. After their first melancholy impressions, they suddenly slumped to realize mountains stood between them and Gibraltar.

Manuela's shoulder blades ached. She'd carried José too long and a pain caught in her chest. She struggled some moments before Rita saw her weariness and reached for José. Her relief was evident but her face was pale.

Manuela could hold her bag but her slight body could not bear the weight of the agile child. She fought tears and watched her father grip the largest suitcase while balancing *el bombo* on his hip. She sniffed in a deep breath and wiped her face with a sleeve before following her family toward the mountain.

That night, the women pulled out their cooking things and made a large pot of *sopa de ajo,* garlic soup. It was made with garlic, the eggs they'd recently traded some left-over apples for and bread. It was known as peasant soup. The aroma was strong, but subtle, and everyone took turns filling their bowls after ripping off a portion of bread. The exhausted group ate before the fire, too tired for conversation and soon slept despite *Pepino's* snorting.

SAN ROQUE AND SURPRISES

At dawn the next morning, they trudged away from *Los Barrios* and the mountains, walking nearly twelve miles to *San Roque*, a small town still in the province of Cadiz *San Roque* is situated a short way inland just to the north of the Gibraltar peninsula. Almendra trees and a large convent nestled nearby, where nuns made exquisite handmade sweets. They knew this because the sign erected in the corner of the shaded area showed subtle drawings for passersby.

Manuela studied the convent as they walked along the narrow lane through the town, missing for the hundredth time her Santa María church in *Fuentesaúco*. Agustín reached for her hand as if needing a lead like a pony at the end of a rope. She grasped it and held his warm fingers tightly with her own. It was getting very dark.

Another campfire. More soup from a pot. Sore feet. Dirty stockings and dresses. Night noises. Aches. Pains. Blisters. Mixed emotions. José's whimpers. Manuela felt drained, limp. She wanted to lie down on the soft rumpled bedding and sleep. For a long while. For a long rest. She dreamed. She felt the sweet sensation of a soft mattress enveloping her. Why couldn't every night feel soft and secure?

Manuela slept badly, rising up from ragged dreams again and again to listen for movement from the others. She woke for good near dawn, cocooned in blankets damp with dew. She woke overwhelmed with wanting to hear her grandmother's voice, see her cousin's smile, the olive trees behind their house, the sound of pigs rooting in the yard. Time stood still for several heartbeats. And then she heard her mother talking quietly to Gus and knew she could lie quietly no longer.

~

Juan ticked off the days on his fingers, knowing the boat would sail at the end of the week from Gibraltar. Victorino sat near the fire studying their papers and the road that lay before them. They were bone tired. The foot of the mountains had made it a gripping ordeal. Felix watched his boys as Lorenzo drew a map in the soil near his feet with a stick.

They were thankful the weather was kind; slogging through rain, mire and mud would have made their journey more of a nightmare. There was that to be thankful for but there was some dissention as they stood on the shoulder of the mountain with the whole valley spread out before them. Should they head directly toward *La Línea* or move toward the beach and follow it around to make it easier to sit and rest with the ocean at their feet?

Juan and Felix chose the closest route but Victorino and Lorenzo held out. It was an easier road, they argued; they'd spoken with someone in the last city and he'd been adamant. The railroad tracks led through the city. Why get off the tracks now? Victorino produced a scrap of oilcloth and a bit of stone from the ground. Placing the oilcloth on his knee, he sketched rapidly to prove his point.

So they meandered toward the edge of *San Roque* and the beautiful haven of whitewashed houses and another church with a bell tower topped with a cigüeña nest.

It was near the church that Manuela saw two old women beating rugs over a porch railing. Impulsively, she waved at them. They stared at the drooping visitors a moment before beckoning them forward. Manuela grinned and glanced over her shoulder at her parents, who stood apart and undecided.

"*Hola, amigos*," the red-haired woman called out. Hello my friends.

"*Hola*," Juan answered, holding tightly to his baggage.

"*¿Van muy lejos?*" Are you traveling far?

"*Sí. Vamos a La Línea.*" Yes, we go to *La Línea*. Victorino responded, lowering his box.

"*Sean bienvenidos. Nos gustaría que vinieran a comer con nosotras.*" We have come to invite you to share dinner with us. You are welcome.

The family was astounded.   Manuela, proud she'd initiated the encounter, glanced at her parents and saw them busily gathering bags, boxes and children before shooing them forward. And she felt ashamed for expecting praise but excited.   She was hungry most days and the thought of eating as a family at a real table made her begin to shake.   Scampering after their father, she pulled Agustín along behind.

The house was small but big enough to seat everyone outside in an open courtyard.   A bare wood table was set up beside long benches.   They introduced themselves as María and Lourdes Mercado, sisters who'd lived in *San Roque* all their lives.   They smiled, eagerly listening to the family story as they trundled back and forth between their small kitchen and the courtyard table. They shooed the women away when they offered to help; Rita, Ramona and Crescéncia sat tiredly as they served the golden, *sopa de molinera* with cumin and chili peppers that would be gazpacho[29]

---

[29] Gazpacho: Cold soup of tomatoes, bell peppers, cucumber, garlic and spices served in hot weather

when summer arrived a few months later. They explained that for dessert, they would serve sweets from the convent of the *Order of St. Clare*.

Teodora, Felisa and Manuela stared at one another, their lips smiling broadly. *Un plato de postre?* Dessert?

The sisters offered their outbuilding to the travelers for the night and directed the men to move wood, boxes and tools to accommodate their blankets. Felix spread straw around to soften the wooden floors. José and Juan were already asleep on their mother's shoulders; Agustín and Alejendro's eyes both drooped and their little bodies could barely sit up. The girls helped the twin boys get settled and then laid down together. The night air was still, as it had been during the day. They slept to the soft strumming of a guitar amid Pepino's barrage of grunts.

They'd missed the First Sunday of Lent and mass.

THE FOLLOWING MORNING cups of thick, steaming Spanish chocolate[30] and *churros*[31] greeted them and brought their eyes more fully open. Disbelief etched their faces again as bowls of steaming rice porridge mixed with cinnamon sat before them. For the adults, hot coffee. There were eight miles of road between them and *La Línea*.

They did not want to leave the warm house or the sisters within but they had no choice. As they gathered their burdens for the last leg of their trip, Lourdes offered an apple for Pepino and patted Manuela's shoulder, handing her a small cloth napkin.

---

[30] Spanish chocolate is the "thickest, creamiest and richest hot chocolate in the world" as far as Spain is concerned. When you melt their chocolate into simmering milk using a solid dark chocolate bar, the chocolate brew is amazing

[31] Churro: crunchy deep-fried fritters dusted with sugar and cinnamon

"Esto es para más tarde." This is for later.

Once on the road, filled with expectation and wondering constantly at the napkin-filled surprise, Manuela grinned at nothing. It was only later when her father and uncles stopped for *la almuerzo*, a cold lunch, that she pulled the fabric open while her cousins and brothers watched expectantly. Apricots! Dried, succulent orange-colored pieces of fruit filled her hand. Manuela uttered a cry of delight. When she extended the fruit toward them, they popped pieces into their mouths quick as lightning. José and Juan reached for one but their mothers shook their heads, sure they would choke. For the other children, a thrill of sweetness touched tongues and taste buds sang.

In the late afternoon, they came to a forest, a long, cool stretch of green leafiness. It smelled sweet and humid. They left the road, hoping they might find wild strawberries but it was too early in the year for that. After a while, they came to a massive stand of fruit trees, lined up like tooth picks as far as the eye could see.

Manuela and Teodora both remembered picking fruit with their fathers, when they had spent those lovely days near the olive orchard with the fruit trees bursting with fleshy globes, such a long time ago. They would miss their sweet-smelling garden. Would there be gardens where they were going?

And then it was morning again. They awoke early. Feeling lost and confused, she could not remember where she was. Manuela's cousins groaned around her, each pulling at their blankets and replacing their shoes, ready for another long walk --- clearly not enthused.

"Hoy es nuestro último día caminando." Today is our last day of

walking.

The children groaned with gratitude.

The food was bread, sausage and winter apples. Everyone washed their breakfast down with water from the urns lodged inside the wagon, thinking about never walking again.

Pepino's straw was nearly gone and so far, he had pulled the cart steadily without a burro's stubbornness most of the time and the bribery helped but even those apples were nearly gone.

The day started crisp and cool but everyone knew the walk would soon warm them up again, sometimes beyond comfort. So, they wrapped their coats around themselves once again like they had every day since getting off the boat in Sanlúcar.

They tried not to think about the lack of privacy they'd endured, the sober faces of the children as they whimpered from hunger, the regimented stopping not necessarily when their strength waned but when the men allowed it. They could not lag behind and they were not allowed to complain. Their daily burdens and impatience generated some impatient arguments.

But now the walking trip was nearly over.

The girls reached for their bundles again, plopped them on their heads and watched their mothers calm the smaller children, wrap them close.

Juan hooked Pepino up to the wagon again while the others rearranged the trunks, bags and the drum case. Crescéncia's basked now rode in the cart, with the dried chorizo, jugs of water and half-filled bota.

The panoramic view that last day when the harbor could be seen miles away seemed to perk them up even if it didn't last long enough for them to put one foot in front of the other. It was a sight they could never have imagined from Fuentesaúco and a sight that they would long remember.

They knew a ship was waiting.

And they wanted to be on it when it sailed away.

Relief etched their faces, their bodies sagged with it, but a magical calm invaded their thoughts as they marched toward Gibraltar.

LA LÍNEA and GIBRALTAR

February - 1911

The Rock of Gibraltar overlooks the Strait of Gibraltar and the northern coast of Africa, less than nine miles away. The rock itself is a mass of Jurassic limestone, 200 million years old, running from north to south for a length of nearly four miles and a width of less than half a mile, about 1600 acres. Gibraltar is a colony of Great Britain, their inhabitants British citizens and their laws based on the English law system. The official language is English although Spanish is widely spoken; most inhabitants are actually bilingual. Gibraltarians have nothing against the Spanish but wish to remain British.

IN TWELVE DAY'S TIME, the trek had been accomplished and the Silváns were safe at their destination at *La Línea de la Concepcion*, known simply as La Línea, the border line between Spain and British Gibraltar. The men's shoulder sockets screamed.

The women's bodies ached and the small children were quiet with exhaustion.

They followed the huge rock island that jutted out of the ocean, a perfect landmark. A large building and stone walkway greeted them at *La Línea*; a very large sign pointed to Gibraltar's wharf. The same poster…the catalyst bringing them to where they stood that day, guided the families and moved them into the sea of humanity beside and around them. The Silván family stood still as the throng of people edged along the water's edge and the massive rock rose above.

The crowded wharf caught them unawares and they were clearly flabbergasted. It was filled with families juggling oversized lumps of belongings. People were perched all over the harbor wall. If they'd been surprised in *Sevilla* at the foreignness of boarding the ship, this was beyond belief. There were so many people standing seven and eight deep or sitting on their luggage or the sea wall, it took their breath away. The startled mothers instinctively grasped children.

On the Spanish side of the border at Gibraltar, a line of men stood ready to purchase any goods or discarded possessions from the immigrants. They knew money was in short supply, but offered the travelers a mere percentage of the value. Our families had no choice; they sold the cart and Pepino. The children hugged the burro as the buyers unloaded the trunks and placed them on the ground. Juan ran a hand over Pepino's back and reluctantly gave his lead to the man before they trundled away.

They found an area for the women and children, and then the four men fought their way through the crowd to ask questions and get their bearings. They found *Fuentesaúco* friends lined up, waiting for physical health exams; one more reason to be apprehensive. If a family member couldn't pass the exam, he or she would be turned away. They refused to think of it. Striving for optimism they forced their way through the crowd to their families. They must all go!

The exams were curious; scars were recorded as was weight, height, age, place of origin, and number in family, color of hair and eyes, amount of money in their pockets. And the name of a family member and village the immigrants left behind. The ship's manifest reflected the information in detail and it took hours and some days for the entire process.

Unsettling conversations ran rampant. The ship's doctor must examine them for disease; to be sure they were sound of body, before they were allowed to board. Strict requirements must be adhered to; Cuba's and South America's (ie. Argentina and Brazil) rules were more lenient than the plantation's in Hawaii. After their rugged journey, they refused to listen; refused to muddy their focus on Hawaii.

Lorenzo was last in line. Arms out. Mouth open. Eye lid poked. His exam took longer than the others. The examiner told him to stand aside as he motioned to another man who watched nearby.

Behind her, Manuela could feel her father's tension spiral up and then fall off when the man finally looked away with a shrug. But that wasn't the end of Lorenzo's exam. The family saw him led to a group lolling against a building near the registration tables, frowns on their faces, exasperation in their postures.

Juan, Victorino and Felix gathered their families but kept an eye on Lorenzo, all equally anxious. Soaring with relief, their own dreaded physical exams approved, they tried to talk above the noisy crowd; so many trying to speak all at once, each screaming words above the other.   They were relatively safe and in plenty of time for the ship's sailing.   No more walking!   Now, if they could just keep their families together!

So many people cluttered the cobblestone avenue.   Rita saw an old woman near them who looked much older than most others. She was a little pile of a woman, wrapped tight in layers of sweaters and scarves.   From the bottom of the lowest skirt hung what appeared to be the hem of a dark slip.   Over everything, a heavy overcoat, unbuttoned, hung open.   She caught the old woman's eye, smiled.   The woman barely nodded, on the verge of tears. Rita gave her a look, feeling everything that the woman's old eyes portrayed.

The steamship loomed above the vibrant, noisy crowd like a whale at bay.

Photo: Port of Malaga. Photo credit: Internet ~ Spanish immigrants
waiting to board the SS Heliopolis in 1907

The women gripped little ones and it was a miracle they didn't plop into the sea.   Being children and never seeing the ocean before, the first thing they wanted to do was walk along the sea wall.   Drooping but unable to relax their watch even for a moment, the women had their hands full until José and Juan fell asleep on top of the piles of belongings and Alejendro and Agustín were packed off with their fathers.

Manuela, Teodora and Feliza sat on trunks near a group of children chattering about *monos*[32].   Monkeys?   What were they?   The girls were intrigued and listened.   Their families had arrived three days earlier and were given permission to walk across the border into Gibraltar for exercise.   They were warned to avoid the monkeys. The girls mimicked them, jumping around and laughing delightedly. Clearly eavesdropping, they learned the monkeys were tailless animals high on the mountain above them. Oh! She'd like to see them since she had never seen one, nor heard of them.   Then the girls talked of dolphins swimming in the ocean beside the ship. Manuela hoped to see them too, but she was so very tired.…   She closed her eyes.

The men learned from their countrymen that many families arrived early and were obliged to spend nights squeezed into one room, all of them sleeping on the floor, fully clothed without privacy.   They couldn't sleep on the wharf.   And that was a hardship they hadn't planned for; everyone was relieved they arrived at Gibraltar within one day of departing.   They would sleep *near* the wharf – outside --- one more night as their coins were nearly gone.

---

[32] Monos   They were called Barbary Apes but were really monkeys (Macaques).   In Gibraltar, are the only free living primate in Europe

Lorenzo slouched against the building where he could hear others whisper their fears. Lorenzo's gut clutched. After several hours, he was summoned; his paperwork was returned by a clerk with a sad look. He did not pass his exam for Hawaii. He could not get on the boat. Then, he was given directions to the kiosk for ships headed for South America and Cuba.

Numbed, he turned to search for his brothers. Lorenzo might have cried.

"Cuba. They will take me in Cuba. And......then I will find you later." His hands shook but his eyes were steady. He had no choice. He would not return home, he could not accompany them to Hawaii but he could work hard in Cuba where the language would not be foreign and Spain was still in control.

His brothers stared at him, stunned expressions flitting across their faces and no words would come. The children squeaked, their round eyes widening in surprise and distress. Tears came in a hot rush, but Manuela dashed them away furiously with the back of her hand. No!

Just after dawn, the families wove through the crush of people toward the portal for embarkation. They were all weighted down with bags as they joined the long queue of travelers waiting, legal documents in hand. The ship creaked and groaned at anchor, massive and foreign. The water slapped against the pier and gray and white birds screamed above them. The girls were told they were called *los gaviotas*. Seagulls.

The crowd of people generated a sweating mass of humanity, pushing and shoving the crowd in different directions. It was shocking and amazing. The Silváns fought to retain their footing in the mad rush. Juan wondered if he should tie everyone together with a rope….. He was quite afraid of losing someone in the crush.

Juan and Victorino's families lost sight of Crescéncia and Felix at the gates. They seemed to float away in the stream of humanity into several very long boarding lines and their sister disappeared. Manuela and Teodora strained to keep their aunt in sight, but the girls were too short and the crowd too thick. As a result, Crescéncia, Felix and both boys were listed in manifest group #19.

Form 562
Department of Commerce and Labor
IMMIGRATION SERVICE

Name: *Hernandez Silvan* *Cristencia*   Age: 26

Sex: *F*   Citizen of   SPAIN

Steamer   ORTERIC   Line

Date   APR 18 1911 APR 24 191 Port of Honolulu, Hawaii

Group No. *44*   List No. *25*

Incomplete paperwork from some immigrants delayed Juan's and Victorino's boarding; they were in group #39 [33]. Enrique Martin's family was in the middle group in #25. If they'd known what waited, they may have turned around and gone home again.

Everybody was happy and also a little sad. Lorenzo should have been with them! Juan and Victorino had never seen so many people in one place. They lined the quay, trembling with emotion, coats and scarves fluttering in the breeze, seagulls hopping around their thin-soled feet. Many immigrants seemed afraid they might be left behind; when they saw an opening many rushed inside, arriving clearly out of breath. The Silváns watched them knock others aside and held their children tightly to avoid being trampled.

With the huge expanse of gray limestone rock looming above, they edged toward the ship's gate on February 24, 1911. Pulling out their required documents again, Juan watched until the man smiled, returned everything and invited him to board the ship. Victorino followed. Hugging their belongings, these Spanish families took their first step into the mysterious confines of the ship.

---

[33] Listed on Orteric ship manifest

PART TWO

A WATERY VOYAGE

The S.S. Orteric[34] was a large vessel fitted with accommodations for about twenty cabin passengers, and was a large cargo carrier being able to accommodate 10,000 tons dead weight. She could steam twelve to thirteen knots an hour and had 3,000 horsepower. She belonged to the Weir line and was on her maiden voyage having been launched at Greenock, England on January 28, 1911. The Orteric sailed from London on February 18 toward Portugal and at Oporto, picked up a batch of immigrants, taking on 305. At Lisbon, 329 people were taken on, and at Gibraltar 960 Spaniards were added on the vessel. She had a length of 460 feet and fifty seven feet in breadth. The vessel logged an average of 11.6 knots on the voyage[35].

---

[34] There is a transcript of the Orteric's manifest available. See *Genealogy* tab of my website
[35] Hawaiian Gazette, April 14, 1911

THE ORTERIC & HAWAII

Finally on the ship[36] after passing through the hatch, they found themselves standing in steerage, cramped with hundreds of others.   It felt like a floating barracks immersed in a dimly lit scene of confusion.   Many would become seasick and nauseous, and the steerage section would soon be transformed into an intolerably foul smelling cage.   The quarters were noisy and privacy would be nonexistent.

Manuela and her cousins followed their parents.   Boys went with fathers, girls with mothers.   Only the boys, José, Juan and Alejendro were allowed to remain with the women since babies stayed with mothers.

In the men's portion of the ship, many passengers were kneeling before chests, playing cards or sitting in groups.   They had time to get acquainted with the boat, ate some meat rolls with a scant bottle of red wine, and unpacked their bag in the small area reserved for them.   Even though space was tight and claustrophobic, *el bombo* was safeguarded and stowed carefully among the bulky boxes.   The boat smelled steamy and the air was

---

[36] The Uprooted / Pau Hana, by Ronald Takaki

thin in the lower confines.   The scent of strong disinfectant permeated the ship. It also smelled of sweat from so many people and it had yet to leave the dock.

Without partitions for privacy, many women hung blankets to designate their personal areas.   Rita and Ramona strung their shawls for protection from prying eyes.   Space was based on the size of their family and they were instructed to keep it clean.   Rows of dark bunk beds were three high in the wide-open area, so most of the time, they would undress after the lights went out.   After sleeping beneath the stars off and on for two weeks, confined to the dark cellar of the vessel unnerved them and the grimness of the place made their spirits fall.

It was so noisy! Various Spanish dialects fought with each other.   Their voices rose in a crescendo of clamoric proportions as Spanish conversations mixed with Portuguese.   Sleeping would be difficult when sharing one's bedroom with hundreds of strangers but they were more ill prepared for the stifling heat, bedbugs that would bleed them and the lice that would soon thrive and run amok.

ancestry

Honolulu, Hawaii, Passenger Lists, 1900-1953

Name:	**Manuela Silban Trascasas**
Age:	9
Gender:	Female
Birth Year:	abt 1902
Port of Departure:	Gibraltar
Departure Date:	24 Feb 1911
Ship:	Orteric
Port of Arrival:	Honolulu, Hawaii
Arrival Date:	13 Apr 1911
Ethnicity/Race/Nationality:	Spanish
Last Residence:	Spain

Source Citation: Repository Name:*National Archives and Records Administration (NARA)*; NARA Series:A3422: Roll 29.

Source Information:
Ancestry.com. *Honolulu, Hawaii, Passenger Lists, 1900-1953* [database on-line]. Provo, UT, USA: Ancestry.com Operations, Inc., 2009. Original data: ; (National Archives Microfilm Publication A3422, 269 rolls); Records of the Immigration and Naturalization Service, Record Group 85; National Archives, Washington, D.C.

Description:
This data collection contains inbound passenger lists arriving at Honolulu, Hawaii from February, 13, 1900 to December 30, 1953. The lists include both alien and U.S. citizen arrivals. In later years passengers may have arrived by airplane rather than by ship.

After securing their places below, our ancestors scrambled up the narrow steps from the depths of the hold below the S.S. Orteric's deck and watched Spain's skyline fade into the distance as they clung desperately to the last sight of the craggy rock. After the monstrous ship slid out to sea, all they saw was open water as far as the eye could see. They had a long way to go and no map to get there and their throats clogged as they repeated the mantra, *"Tenemos que ir. Tenemos que ir. Tenemos que ir."* We have to go. Their lives had taken a hairpin turn and there was no going back[37].

---

[37] An excerpt from the Pacific Commercial Advertiser, State of Hawaii Library on microfilm, State of Hawaii Archives: The SS Orteric was a British steamship and the travelers were crammed into the upper deck and in steerage. The Portuguese embarked from the agricultural districts of Lisbon while the Spaniards were from the district of Sevilla and from the mountain

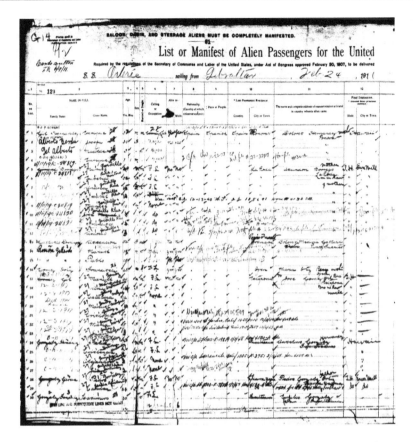

Ship's Manifest ~ S.S. Orteric sailing from Gibraltar Feb 24, 1911
(Gonzales family: Line 24-27)

Seen from a distance, the *Orteric* presented a pretty spectacle and cut a swift, hissing path through the clear blue water.   But

districts.   The Portuguese were embarked from Lisbon; the Spanish embarked from Gibraltar.   The SS Orteric took in 305 immigrants from Oporto and another 260 from Lisbon.   There were 960 Spaniards embarked who were sent into the ship.
Lines 1-5 list Juan Silban Hernández and family
Lines 6-11 list Victorino Silban Hernández and family
Column 11 shows the relative they left behind: Agustína Hernández, mother, Fuentesaúco

within the bulk of the ship, their temporary home, the family had to pick their way through the throng.   Cramped and uncomfortable, the galleries were thick with bundles, bags, mattresses, small cribs; the ship's hold was dark with people jostling for space.   How many, she wondered, how many people were here?

The women blanched at undressing in a sea of strangers. Following other women's examples, they quickly learned to wait until dark where they could create their own privacy after the lights went out behind shawls they hung around the bed frames like curtains.

In an effort to acclimate themselves to the strangeness, the children stayed near their parents.   With Juan beside them, first they looked for the toilets.   An unimaginable stench greeted them. There were too few toilets for such a crowd, and these were soon leaving the immigrants breathless from the disgusting odor. Manuela squatted first, and then held Agustín against the flat open seat as they relieved themselves; fighting against the overpowering urge to vomit, their hands clapped over their mouths.   It soon became a filthy area.

That first night, Manuela couldn't sleep; she needed her mother's reassuring touch.   Her stomach hurt her; she felt it knot with pain.   She knew she couldn't leave her bed in the dark.   But the toilet was up those narrow stairs. She couldn't see a light. She clenched her teeth, wrapping her arms around her belly.   Then the pain grew worse.   Slowly, she got up....   Some children whimpered in their sleep.   She could hear a woman sobbing close by.   She turned to the stairway and worked her hands along the railing, pulling her feet up carefully, quietly.   She hated the dark but she told herself to keep moving.   Once inside the toilet room, the air was stuffy and foul.

Afterward, she examined the clothes she was wearing. A white night dress, a little too long. It was simple but comfortable. Her toe was slipping out the edge of her right shoe; she was afraid if she removed them to sleep, they might be missing the next morning. She held her bundle close and used part of the bulk to pillow her head. And she slept.

As the days passed, little by little, she came to know many of her neighbor's names and ages, but some of them spoke differently; they could hardly answer her. There were children everywhere. Manuela, Teodora and Felisa were relieved to find Juliana and Antonia Martin. The girls helped with chores and met other girls their age around the boat, trailing after them like scruffy sparrows. The boys chased each other and played hide and seek around the deck, wildly trying to avoid the men, who didn't always take it kindly to have a child bombard them as they stood at the railing or moved through their work.

Not only the food, but riding the water turned their stomachs. All that water stretching around them until it seemed that was all that was left in the world. It seemed to swallow the sky. Each watery day ran into the next like a fixed blur before spring laced its way into the calendar, making the voyage difficult and overly long. The lurching ship spawned personal discomforts that touched everyone; so many children to care for, sea sickness, turbulent wind, storms filled with sheets of rain, fog, cold, then hot sun. The foreign weather and winds often buffeted passengers, forcing them below deck.

Manuela's stomach wobbled. She gagged on the vinegar water she was given to calm her belly, just as her cousins did.

155

Still, she preferred to be up on deck, facing the sea in the fresh air, rather than hugging a pillow on the makeshift bed, sickly warm, lurching.

Impatience warred with boredom. Babies cried. Diaper rash ran rampant and diarrhea was the norm. Mothers carried the brunt of the caretaking and many became mothers to more children than just their own.

Not only did the Hawaiian government pay their fare, but their food as well; strange food that slammed into their systems causing their bodies to rebel in response. But it was the only food available. Downstairs, an elongated table sat in the massive hall's central area where food was brought from the galley and spread for meals. Typically, the passengers carried their dishes and served themselves. Sometimes kitchen servers would ladle stew or soups when it was safer to do so. Some families would take their food to their private areas. The first night on the ship, they'd been served *arroz con pasa,* rice with raisins[38]. Since their food was so different from their Spanish and Portuguese diets, many were disappointed and some tossed their dinners into the sea with disgust. To ease their discomforts, a weekly inclusion of prunes and crackers helped when the strange food catapulted their digestive systems into chaos.

Most passengers kept busy. Most were overwhelmed with discomforts. Many volunteered for daily jobs such as carrying pots of food and urns of hot coffee from the galley, washing the ship's deck or tossing sawdust on the floors to cover the nasty smell of vomit and other unmentionables. Some passengers were taught to perform duties for the safe operation of the ship. Fire drills and

---

[38] Source: Memories of Spain, by Anne Aguilar Santucci 1997

abandon-ship procedures were practiced and everyone had to know their assigned places.   Others worked inside the galley and helped the cooks prepare the food or served tables or washed dishes or crusty pots and pans.

One specified daily chore included dousing the ship with a healthy dose of pine cleaner but the stink was part of their discomfort!

SENSELESS DEATHS STALKED THE SHIP.   The Spaniard from Jimena was preoccupied when he started down the dizzyingly-steep steps on the narrow stairwell from the galley kitchen.   The coffee was hot and it was his daily job to transport the large coffee urn to the eating area for the immigrant's meals.   And the woman was distracted.

In my mind's eye, I imagine he held the unwieldy urn with difficulty as he walked down the stairs.   On the same steps, climbed Alejandra Saez Galache from Fuentesaúco; a young woman, a new bride seven-months pregnant....She'd been bedridden with seasickness and rarely at with the mass.   Her husband took her food and drink.   But this day?   Why was she coming up to the galley?   Nobody could guess.   In a heartbeat, man, woman and hot coffee spiraled down the rocking ship's steps. Friends of the Silváns, Alvas, Corrales, Gonzales and Martin families, she was immediately lifted and gently carried to the Orteric's hospital room.   Her baby died[39] and she barely survived the fall while she and so many grieved for the senseless loss of her unborn child.

---

[39] Source: Memories of Spain, a story by the family of Frances Blanco DeFuentes, Fuentesaúco. Careful study of manifest notes confirmed the woman's name

The immigrants adapted to bathing, toilet and laundry facilities, though crude and lacking privacy. But the showers! Smelling their own skin, salty and rank, Ramona, Rita and Crescéncia held babies and led the older girls to the bathing room. Several other women and children waited, taking turns. Naked in the room, and without privacy, women and girls were sprayed with water from above, through a steel-grated opening by men holding hoses. It was embarrassing, even humiliating, but the ship's doctor and nurses told them showers would help avoid any kind of epidemic on board the ship. Many women kept their aprons on...... Otherwise, they had to wash in basins in public washrooms in full sight of everyone.

The laundry area was in the hold of the ship. There were tubs, washboards and running water; women were given soap to wash laundry; after scrubbing, they hung their clothing to dry on rope lines on deck. They learned quickly to gauge the wind first and often hung the clothes in their *bedroom* as some of their clothes had blown into the sea.

They often opened tiny port holes near their sleeping areas to air out the beds. Unfortunately, many smaller children peed in the living areas. The closest toilet was up that steep banc of stairs where Manuela had crept that first night. An adult usually held small children for fear of being tossed overboard by the strong winds after they traversed the steps. The toilets were flat, like a small table, smooth and wooden with a hole in one and three holes in another. No flusher handles; instead, they were hosed down each day and the waste was pushed into the ocean.

A SHIP'S WAY OF LIFE

Life on the ocean contained some good times and some bad times as the travelers lived on the cramped ship. Never having spent so much time with so many people, the constant noise was grating --- someone always talking, complaining, and machinery loudly whirring. They couldn't change out the stale air any more than they could muffle the sounds; yelps and cries could be heard on any given day just by walking along the tiny, tight corridor between the beds. They had little ventilation from the living conditions and the area reeked from buckets used for toileting where they slept.

With little semblance of privacy, and sometimes less camaraderie between the two nationalities, they forged through the days. But in spite of their trials and tribulations, their Spanish spirit prevailed even when their children became anemic.

The doctor, John Hopkins Pugh, argued the law required the immigrants to take their mattresses on deck to be aired periodically but nobody listened and he worried about their health and his ability to care for them when they sickened. He was also frustrated because even though there was electricity on the ship, there were no fans in the immigrant's sleeping area. When they battened down the hatches during storms, the ventilation need was worse and infant mortality increased.

In the midst of his worrying, our family roamed the ship and made new friends or visited with old friends from their villages. Sometimes they relaxed on the ship deck in good weather; the children used the ship as a playground. Jacinto and Celestino played tag with new friends. They found hiding places and learned which area was taboo. Sometimes they watched the older boys fight and throw dishes at each other, watching china plates break into little pieces and later saw the boys slapped for it. When they weren't watching other boys getting into trouble, they were inventing new games of their own. The twins were inseparable; where you saw one, you saw the other.

The evenings were the best part of the voyage; the immigrants enjoyed created entertainment like fiestas; they talked and sang, told stories and argued and danced to keep tediousness to a minimum.   Spaniards learned Portuguese songs and the Spaniards taught their songs in turn. Although both cultures clashed at times, during those festive moods, disagreements were temporarily forgotten.   And when the guitars, drums and accordions sat in the hands of these immigrants, the music gave life.

Juan played his beloved drum and many others had accordions, guitars, violins and mouth harps. He often sang his favorite song written by Juventino Rosas, *Sobre las Olas*, Over the Waves.   Castanets were pulled from small bags and flamenco tunes were picked on guitars. And they danced la *Sevillanas*[40].

Music made Felisa Silván drunk with happiness. She wanted to dance *la jota*. She loved to dance and keeping still when music throbbed was impossible. Instead, she tapped her feet while

---

[40] Sevillanas = a type of folk music, sung and written in Sevilla, Spain. Historically, they are a derivative of Castilian folk music.

listening to Manuela's music, tapping spoons.   And she enjoyed laughing at Juliana when she laughed at Manuela.

The staccato beat from the guitar, the hand thumping on its face and fast-paced violin spelled flamenco.   The singing, dancing and guitar resonated with the crowd and hand clapping accentuated its music like no other.   Their eyes sparkled, their hips swayed, feet tapped and their heads shook in the same staccato beat.

The little girls jumped, tapped and danced their way through the music like a living play.   The violin strings dueled with the guitarist's tremolo[41], where his fingers picked the notes so quickly, it rolled across their minds like a feisty waterfall.

And the dancing was more than entertainment.   Often, Manuela and other girls her age would go en masse to the dirty kitchen and dance *la Jota* for the Chinese cook in exchange for extra roasted potatoes for their families.   Frequently, they danced first and then were told, "Finne…" (no roasted potatoes left over). So they dubbed him, '*Capitán Finne.*'

The women sang, embroidered, crocheted, sewed and kept the living quarters as clean as they could manage.

Juan's daily job, along with a few other men, was to haul five-gallon cans of meat and potatoes to the great hall for lunch. With over 1,500 mouths to feed, it was a daunting task but hunger was mostly appeased.   Their jobs filled the watery journey with busy work.   It also gave them strength through exercise rather than thinking about the rumbling nausea in their bellies as they tried to control their sea legs.

---

[41] Guitar picking on a single note at a high speed.   Tremolo means a modulation in volume; in the context of stringed instruments, usually refers to repeatedly striking or bowing a single string in a steady rhythm, especially the fastest rhythm the player can maintain.

And the men played dominoes and cards called *la brisca*. The men were never too tired to play their card games, sometimes late into the night. Some of the women played also, but watching and caring for their children and the pregnant women on board kept them more than busy. The Portuguese called the same game *la brisca*[42] and removed the 8, 9 and 10 in the deck.

Once a week, everyone lined up with tin cups for their portion of wine to accompany their meal. Several times, fights erupted when someone took more than their share causing havoc between the Portuguese and Spaniards.   Furniture was broken, hair was pulled, bruises appeared and many fought in ways that often explode in close quarters with two nationalities striving to best one another[43].

Cramped quarters on cargo ships not built to accommodate passengers also created breeding conditions for the spread of measles, small pox, scarlet fever and other contagious, epidemic diseases such as cholera.   After long hours spent in the depths of the steerage areas, some nights many people walked the deck just to inhale the fresh salty air.

Huddled against her mother, Manuela watched families slowly lose their sanity.   There was not enough to drink and they missed their familiar food; no chorizo, no garbanzo beans.   The heat was stifling.

---

[42] La Brisca, a Spanish card game that is a variant of the Italian card game Briscola

[43] From an excerpt taken from the Pacific Commercial Advertiser, State of Hawaii Library on microfilm, State of Hawaii Archives. "There were ailing babies, seasick immigrants, and distress among the vast majority of the travelers, for they were not used to the cramped quarters of the big vessel and unaccustomed to the food served. They appeared to be a fine lot of people, said Secretary of the Territory, Mott-Smith to the Immigration Doctor, Victor Clark.   There were many disagreements between the Spanish and Portuguese immigrants; so much so that they had to be separated.   The women seemed to always be part of the acts of disagreements.   They went so far as hair pulling

"*From almost a semi-tropic climate, such as prevails in Portugal and the south of Spain, across the southern Atlantic down to the verge of perpetual floating ice and cold storms is bound to prove a shock to the constitutions of those unused to such sudden climaxes of weather, especially the children, and it was these little ones who suffered most. Then up again and across the equator for the second time the ship sailed its course under a blazing sun, until it reached the area of the cooling trade winds near its destination. But the changes of climate, for which probably few if any of the passengers were prepared in clothing or accommodations, were bound to have its effects on their health, even if the contagious diseases had not been present.*"

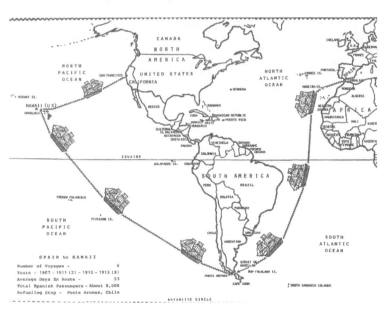

The skilled captain steered the S. S. Orteric on a route that continued southwest traveling past the northwest coast of Africa, across the Atlantic Ocean, down the east coast and into the Strait of Magellan, a sea passage around the tip of South America. It was known to be quite dangerous due to the narrowness of the passage at certain points, making it difficult to navigate. Winds were unpredictable, and the water was rough, but a resupply and refueling stop was necessary at *Punta Arenas, Chile*, which was the halfway point of the voyage to Hawaii and lasted two days. The sea was turbulent where three oceans met. And sailing through the strait, caused many to become seasick and bedridden as the ship rounded the cape; immigrants were confined below deck. The Panama Canal would not open for another three years.

During this time, the immigrants still managed to celebrate Palm Sunday on March 25, Good Friday on March 30 and Easter on April 1, 1911. A cleric was aboard and mass was held on deck, weather permitting. Other times, mass would be offered in the great hall. Lowering their heads to their hands, they prayed more fervently. As they'd been taught all their lives, they prayed for the grace to accept whatever trails were ahead of them.

Seasickness kept many passengers in bed. A serious epidemic of lice infested the hold and fumigation was a nasty affair. The medics separated the sexes, took their clothing and forced everyone through a maze where disinfectant was showered on them from above, below and both sides at different heights in the bathing room. While delousing took place, their clothing was placed in huge ovens of burning sulphur. Men's pants shrunk, women's blouses tightened, children's clothing was handed down to younger siblings.

Without proper toilet facilities, many immigrants dirtied the deck in corners, beneath stairwells and in other unobtrusive areas. In response, the deck's filth was covered in hot, stinking tar instead of cleaned and strewn with sawdust. The smells of hot tar, dead fish, and sweating passengers were nearly overwhelming.

And that wasn't the worst of it.

DEATH ON THE ORTERIC

Once the ship left *Puente Arenas*, disease spread among the children like a wild fire. Dr. Pugh took charge and roamed out to examine every person on board, whether they consented to such probing or not. He tried to segregate those with fever from those without.

Jacinto Silván became feverish after rounding the cape, his small face became flushed and he wasn't hungry. His eyes were half open, but fixed in a fever-stare like a dream-soaked daze. His twin, Celestino, urged him to play, but Ramona shooed him away, his brother was sick.

Dejected, he turned away and watched her bathe Jacinto's forehead with a wet rag after sending Teodora for their father, Victorino, with an urgent message to get the doctor. He heard the word, *measles*, but did not know what it meant. He tried to inch closer to his brother only to be pushed aside when the doctor pulled Jacinto into his arms and took him away. Teodora and Felisa held tightly to Celestino and the girls felt him quiver under their hands. They were instructed to stay put and they did as they were told. Nobody fully understood the seriousness of measles.

In 1911, there weren't many drugs to treat diseases. Jacinto was only one of many sick children. Many were contagious and many children started getting sick. Too hard to isolate them, an epidemic grew in proportions that were hard to tally. Fear struck at the hearts of parents, especially those with children in the infirmary, but for the healthy ---- life was a nightmare in waiting.

Celestino waited like a ghost for his brother to walk down the steps again. Teodora and Felisa waited for their parents to say their little brother was well again. Agustín and Alejendro missed following after him and wanted Jacinto returned to the family group. Juan was too young to understand and his mother, Crescéncia, kept them secluded from the bulk of the passengers as well as she could. The women walked among sick children, as if on egg shells.

Along that vast ocean trip, sadness slammed their hearts. Jacinto, Victorino's five-year old son did not come down those steps to the hold ever again. Measles stole him from their family and shock settled among the Silváns. For the Silváns, Gonzales', Martins and their friends aboard the ship, the deaths were stunning and totally unforeseen.

Celestino stared at his mother. She cupped her hands around his face. *"Debo decirte algo terrible."* I must tell you something terrible.

"Terrible," Celestino whispered. *"Jacinto?"*

"Jacinto se ha ido, niño." Jacinto is gone, child. Her voice broke and she had to stop. She tried again. *"Jacinto está......."*

"......muerto. ¿Quiere decir que está muerto?" Dead, you mean he's dead.

She nodded jerkily. *"Si, eso es lo que quiero decir."* Yes, that's what I mean to say. Ramona shivered uncontrollably.

The boy stared at her in disbelief and pulled his eyes away to beseech his father, who opened his arms and the now-twin-less boy threw himself forward to be swept up into Victorino's arms.

Manuela sat down next to Teodora who had gone quiet. She took her pale hand and squeezed it; her cousin did not respond. She couldn't move or think or believe the news. Horror froze her mind and she was angry. Why!? She wanted to go home and have their life as it used to be. Teodora turned inward and held her arms tightly wound around her body, swaying with her eyes closed. She could not remember ever hurting so much.

Like other grieving mothers before her, Ramona lovingly wrapped her little son's body in a blanket and stood beside Victorino as their boy was placed on a wide board. She stood like a stone. The shine of tears was in her eyes as she watched her little boy's body lifted to the railing and slip over the edge into the wine-dark sea. Rosary beads twinkled in the sun as she imagined the splash in the water. An involuntary sob issued out of her throat, stopping the words of her whispered prayer. She knew she would never be the same[44].

Her heart heavy with grief, Ramona blamed the boat, the move, the ocean and her husband. She vowed never to get on another boat and swiped tears until she could cry no more. At night, Ramona and other grieving mothers sobbed into their pillows for hours but nobody had the words to relieve their sadness. They tried to focus on their faith but it was sorely tried during that voyage as their cramped lives and sad hearts counted so many days and nights when they felt the boat rocking and grinding beneath

---

[44] In all, during the trip, there were forty eight deaths from measles recorded in the ship's log among the children on the voyage. Ten other deaths occurred due to various reasons and fourteen (14) new babies were born at sea.

them.

Many rosary beads clicked together as women often repeated the Hail Mary prayer..... *Dios te salve María. Llena eres de gracia. El Señor es contigo. Bendita tú eres entre todas las mujeres y bendito es el fruto de tu vientre, Jesús. Santa María, Madre de Dios, ruega por nosotros, pecadores, ahora y en la hora de nuestra muerte. Amén*[45]. They gathered in their grief, trying to gain some succor from one another as the finality of their children's deaths numbed them.   They also learned what *eterno* and *nunca* meant.   They could *never* kiss those tiny brows again ..... for all *eternity*[46].

Victorino blamed himself and stared at the wet horizon for days without speaking to anyone as endless pain engulfed his family.   He fought shame and guilt for bringing his family to this blackness and ill-begotten voyage across the watery miles to a place nobody was sure of.   He couldn't make words and shifted his gaze to the floor, to the slick and dirty area beneath them and knew he would always remember that day with the smell and dirt under his shoes.   Eyes filling with fresh tears, his face a mask of pain and disbelief, suddenly he wasn't sure at all.

The dark silences and who-to-blame mentality only began to ease as rumors of land reached his ears.   He pulled his chest tight, closed his eyes and gripped the railing.   He scrubbed his face with both hands, smearing the wetness, as if to remove the scene of that small bundle on its last trip to the choppy sea.   Then he went in pursuit of Ramona.   They must talk about the life ahead even though Jacinto's ghost would lie between them for a long time and

---

[45] Hail Mary, full of grace, the Lord is with thee, blessed art thou amongst women and blessed is the fruit of thy womb, Jesus. Holy Mary Mother of God, pray for us sinners now and at the hour of our death. Amen."

[46] Eterno = eternal / Nunca = never

leave a vacuum in their lives. She couldn't say Jacinto's name without it getting stuck in her throat; a small fresh grief tightening like a band around her chest.

And then tragedy struck again.

Little Simon Martin Sesmilo stopped eating, became feverish and was covered in a red rash. The doctor could not keep up with the ailing children as they became ill. Whether it was smallpox, measles or scarlet fever, he was hot and disoriented and could not be soothed. He was just past two years old.

Felisa was so frightened after losing her brother, Jacinto, that she held tightly to Juliana and whispered prayers and promises that Simon must get well. Little María Martin Sesmilo, Juliana's five-year old sister, had already lost her playmate and cousin, Jacinto, and couldn't fathom the loss. It was like a bad dream. God couldn't take another child from their family, surely not!

Enrique Martin Gonzalez watched his wife and son helplessly, feeling tension along the back of his neck spring and harden. Felipa mopped the boy's brow and cradled him closely, lying with him on the lice-infested bed, refusing to let go of him. Sitting beside Antonia, his older sister, the girls watched Felipa's terror-ravaged face from the edge of the huge room listening to his mother sing to her baby boy.

The day lengthened and grew dark; Felipa begged Simon to respond to the wet cloth she pushed to his small mouth. Then she sang softly, patting his small back and rubbing it softly in slow, circular motions. Her humming notes quieted the little boy; the women listening were swamped with pain.

Felisa squeezed her eyes shut and opened them only when she felt Manuela's hand on hers. Tears trickled from the girl's eyes and they couldn't speak because their voices were thick. Fear of death was too real for them on this water-logged giant of a boat and fear was a terrible thing.

During the night, Felipa knew her only son was gone as she pressed her cheek to his mouth and felt not a breath of air from him. She gripped him tightly and glanced around her; the vision of Jacinto being placed on that board wrapped in a little blanket and then slipping into the ocean was beyond her comprehension. She struggled and cried softly. The doctor was busy with many other sick children; she prayed he wouldn't take Simon. Not yet.

Broken hearted and without the slightest notion as to what moved her to do it, she managed to hide his small body for two days before the throbbing in her head built to a roar. Something vital had been plucked out and uprooted from her chest...By the time they took little Simon from her arms, the pressure in her breast was so strong she had to consciously school every breath[47]. And she wept violently in her hands.

The day was bleak. Simon followed the way of Jacinto along with four other small blanket-wrapped bodies amid more prayers, more tears, more clicking rosary beads, and more grieving parents. He was just one many children to be lost along the way that included their good friend's baby girl Balbina Ramozal Corrales and soon afterward, María Magdalena Corrales, both from *Fuentesaúco* and they still had not reached the promised paradise of Hawaii.

No one understood the joy a mother has from giving birth to a child, nor the devastation upon losing one. Grief clogged their lungs; they ached for solace amid anger and loss, sometimes shutting down pieces of their heart.

---

[47] Source: Julie Elliott, granddaughter of Juliana Martin Sesmilo

ALOHA AND PROMISED PARADISE

Birds!   Seeing birds meant land! Three weeks later, the news at the break of day was most heartening.   The passengers were told that they would soon see the land of Hawaii.   Eager for the first glimpse of their destination, they lined the rails in anticipation of that long-awaited moment.   They had been on the ship 45 days. Small wonder that such a glimpse would create such a stir.   And when they saw the outline in the far distance, cautious excitement was everywhere, albeit along with a ribbon of anticipation.

The next morning, the islands of Hawaii and Maui were clearly visible at dawn.   Gathered at the prow were many passengers who thanked God for His kindness to them even though they experienced the communal sorrow that afflicted the parents of all who had lost loved ones on the long voyage.   On the morning of April 13, 1911, the island of Oahu appeared in view.

Juan Francisco Silván did not know which was more shocking: the notion of riding over the sea to a land of the unknown or the slow, deep sense of astonished pleasure that began to rise in his chest as the tuft of land grew in the distance.   Turquoise water shimmered and danced toward white sandy beaches in mesmerizing waves of white foam; more beautiful than any piece of paper could have expressed. His face came alive with surprise and his blue eyes stared in fascination at the palm trees that appeared two inches tall from the distance; growing in height as the boat lumbered towards the shore. A gentle breeze turned warm and caressed his smiling face. He could just make out a water tower, a white church steeple and rows of houses. *"Será bueno,"* he whispered. It will be good.

The Titanic would sink on its maiden voyage almost one year later, April 12, 1912, killing more than 1,500 of the 2,228 passengers and crew. It would sit on the North Atlantic floor about 400 miles off Newfoundland and not be found for seventy three years. Juan couldn't know how very lucky they were to arrive safely but would undoubtedly think about it when news of the sinking Titanic was broadcast within a year.

He gazed at his wife, Eustoquia Rita Trascasas Marzo Silván, and smiled as he noted her cinnamon-brown hair pulled into a gentle twist at the back of her neck, a tendril slipping out of the scarf wrapped around her head. It filled his heart just watching her. She raised her gentle eyes, brown as coffee beans, and gave him a look. Since Jacinto's and Simon's deaths, he was never far from his wife or his children; they shared that special blessing that comes when a life is snuffed out and your children are missed in death's roll call.

Manuela saw her father and mother exchange glances and the communications that passed between them.

Rita felt humbled by the oncoming island. She wanted to

172

hold her children close and she wanted to feel unafraid.   And now that little José could walk nearly unaided, she held him to her breast and soothed his unhappiness.   He wanted to run freely around the deck.   His first few steps had been a major source of entertainment for everyone as he'd wobbled across the moving deck, entranced with his new-found ability.   He was gaining strength and wanted to walk without restriction though his legs were bowed and thin. Squirming to get down, his mother patted his bottom and whispered, *"No, mi hijo."*

Manuela glanced at her mother's expression, somber with worry.   One of her braids had come undone and the wind whipped hair against her cheek; her small hands gripped the railing and her mind went walking.   Barely reaching the top, she pulled herself higher and her brown eyes squinted in the sun, clearly enthralled with the sight before her.   Her small mouth formed an O in delight as Agustín tried to walk up the side of the boat beside her.

"Deseo ver!"   I want to see.   His well-worn little shoes scraped the ship's inner wall as he jumped to grab the railing. Unable to peer over the top, he yanked on her skirt and started to cry.   Manuela reached down excitedly and stretched her small arms around his middle and lifted him as high as she could while he squirmed and she danced around unsteadily, trying to lift him.

When her godfather, Victorino, saw Manuela struggling, he came to her rescue by swinging Agustín high in his arms.   His uncle laughed at the surprise on the boy's face, turned him around and held his butt in both hands, swaddled like a chair.   He grinned at him and squeezed Manuela's shoulder.   And then he threw his hat in the air and laughed when he saw the coast of Hawaii and felt the sight temporarily knock him out of his grieving stupor.   Young

Celestino, his son, caught it before it could fly over the railing and everyone laughed; the first laughter or smiles since little Jacinto died.

Crescéncia stood nearby and felt the first stirring of excitement after the difficult days aboard the ship as the anchor chain rattled.   The frown between her brows eased and a flicker of light came back into her eyes as they neared the pier.   The strange trees greeted them and her breath caught at the island's beauty. And she felt like a child, filled with wonder and awe, as she tipped her head back…far, far back, to stare upwards into the palm trees.

QUARANTINE

Just before the S.S. Orteric neared the *Honolulu* pier that morning, Dr. Pugh diagnosed a child's death due to scarlet fever and raised a yellow flag high on the mast.   He immediately radioed the ship's offices so appropriate steps could be followed upon the immigrant's disembarkation while the immigrants, blithely unaware of the flag's import, dragged their luggage up to the deck pushing, pulling, hugging each other and yelling, for once oblivious of the stench and tar beneath their feet.

Because of the fever, the *Orteric* was promptly quarantined[48] and lay anchored at a distance like a banished leper, gazing at Honolulu and the crowd on the pier waiting for their arrival.   The harbormaster pulled up alongside giving instructions, although the immigrants knew naught what was happening around them.

When the S.S. Orteric [49] eventually landed in *Honolulu* harbor, my grandmother, Manuela Trascasas Silván, was a mere heartbeat from turning ten years of age, a little girl who'd left everything she held dear.   It was a moment she'd imagined so many times, dreamed of both waking and sleeping.   Now Manuela couldn't believe it was real.   When she heard the ship grind along the quay beside them, she lifted her face toward a flock of birds flying in tight formation.   They settled on the branches of a tall tree

---

[48]   Compulsory isolation, typically to contain the spread of something considered dangerous

[49]   The exact time of arrival in Honolulu, Hawaii was 9 o'clock a.m. April 13, 1911

stretching skyward toward the spring sun. The birds chattered noisily, sounding like children gathered around the food table on the *Orteric* just the day before.

Her coat hung over her arm and she smoothed out the wrinkles of her dress. Hawaii. She stared at the tiny flowers on the blue background of the fabric, dancing under her fingers, so familiar and soiled. The waist of her dress moved freely and hung loosely. Excitement bubbled in her mind and body as she waited for her turn to disembark. She was not sure what she would encounter on the beautiful island but her mind twisted in every direction with thoughts running wildly.

The crowd from the ship moved like molasses until it was finally her turn, along with her parents and two brothers as they were herded down the landing incline. Her cousins and aunts and uncles were pushed along in a sea of bodies and then the group narrowed to two abreast to walk onto the wooden pier.

Her dress was filthy, a distinctive odor clinging to her as was everyone around her. The smell gagged and stupefied and she had been anxious to get off the boat floor that had been recently mopped with hot black stuff called tar. The smell had lingered and made her sick. Before that, it was so nasty that she didn't want to walk on deck at all. Children peed sometimes where they stood and there was no place to wash their clothes or their bodies except a very tiny area if one could get water for the buckets or stand in that room and get water dumped over you.... Finally arriving at their destination promised clear breathing and she wished she could sprout wings and fly over the railing and onto the ground. She needed to get off!

Rita guided her along, feet on the floor. The flow of passengers had become a stampede toward the terminal. So much for the wings... Her heart nearly bounced out of her chest as she padded alongside her mother, wondering what would happen next. Would they get a house? Would they eat Hawaiian food now? Would her father play his drum and would her mother dance *la Jota* just like at home? And singing... Would they sing? Would their lives be the same, different, better, worse? She had been too excited to sleep the night before; she and Felisa had whispered their fears and anxiety but they had little time to worry...

That morning, a breeze blew strands of hair across her cousins' faces. Each found a ribbon in their pocket and tied their hair back. They inhaled deeply, smelling foreign scents around them. It amazed them that they had made it to this point. Their hearts continued to beat as they'd gazed across the water to the lush green land beyond the ship's railing.

As their feet hit Hawaiian soil for the first time, their legs felt rubbery and threatened to drop them where they stood. After listing on the ship for nearly fifty days, the ground wavered beneath them still.

Manuela, Teodora, Felisa and Juliana stood amid their families and laughed as they watched a husky-looking Spaniard leap from the gangway to the wharf, shouting *"Viva la Republique!"* His exultant shout resounded within the shed. He sped through the building, reached the open air and felt solid soil beneath his feet and tossed his hat. The resulting laughter was a much-needed boost to the end of their journey.

Virtually everything ahead of them would be foreign and strange. Most of the immigrants had lived in a world of the farm and the village. They had overcome the noisy port cities that were frenetic and crowded. They had overcome, mostly, the terrifying journey traveling across seemingly endless watery prairies toward the islands and they now stood in Hawaii --- a place that a poster had described as the Paradise of the Pacific.

However, relief soon warred with impatience. Immediately, the immigrants were guided in two directions. Baffled, our families watched men separated from women again;

mothers from their older male children, husbands from their wives.

Chaos followed. Manuela couldn't understand why they were pushed and shoved into a huge room with showers. Foreign voices were raised to epic proportions and she understood not a word until a woman shoved her way forward.

"Debe quitar toda su ropa y ponerse rápidamente en las duchas." You must remove all your clothes and quickly get in the showers.

¿Qué? What? Pandemonium ensued.

¿Por qué tenemos que ducharnos con todas estas mujeres?" Why should we take showers with all these women? Rita and her sisters-in-law were horrified as they gripped Manuela, Teodora and Felisa closely, demanding answers. Felipa Martin glared at the woman as she circled her arms protectively around her three daughters.

"Escarlatina. Ustedes están en cuarentena." Scarlet Fever. You are in quarantine.

Stunned disbelief turned the women into stone for a hushed moment before pulling their girls against them; as if to ward off circulating germs of the dreaded fever. Ramona's and Felipa's hearts screamed at the thought of losing another child and their eyes pooled with tears. Their chests constricted and they stared at the woman with grieving-mother hearts.

Strong soap and thin cloths were distributed to the women. And under the watchful eyes of the matron, our ancestors and the other women set about the humiliating task of undressing in a room full of strangers. Manuela put her dress in the big basket and stepped out of her shoes. While she hurried to tug the long-sleeved sweater over her head, she unbuttoned her dress and let it pool at her feet.

When some women refused to comply, their clothes were ripped off and steaming showers were sprayed over them. Nobody avoided the cleansing. Their clothing and shoes were removed, placed in a sack with name tags and placed in an oven for fumigation, later returned dry and shrunken beyond redemption. This, of course, brought the distressing flashback of the ship's de-lousing regimen in stark remembrance.

Manuela stood still, shocked and scared. What were they going to do to her? Put her in jail? Send them back to Spain? Both were frightful prospects; the sea voyage had exhausted them. Watching her father and brothers leave with other men while she remained behind barred windows was like a stab in her head. What was going to happen to her? The thought chilled her to her bones. This was Hawaii? She was too young to understand what quarantine meant and when she questioned the adults, their response was garbled. She would live her entire life thinking the women in charge destroyed her clothing and made her stand naked among the women as Hawaii's Aloha --- welcome.

Everyone was soapy clean but the clamor of Spanish and Portuguese voices increased to a screaming frenzy. The frightened women began talking so fast to one another, nobody could understand, nor be understood. The air fairly crackled with electricity, the mood set on panic. Manuela saw soft-spoken women she'd grown friendly with on the ship change from ladies to manic strangers. Their upraised voices sprang a well of eerie fright to those around them, especially the children. No matter how she tried to understand the people in charge, the words were gibberish. Looking at her mother for understanding didn't seem to help.

Rita was clutching Ramona's arm and Crescéncia clasped

Felisa and their cousin, Juliana Martin. Felipa Martin crushed Antonia and María to her tightly as Manuela looked around for Teodora. Their eyes met in the briefest moment before they moved toward their mothers, hoping for resolution and balanced judgment.

Teodora whispered in a breaking, hopeless voice, *"Bienvenidos a las hermosas Islas hawaianas."* Welcome to the beautiful Hawaiian Islands.

In the other part of the building, the men and boys were treated the same, but did not fight the instructions like the women, realizing they had no choice. They'd already gone through too much to let this bizarre welcome slow their stride into their new life.

Quarantine! [50]

In the early days, when there was quarantine for ships coming into the harbor, people were quarantined on what was called Quarantine Island. It was a small tidal island that sat on the reef just outside of what we call Downtown Honolulu.

---

[50] Located at the entrance to Honolulu Harbor, Sand Island boasts a fine view of the Honolulu coastline from the harbor to Diamond Head and is noted as a place to view Oahu's stunning sunsets. Palm trees line the long, uncrowded sandy beach. The sand is coarser there than at other Oahu beaches, and the offshore bottom is rocky and uneven. Sand Island was once known as Quarantine Island during the nineteenth century when it was used to quarantine ships believed to hold contagious diseases.

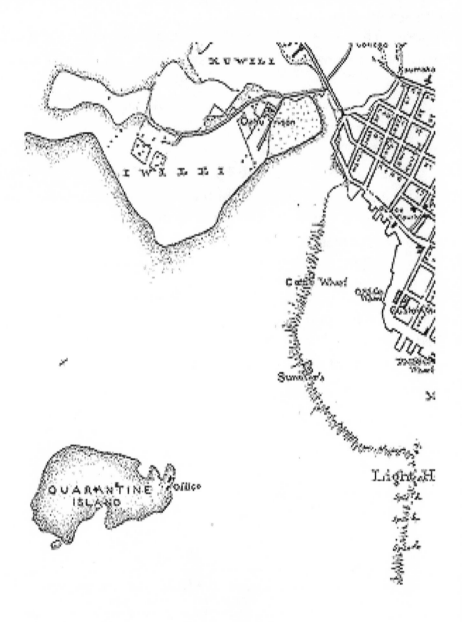

Transcript of Historical Newspaper

Hawaiian Gazette

Vol. LIV No. 30   Honolulu, Hawaii Territory, Friday,
April 14, 1911 – SEMI WEEKLY   Whole No. 3534

ORTERIC ARRIVES WITH MANY LABORERS

Death Busy Since Ship Entered Pacific –

Fever and Measles

ALL IN QUARANTINE

Majority of Fourteen Hundred Are Spaniards.

Death stalked among the fifteen hundred Spanish and Portuguese immigrants aboard the British immigrant steamer, Orteric, which arrived yesterday after its long voyage from Spain and Portugal.   Fifty-eight deaths were recorded among the children during the voyage.   Measles was the cause, as entered on the ship's log and in all but one instance, the bodies were consigned to the sea for burial but the federal quarantine officers detected evidences of scarlet fever, and the territorial board of health which looked after the body of the child who died just as the steamer was about to enter the harbor, announced last evening that death was due to scarlet fever and the immigrants were ordered sent to quarantine island.

The vessel arrived in port shortly after nine o'clock yesterday morning and went to the channel wharf.   At one o'clock, the United States Immigrant authorities began looking after the disembarkation of the newcomers and sent them to the federal station.   There they were preparing for a comfortable night, the first that many have had since their departure from continental Europe, nearly two months ago when the order was made to send them over to Quarantine Island.   The transfer will take place this morning at seven o'clock.

Inspector-in-Charge Brown on the federal station has not passed upon any of the immigrants yet and this will be deferred until after the quarantine period is completed.   Meanwhile they will be considered as aliens and be under the direct authority of the health officials on the island, although the expense of quarantine will fall upon the Territory.

Glad to Be Home

The immigrants are decidedly glad that their journey has ended.

"Viva la Republica!" shouted one husky-looking Spaniard as he fairly leaped from the gangway of the steamer to the wharf.   He shouted so that the shed resounded with the exultation.   He leapt as he sped through the shed, and when he reached the open air and felt the soil of Hawaii under his feet, he waved his hat.

Another, a Portuguese, middle-aged and carrying heavy bundles, ran down the gangway, his eyes almost glittering as he ran through the shed knocking his countrymen right and left, shouting: Away from that jail ---- away from that jail.   He turned a look of disgust upon the ship, and it is little wonder he wanted to leave it as death and filth had full sway upon the vessel for nearly fifty days.   The decks fairly reeked of filth, much of the latter being accumulations of litter due to the ignorance of the passengers.   The others, as well, heaved a sigh of relief as the last immigrant left the vessel, for then, and then only, did they have a chance to clean the vessel.

Fourteen Births

There were fourteen hundred and [51]ninety four immigrants on the vessel when it came alongside the wharf.   Fourteen hundred and fifty two were aboard when the vessel left the continent of

---

[51] Numbers transposed since the higher number left Gibraltar and lower number entered the harbor.

Europe behind and started across the Atlantic. Fifty eight children died and fourteen little ones were born at sea.

It was no pleasure[52] which Doctor Pugh, the surgeon, held on that trip for sickness was rife on nearly the entire voyage. There were ailing infants, seasick immigrants and distress among the vast majority of the travelers, for they were unused to the cramped quarters in the big vessel and unaccustomed to the food served.

Two hundred and fifty gallons of oil and a large quantity of wine were aboard and this was doled out slowly to the crowd, but even these adjuncts to home meals were insufficient to make them feel entirely at home. To make matters worse, measles broke out and decimated the ranks of the children and then at the last moment, scarlet fever made its appearance to add to the miseries of the people because of the long quarantines they will now have to undergo. All this tried the patience of Doctor Pugh and the trained nurses, one of whom has made three trips with immigrants from Portugal and Spain.

Fine Lot of People

"They appear to be a fine lot of people," said the Secretary of the Territory Mott-Smith when he went among them.

Doctor Victor Clark, head of the territorial immigration board, agreed with him. The doctor stated that the Portuguese came from agricultural districts back of Lisbon, while the Spaniards came from the districts of *Sevilla* and mountain districts. The Spanish were embarked at Gibraltar and the Portuguese at Lisbon and Oporto.

The Spanish were easily distinguished from the Portuguese because of their headgear and corduroy clothing. Their hats were wide brimmed, full crowned affairs and the corduroy of many colors ranging from dark brown to snuff-yellow showed hard usage and age in nearly every instance. They all looked, with a few

---

[52] Text indecipherable – I guessed 'pleasure'

exceptions, to be people from agricultural districts. One or two were dapper, as if they hailed from some city.

Few Belongings

Poverty was the badge of nearly all and their belongings did not amount to much. When a family came ashore, the father carried the largest bundles, the mother came with a bundle or a baby or two in her arms, often balancing a package or two on her head. The children carried buckets and rudely-fashioned toys, mainly little barrows. They clung to these toys and cried if they were taken away from them. The little people were mainly sturdy and strong, although the infants, as a rule, looked sickly and some could barely stand. As many of the women landed on the wharf, they crossed themselves and they smiled. They were back on land. Possibly some smiled because they were in a new land.

Wanted a Bath

The immigrants passed through a lane of officials and employees of the federal and territorial governments and into the big building of the immigrant service. Once within the building and finding a place to stow their belongings there was a rush for the bathrooms and some bathing was the rule of the day. Many congregated in the yards and were soon in the enjoyment of leapfrog and other games, while others peeked longingly through the fence railings at the preparations going on for dinner. Huge caldrons containing a stew of meat, onions, potatoes and carrots had a tempting smell and looked tempting when the great lids were taken off and the contents stirred.

The newcomers were interested in the great marquee erected in the grounds, within which were long tables and places set with the cups and platters, where nearly a thousand could be accommodated. The Japanese attendants were a source of interest to them, for they were probably the first Japanese the majority had ever seen.

An excellent dinner was served at the station and the change from the ship's feed to that prepared under the direction of Caterer Kishi caused a great rush upon the supplies. It was a fine meal, well cooked and thoroughly enjoyed and there was plenty of food for all. Then the new arrivals disposed themselves for the night, and morning at seven they will cross the harbor.

Spaniards in Majority

The Spaniards are in the majority numbering over nine hundred. On the voyage here, they and the Portuguese had many disagreeable clashes and had to be kept in separate portions of the ship. Shortly after the ship left the European continent trouble began to brew and it was one sided, for the Spaniards greatly outnumbered the Portuguese. As usual, the women were the cause, flirting with the men. The ladies differed and after a little hair pulling, the men entered into the fray. That battle is now referred to among the ship's officers as the "Battle of the Equator." It was quelled by Captain Findlay and the ship's officers.

But it was not all fighting on the voyage, for most of the time was occupied by eating[53] and the various sports. Many of the Spaniards are very graceful dancers and quite musical. One woman came ashore yesterday carrying a trombone while many had guitars and other queer-looking musical instruments.

Long on the Eats

It was a great task to feed this army of people. When the ship sailed, she had 120 hundred weight of sugar; sixty tons potatoes, 240 gallons salad oil and 290 gallons pickles as dainties. About forty head of beef cattle were carried on the forward deck. In feeding the people, the ship's people used one bullock, two barrels of salt pork and several pigs to a meal. On the store list was 200 pounds of tobacco, 60, 900 packages of cigarettes, 250 cases of

---

[53] Text indecipherable – I guessed 'eating'

condensed milk, 560 pounds of tea, three tons of salt. In the bakery, three thousand pound loaves of bread were made every day.   There were also immense quantities of crackers, biscuits and flour.   Wine was served once each week during the trip and when approaching the Islands, was served twice in seven days.   At Puente Arenas sixty sheep were taken on board.   The work of peeling onions and potatoes and carrying food to the immigrants was large and many of the immigrants were employed for this duty. As the vessel approached the Island, a vast quantity of straw was thrown overboard, the remnants of the bedding which had become very much soiled during the voyage.

Veteran Crew

The ship is handled by veteran sailors from Captain Findlay down to the ordinary seaman who so willingly carried babies down the gangplank to assist overburdened mothers.   The officers are: Arthur Atkins, first officer, Maurice McNab, second officer, Peter Tait, chief steward; Thomas Buchanan, first engineer, with George Perry, John Bailee and William Bowie as assistants in the engineering staff.

Territorial Quarantine

The quarantine ordered imposed on the immigrants today, is territorial, not federal as scarlet fever is not a quarantineable disease under federal health regulations.   The federal authorities are to look after the people on Quarantine Island at the request of the board of health and at territorial expense.   Doctor Hamus, head of the United States quarantine service, stated yesterday that undoubtedly some of the deaths during the voyage were due to scarlet fever.

The vessel is to be fumigated, and then her cargo of 500 tons of sulphate of ammonia will be unloaded at the railway wharf.   She has 5000 tons of cement for Vancouver and Victoria and will sail for the coast tomorrow or next day.

On Maiden Voyage

The Orteric is a large vessel fitted with accommodations for about twenty cabin passengers, and is a large cargo carrier being able to accommodate 10,000 tons dead weight. She can steam twelve to thirteen knots an hour and has 3000 indicated horsepower. She belongs to the Weir line and is on her maiden voyage having been launched at Greenock, England on January 28, 1911. She will probably join other Weir liners between Seattle and Orient ports. She has a length of 460 feet and is fifty seven feet breadth. The vessel logged an average of 11.6 knots on the voyage.

The Orteric sailed from London on February 18 and at Oporto picked up a batch of immigrants, taking on 305. At Lisbon, 329 people were taken on, and at Gibraltar 960 Spaniards were added on the vessel.

It was after the vessel had left Puente Arenas that disease began to spread among the children.

Transcript of Historical Newspaper
Hawaiian Gazette
Honolulu, Hawaii Territory, Friday, April 25, 1911
SEMI WEEKLY

PLACE CHARGES AGAINST VESSEL
Summary of contentions of government over Orteric
(From Saturday's Advertiser)

~~~~~

If there is any provision of the United States passenger carrying law that the Weir liner Orteric has not broken it is not officially known. The finding of the federal grand jury and the others that have been camping on the trail of the Orteric defects for the past week (and which have not yet been officially made public) seem to point to the fact that that same passenger law is a sorry looking object now that the Orteric has gone through it.

In the lack of hospital space, in the lack of sanitary accommodations of the most urgent nature, in the lack of ventilation, in the lack of cleanliness, and is the failure to separate the sexes, the government contends that the Orteric has broken the law. The vessel itself, through its agents, officers or attorneys, deny these charges and are said to admit others.

The conclusions to those who have been on board investigating are that while those laws have been broken, it has been the result of carelessness rather than an attempt to save money on the part of anybody concerned. It is conceded that the immigrants have probably been treated better on board the vessel, in the way of food and courtesy than they have ever been treated before in their lives. But, says the government, they were not treated sufficiently well with the demands of the government.

Hospital Lack
The vessel, claims the government, violated the law as to hospital space insofar as the hospital space required by law was not

furnished.   The "ship" is said to admit the allegation.   The vessel also admittedly violated the provisions of the law relating to her manifest, is having been lacking in several features.

These were probably the lesser violations, although they were sufficient in themselves to get the ship into trouble but the most serious points were her being the lack of decent cleanliness.

While the officers of the vessel assert that the lack of cleanliness was the fault of the immigrants, the United States will claim that no means of being clean were afforded them.   Twenty days before the ship arrived, it seems a bath was fixed up and not before then.   This bath consisted of just a faucet where one of the immigrants could, if he or she chose, to get under it and utilize it in full sight of everyone.   There were wash basins in the public wash rooms but it was also impossible to use these for bathing outside of the use for which they were intended.

Insanitary

As to the sanitary arrangements, these appeared to be equally bad if not worse.   There were accommodations on the upper deck but there were none on the deck below where some passengers were kept.   Anyone desiring to use the lavatory had to walk up two companion ways if they "lived" on the lower deck and one, if they were quartered on the deck above.   Those too sick or otherwise unable to make the climb were seriously inconvenienced as there were no substitutes for the lacking accommodation except those made by the passengers for themselves, with the result that the decks, according to the allegations, became filthy.   No buckets were provided and the maternity hospital ward is also said to have lacked the necessary requirements to the same degree.

Tarred the Deck

The method of cleaning the deck was a smothering one.   At no time, according to the government inquisitors, was the deck washed, but tar was spread over the filth and dirt and this in turn was strewn with sawdust.   The second doctor of the ship is said to have complained frequently to his chief over the stench which arose from this method which is said to have been simply sickening.

The captain and officers were given authority by law to muster the passengers and their mattresses on the upper deck, and are indeed, required to do so. They claim that the passengers refused to answer the calls but the fact remains that from the time the vessel left until she arrived at Honolulu, ninety-five percent (95%) of the mattresses were never aired.

Ventilation

The law requires that these things should have been aired and also requires a specific standard of ventilation. The ventilation of the Orteric, according to the charges being defective is the ventilation law was not being complied with. The ventilation was particularly not sufficient when it became necessary to batten down the hatches and where this necessity arose; it appears that the percentage of infant mortality invariably increased. There was an electric plant on board but there seemed to be no electric fans.

"Battle of the Line"

It appears that when the ship was in the equatorial waters, a scrap appeared between the Spanish and the Portuguese who have never been known to possess very much aloha one for the other and this affair is jokingly referred to by government officials as the "battle of the line." Too much wine is described as the cause of this little scrap but there were apparently no casualties for the records are silent in this respect.

The law making the separation of the sexes in certain respects mandatory never seems to have been greatly complied with but the government alleges that after the battle of the line, there was hardly any attempt at all in complying with the regulations claiming further that the construction of the vessel itself violated those laws.

One of the things said to be admitted to that after the scrap,

194

the Portuguese and Spaniards were kept apart, which resulted in the indistinguishable singling of the men and women contrary to the statistics.

Food Good, but.....

The food appears to have been good and wholesome and the inquirers can find no fault with it.   But although the government is in every way satisfied on this point, the immigrants were not and say they did not like it.   The absence of garlic and the general absence of the other relishes demanded by the Latin people was probably the reason.   The government, however, claim that the facilities for cooking were not up to the requirements.   There is also some conflict with the condensed milk for the infants.

Nobody Knows

There appears to be a strange ignorance on the part of everyone concerned as to how many people there were on the ship. The federal immigration authorities, according to their papers, state that they suppose 1514 souls on board.   Collector of the Port Stackable, from his official papers, unofficially supposes that there are 1342 while someone else officially supposes there were 1549. The territorial people seem to have no number at all.

It is claimed that there were 456 infants under the age of eight years on the vessel but neither this figure nor the others have been verified by the immigration officials as these do not step in until the quarantine is raised.

The 56 or 58 deaths, with the exception, were from these 456 infants and the scarlet fever or measles or whatever it was seems to have particularly swept through the entire number, none of whom escaped although half a hundred died.

The present anemic condition of the children is supposed to be due to this disease, whatever it may have been.

Orteric at Outer Anchorage

THE UNITED STATES passenger regulations under the act of 1882.... It should largely rest with Agent A. J. Campbell of the territorial board of immigration who inspected the vessel whom he chartered to bring the immigrants from Spain and Portugal and is reported to have gone through the vessel before an immigrant was aboard.

The question has now arisen as to who is just to blame for the oversight --- the ship's people or the Territory's immigration agent[54]. Orteric may not sail for several days[55].

---

[54]December 9, 1911 – Regarding unsanitary conditions on the S.S. Orteric, "The Department of Commerce and Labor yesterday announced that the modified fine assessed against the British steamship, Orteric, would be $7,960 for neglecting the sanitary conditions in connection with bringing immigrants to Hawaii in the steerage. The original find assessed was $10,000." Source: Pacific Commercial Advertiser newspaper, Honolulu, HI

[55] Some of the bottom of the newsprint is too blurry. It looks like the ship was sent to a place to be thoroughly cleansed but it is still in quarantine....

MORE DECISIONS AND *PLUMERIA*

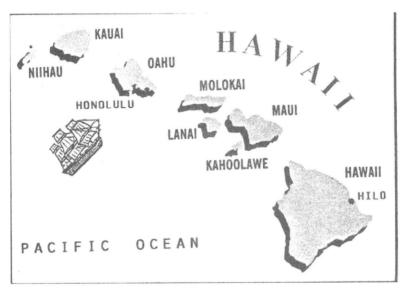

AFTER RELEASE FROM QUARANTINE to immigration service after nearly a month, the worst was over, and the processing to establish the immigrants in their new homes began. The shed of the Planter's Association was a big immigration building that contained facilities for bathing and washing clothes. Interpreters stood ready to answer questions and advise them. Immigrants could engage in whatever pursuits they desired. Some were artisans and tradesmen and remained in Honolulu. But the majority had agricultural backgrounds and proceeded with their plan to work in the sugar cane plantations.   The land owners' plantation representatives were there to register them for work under agreements which prescribed the conditions offered for work and living.

```
THIS AGREEMENT made this .............. day of .............,
A. D. 190 ... by and between ......................... Company,
an Hawaiian corporation, party of the first part, hereinafter
called the "Company", and ........................... party of
the second part, hereinafter called the "Homesteader".
                    W I T N E S S E T H:
     In consideration of the premises and of the agreements of the
Homesteader hereinafter contained, the Company hereby covenants
and agrees to and with the Homesteader during the term of three
years from the date hereof as follows:
     1. That it will furnish employment for the said Homesteader as
an agricultural laborer at its plantation at ..................
for the full period of three (3) years from the date when such
employment actually begins, and also employment for the wife and
able bodied children (of fifteen to eighteen years of age)  of
said Homesteader, paying therefor wages for work actually per-
formed at the following rates:
     To the Homesteader:
          First year ......................... $20, per month;
          Second year ........................ $21, per month;
          Third year ......................... $22, per month;
     To the children of the Homesteader residing with him  as part
of his family:
          Males 15 to 18 years ................ $15, per month;
          Females 15 to 18 years .............. $10, per month;
     To the wife of the Homesteader
          under 40 years ..................... $12, per month.
A month within the meaning of this section 1  to consist of  26
days, and a day to consist of ten hours in the field and twelve
hours in or about the sugar factory.
     2. That during the term of three years from the  date hereof
the Company will furnish the Homesteader free of charge, a house
for himself and family, fuel and water for household purposes,
and at the option of the Company, water for agricultural pur-
poses, when necessary, on the lot hereinafter referred to, and
medical attendance and medicines for himself and family.  In the
event that the plantation of the Company is dependent upon rain-
fall for its water supply, its agreement to furnish any  water
under this section shall be limited to supplying the Homesteader
with a suitable tank to store water for household purposes.
     3. That within six months after the arrival of said Homesteader
at the said plantation, it will furnish to the Homesteader a par-
cel of land containing an area of one (1) acre upon said planta-
tion, and provide thereon for the sole use of the Homesteader
and his family a dwelling house which shall consist of not less
than two rooms and a veranda.


     THE AGREEMENT CONTINUES, AT SOME LENGTH AND DETAIL.
     FOLLOWING IS A SUMMARY OF THE REMAINING SECTIONS:

     4. That upon the Homesteader working, according to the terms
of the agreement, for a period of three years, the Company will
provide him with the deed to the lot and improvements thereon;
with conditions to protect the interests of the Company.
     5. That before the deed is delivered, the Company is responsi-
ble for taxes and maintenance of the property.
     6. That the Homesteader will work to the best of his ability
and be willing to work at night if called upon to do so.
     7. That the house and lot will be used only for the Homesteader
and his family.
     8. That the premises will not be used for any unlawful or im-
moral purposes.
     9. That should either party violate any of the covenants con-
tained herein, the other party has the right to terminate the
agreement.

     IN WITNESS WHEREOF the said parties hereto have hereunto and
to another instrument of like tenor and date set their hands and
seals at Honolulu, Territory of Hawaii, the day and year  first
above written.
```

This is an example of the type of contract used to register a legal agreement between the sugar 'Company' and the 'Homesteader' or head of the immigrant family. Through Section 3, and the last paragraph is a direct copy; Sections 4 through 9 are paraphrased to conserve space[56].

---

[56] Source: Memories of Spain, by Anne Aguilar Santucci 1997

Honolulu immigration building

Soon, decisions had to be made; which plantation? Which island? They thought Hawaii was one island, not a group of islands, so their options were overwhelming. There were several plantations near Hilo on the island of Hawaii; *Kukuihaela* for the Corrales family. Several *Fuentesaúco* families already worked there from the 1907 sailing; an uncle was waiting for them. The *Waiakea, Papaikou* and *Hakalau Plantations* hired many families so another boat to another island…

Once the men demonstrated their prowess in the cultivation of sugar cane, they would receive gratuity and absolute ownership, without any charge, the house where they were living and also that parcel of soil.   Earning a dollar a day was mind boggling and they were determined to honor their contract and prove they were worth the ship's ticket which would have otherwise cost each person 300-500 pesetas.

The immigrants were returned to the main artery of the immigrant holding rooms and led through an outer building. Outside the entrance on an open grassy area, a great marquee was erected with massively-long tables.   Cups and platters sat among groupings of fruit, previously unknown to them: papayas, guava, bananas and mangos.   The aroma from the stew of meat, onions, potatoes and carrots was incredibly tempting after the ship's food. Quite a stir of interest was on the cooks and attendants; probably the first Japanese they'd ever seen.

Residual emotion from the journey and the relentless speculation touched Manuela.   Hawaii's scented flowers wafted toward her on the breeze and she lifted her nose to inhale their exotic perfume.   Tall palm trees swayed above, flowering shrubs and a multitude of trees with bright flowers beckoned.   She would discover a special love for these, the *Plumeria*, and learn to make leis from the sweetly-scented petals.   She held out her arms and twirled around with her face to the sun, bracing against the slight breeze as her nose eked out the scent of the tropical flowers around her and her mind settled.   It was a paradise after all.

SUGAR PLANTATIONS

The men hit the ground running, intent on learning sugar cane farming from planting and cultivation to its maturity. Despite their knowledge of orchardry handed down from generation to generation, they found sugar cane profoundly different.

And they were ill prepared for their experiences as plantation workers in Hawaii. They had come from societies where they labored to provide for their families within a context of traditions and established rules and obligations. They had control over their time, working with family members and people they knew. The peasant farmer followed the rhythm of the day, weather and seasons in Spain. And they lost their names along the way.

In the old country, workers had names that connected them to family and community; names given to them by their parents, names that told them who they were, names that were important in the old village --- but in Hawaii, they became numbers.

Plantation administrators often mispronounced many of our ancestor's names. Since many immigrants could not write, a numbering system was implemented to track them.

Bango ID tags[57] were made of brass or aluminum, a number stamped on one side, not unlike the later social security number except these numbers changed with each plantation job. It was usually worn on a chain around their neck and came in different shapes, typically determined by a worker's race. Every Hawaiian plantation used the bango system and laborers were required to wear the disk during working hours. These metal disks were hard to accept because they put a distance between themselves and their humanity. However, the disks purchased items from the plantation store and if our families were short of cash, credit would be provided, all kept in account books under this bango number system.

Finally the laborers were on the plantations. Many workers hoped they would be able to save enough money to return to the old country, to begin again in their homeland, and to recover their names, there personhood. Others planned to stay permanently in the islands and open their own businesses or plow their own fields. Whether they intended to be sojourners or settlers, a great many of them remained in Hawaii. All of them carried a fierce and tenacious hope regardless of the future they imagined for themselves in the islands, home again or America.

Felix Gonzales Hernández opted for Ewa Plantation, considered one of the most prosperous plantations in Hawaii.

Ewa (pronounced EE-vah) Sugar Plantation, two miles from Honolulu, was incorporated in 1890, its first sugar cane crop harvested two years later. By 1911, the Ewa Plantation Company

---

[57] Source: "Bango Tags: A New Identity." www.hawaiiplantationvillage.org, p.4

community contained over 2,500 people; several laborers camps, a plantation store, kindergarten, clubhouse, hospital and dispensary, and several outlying camps. Approximately 30 miles of railroad track serviced the plantation. Sugar from the mill was conveyed by the Oahu Railway and Land Company to Honolulu Harbor for shipping. There were several artesian wells.

Felix's experience with horses derived from his military days in Spain's cavalry offered him good employment in the Ewa Plantation stables with the horses and mules used on the plantation.

Juan Francisco and Victorino Silván also chose Ewa; they wanted to keep their family together. Victorino would work near Felix, but Juan would work in the sugar cane.

The *Harvey Plantation* on the island of Hawaii lured the Rodriguez Thomas family. The Reguera family went to the *Puunene Sugar Plantation* on Maui. The list of plantations went on and on.

Those who chose neighboring islands, like our families, boarded another boat to be transported to their assigned plantations. They were provided houses, wood and water at no cost by the plantation; typically a four-room cottage that included no less than two bedrooms, situated on a lot of approximately 5,000 square feet, with the necessary wash, bath house, and other sanitary arrangements on the premises.

The houses were not wired for electricity for cooking. In the corner of the house were storage rooms for the wood to fuel their ovens and stoves; inside were cooking grills, outside where they cooked most of their food stood their beehive oven,

Typical plantation house built on stilts, which kept house above high water run-offs during heavy rain. Rainfall is particularly heavy in the Hilo area, where the annual mean days of rainfall is 282.

el horno[58], a mud adobe oven built outdoor.

The sugar plantations were managed by foremen, called *lunas* who provided detailed insight into their new plantation life. And the sugar industry in particular as he handed them their specific jobs and explained the rules for working, the timelines, the payment schedules and their new living options.

Rita found the house just as she imagined it except for the stilts and the several steps to enter inside. It was full of sunlight and smelled of freshly cut timber and strong soap. In the main

---

[58] Source: Wikipedia -Originally introduced to the Iberian Peninsula by the Moors, it was quickly adopted and carried to all Spanish-occupied lands. The horno has a beehive shape and uses wood as the heat source

room there were six six-paned window sashes, two on each wall. From the far side there was a stretch of clear spring sky and the glint of yellow-green on the tall palms that bordered the river. From the door there were the deep shadows of the dense cluster of foreign-looking trees.

Rita was silent, overcome with emotion. She walked through the house again, the floorboards solid underfoot, to stand in the back of the room gazing beyond the piece of soil that now belonged to them. The doorway gave her a view of the bright flowers amid the trees in a small clearing where she could see clumps of Anthuriums blooming in riotous bright red.

And ferns were everywhere. She inhaled the fresh air before turning to smile at Juan who stood thoughtfully behind her. He pointed to the two-hole toilet behind her some feet from the back door, the tin tub beside the door that would be their bathtub and they shared a laugh together.

Several cottages away, Victorino watched Ramona's shoulders relax and felt a settling of her spirit though still deeply mourning Jacinto's loss. He'd believed the dream, sold all they possessed for their passage and his siblings had followed suit. As the oldest in the group who left Spain on the ship bound for Hawaii, he'd felt the burden of decision and he gave a wide, slow smile to watch their faces that day. His doubts eased; if only Jacinto could share it with them...

The women glanced at other houses close by. The spell of warmer weather had brought out washtubs and clotheslines and they heard women call to each other as they worked. It would be easy to imagine living in this country and it was good.

As our families landscaped their yards and planted vegetable gardens, they developed the home feeling in their camps. People began to know and care for each other. They helped newcomers with clothes, food and especially bread. In essence, they raised their families, played, worshipped and transplanted their cultures from the old country to Hawaii. They kept the Spanish traditions but tasted the Hawaiian poi (most often they did not like it.) They cooked *garbanzos, habichuelas, arroz con pollo, potaje, lentejas.* These are soups made of vegetables and beans (usually chickpeas) consisting of cooked vegetables, onions, garlic, tomatoes and peppers. Variations could include egg, spinach, chorizo or bacon. Spices are added such as garlic, paprika, pepper, cumin, oregano and cloves.

The physical organization of plantation housing reflected a social hierarchy. The manager lived in what looked like a mansion with spacious verandas and white columns overlooking the plantation; his foremen and the technical employees were housed in handsome bungalow cottages. The workers of different nationalities were usually housed in separate buildings or camps, seemingly subdivided into racial sections. The formation of separate ethnic camps reflected the wave pattern of labor recruitment and immigration. As planters recruited groups of laborers from different countries, they constructed new camps for them. The laborers themselves preferred camps of their own, so they could practice the customs and traditions of their respective homelands and speak their native languages.

Each nationality group more or less constituted an exclusive group of its own and didn't always mingle with any other. Our families met other Spaniards and had the opportunity to socialize with their friends, family or other nationalities at the various festivals during the different sugar-cane development stages or religious festivals. They adhered to the Spanish traditions made easier as they were placed among other families from Spain, although from various provinces. The inherent sweetness of living in their cultural settlements helped them after the sorrow of leaving their lives in Spain behind.

Their parcel of soil was large enough to plant a vegetable garden, garbanzo and habas (beans), fruit trees and flowers. And they had room for chicken coops and a goat for milk and making cheese, or other small animals, such as pigs, which was a typical plantation camp life in the early 20th century in Hawaii. Mostly, our families grew everything but flour, brown sugar and rice.

Manuela, giddy with excitement upon learning about the chickens and the flowers, talked of nothing else for days but her bliss was short-lived. As the house settled down and their belongings were put in place, the men started their work days very early and the women handed out chores. Their apportionment of wood was stacked by the door and they had made friends in nearby cottages.

And the children would attend the plantation's school. Manuela bit her lip in vexation. She had gone to school in Spain for a short time before they walked out of the only life she had ever known. Now, she wanted to play in the garden, run through the camp, help with the cooking and learn to sew the loose dresses she saw locals wearing outside the camp lines. Pooh! School was for boys, wasn't it?

Teodora and Felisa would also go. It was already decided. *Tio* Victorino was very stern about it when he stabbed his finger at the poster that explained children must be schooled.   The school was free and the children would receive an education!   The fathers brooked no arguments and the mothers solemnly agreed.

Manuela glared at Felisa as she jumped up and down, ever hopeful and cheering the news.   Felisa wanted to learn to read and write in the English so she could learn to speak their language.   She was tired of listening to gibberish.

Teodora sat aloof, while watching her younger sister dance around the room and saw her cousin, Manuela, scowl and shake her head grievously.   Teodora would attend until she turned fourteen, then she would join the women in the fields or earning a wage doing laundry, sewing or cleaning homes.   Two years wasn't such a long time; she might even learn to speak English, write and read...

But not yet.   The cousins explored their new home, walking on and on...listening to the melodic, lively twittering of songbirds. Manuela and Teodora pulled Felisa along and the girls looked up, surprised to hear birds so close above them.   The nearest houses were not whitewashed with plaster like in Spain, but white wood beneath a strange wooden roofline.

The schooling decision made, the men turned to discuss their new lives as the women prepared their evening meal.   They were anxious to make their lists for seeds and a friend promised them seed potatoes to begin the Silván gardens where their fertile fields would be moistened by their sweat.   The women separated their flower seeds from Spain in little folded pieces of paper.   There were starts for green peppers, onions, tomatoes, green beans, garlic, cucumbers and their garbanzo seeds.   Their grapevine starts would take four seasons to mature --- a sign they were planning to stay longer than the three years on their contract.

KILAUEA SCHOOL

Everyone was excited except Manuela. She couldn't seem to capture Felisa's feeling of expectation. She was unsure why. But even in her poor mood, she could not ignore the thought of reading a book or writing her own name. Was it the fear of school that made her heart pound or that she wouldn't learn what she was supposed to learn?

School day arrived quickly. In the bathroom, Manuela washed the sleep from her brown eyes, which in the mirror blinked at her from an oval face under dark hair, long and looped down her back. Her dress was clean, as were her stockings. Her shoes were tight and she ached to take them off and run barefoot as she'd seen the other plantation children do upon arrival. But her mother raised her eyebrows at her and did not speak. Instead, Rita nodded toward the door.

A group of children ranging in age from 6 to 12 were gathering at the edge of their dirt lane. She, Teodora and Felisa ate bowls of hot cereal doused with milk and cinnamon before being handed a cloth-wrapped package with their lunch inside. A clattering wagon appeared and the children were loaded on like little ducklings, before lurching away. Within a short time, after passing green trees filled with colorful blooms and birds of every variety, they stopped in front of a tall, narrow building on Kolo Road with KILAUEA SCHOOL[59] painted in bright letters.

The school was on the edge of the clearing where the Spanish housing spread before it through the fronds of swaying palms, banana trees, cawing birds and the smell of soil with the faintest taste of salt in the morning air. It was a medium-sized wooden building with windows that faced the road and two on each long side facing five narrow steps. The building stood on semi-poles to avoid high tides during storms and its façade looked aged and a bit dark.

The children were herded into the one-room building to find hard-scrabble tables in deep rows waiting for them. There was a cubby hole in the wall for their lunches and outer garments. Manuela was glad to be seated next to Felisa and Juliana, but wished she was across the room with Teodora and the older children.

There were two Portuguese women in the school. One was a young, friendly woman named María, sympathetic to the children's first-day-at-school jitters. The other woman was fierce looking, glaring when María soothed a crying boy at the next table. She introduced herself as Señora Isabelle Palmida. Her round face had puffy clots of skin beneath dark eyes and black bushy eyebrows. Small lines creased her lips like a coin as if smacking them together after sucking a lemon. Her voice was stern as she held up her hand.

"Silencio por favor."   Silence please.

Manuela fought a smile. The room was already silent, couldn't the teacher hear it?

---

[59] Kilauea School in 1911 was a small building; newer school, 1922, is still active.

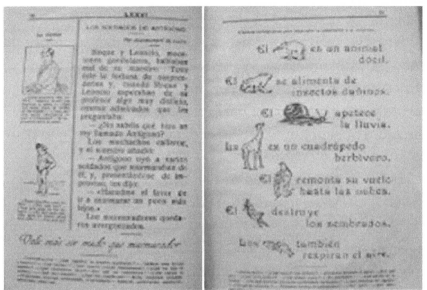

A large, wooden desk faced the students and Señora Palmida stood before it; blackboards lined the wall. Nodding toward María to distribute a reading book, paper and a stubby pencil to each student, she walked around the room and stared at each child. Her hair was pulled on top of her head like a little flower with wisps of dark hair slipping out and hanging in front of her ears. Her dark eyes were sharp and questioning.

"¿*Cómo te llama, niña*?" What is your name?

A little girl stared and whispered, "Encarnacion."

Each child repeated their name and she moved on until she stood up front once again. During the next two hours, she explained the school rules and asked the children to write their names on the paper in front of them.

Manuela's dark head was bent to her paper. She could not read or write so she held her pencil tightly and drew her initials elaborately instead.

Her belly cramped when the teacher walked in the front of her table as she laboriously printed her initials, *M.S.T.*

They listened to the teacher read a story that seemed to have no end. And Manuela was past the need for a toilet break. She squirmed and tightly crossed her legs until she couldn't hold it a moment longer. She raised her hand but the teacher ignored her. Frustrated, she shook it wildly above her head, twisting in her seat awkwardly.

Señora Palmida stared at her with frown lines creasing her forehead. "*¿Qué desea usted?*" What do you want?

"*Necesito usar el aseo.*" I need to use the outhouse (toilet). Manuela's mouth trembled slightly when she whispered the words fiercely. She couldn't wait until lunch break to pee and she felt the spring of tears behind her eyes.

The teacher drew her dark eyebrows together and scoffed, "*Se puede esperar hasta la hora de la comida.*" You can wait until the dinner hour. Without waiting for Manuela to answer, she moved to the next page of the reader and pointed to the picture.

Manuela squirmed again, her eyes wet with frustration. "*Por favor..... Señora Palmida,*" she asked tightly.

The teacher turned toward her slowly, clearly angry for the interruption. Before she could say a word, Manuela jumped up from her chair and stomped one uncomfortable shoe, demanding permission to go to the toilet at once.

The teacher glared at the child, clearly annoyed and then her eyes widened in shock as a stream of pee dribbled to the floor at the girl's feet.

Manuela's face blanched and she fought tears that quickly turned to anger. She thought she might come apart like a puff of wind and she remembered the children on the boat who had no place to pee; now it was happening to her.

Silence dropped between them like a stone.

"*Usted limpia ahora mismo!*" You clean that up right now! The teacher's face glowed red as she started forward.

María hurried quickly from the other side of the room, earnest concern so clear in her dark eyes.

Manuela bristled; before either of the teachers could reach her, having seen the looks of dismay on the other children's faces, she'd turned with the pencil clenched in her fist and disappeared.

Stumbling erratically, she burst out the school door and skipped down the steps, the sound of urgent voices following in her wake. She ran. Her legs propelled her in the direction the wagon had brought her early that morning. Walls of thick vegetation rose up on all sides and arched overhead in a lacy canopy that filtered the light to a soft shade. It had just rained; the air was steamy. Deeper into the woods lay a mysterious emerald world dappled with golden sunlight. She felt enclosed, sealed off from a world that suddenly seemed desolate. Catching her breath for only a moment, she went still, looking over her shoulder to listen before quickening her pace. Manuela didn't stop running until she found her new house. Her hands were sweating and she was breathing hard, shaking and angry. She smelled of urine and sweat. Sounds consoled her – birds singing and voices laughing in the distance. A bright yellow flower swayed in the breeze as if to welcome her to spring. She embraced it all.

The house was quiet and welcoming. Her feet glided over the empty room and she was relieved; her mind and breath settled. Ripping off her dress, stockings and panties, she grabbed a bucket, filled it with rainwater and heaved it inside the doorway. Making sure nobody was about; she quickly doused her clothes and washed herself with the soapy water before rummaging for her old clothes. She promised herself she would never return to that wood building or listen to old Señora Palmida again and that single journey changed the course of her life. She would work like her mother and aunts[60].

The next day was the first day of Manuela's new- found freedom in Hawaii. Unable to hide her dripping clothes hanging from the clothes line behind their house the afternoon before, she'd learned the art of debate as a dignified *confabulator*[61]. She talked herself hoarse and it won her the independence she'd hoped for instead of proving herself *alocada*, scatter-brained.

Rita Silván saw a delicate fierceness in her young daughter that she secretly applauded. Her sons were small and having Manuela to help with them as well as the other women's chores would teach her things in life that schooling wouldn't. It was decided among the women that Manuela would be their personal project and they would hold the keys to her learning and safety without the schoolroom.

The corner of Manuela's mouth lifted in a semblance of a smile. Thoughts chased around in her head like playful kittens. She'd won and gooseflesh pimpled her arms.

The women would teach Manuela to cook soups, grow vegetables, crochet, sew tight seams and bake bread. They would teach her to care for children and allow her to become who she was meant to be without schools or the pressure of regimented classes

---

[60] This story was one of Abuelita's favorites to tell us, laughter filling in where words were lost.

[61] Confabulator = conversationalist

the Hawaiian government prescribed for her. She would, however, be watched over and protected as all young Spanish girls expected and Manuela understood that was non-negotiable.

The women chose not share the dramatic change in the rules with the men. Not yet. They had already made their thoughts known.

The ladies of the Silván family did not have long to wait before their new endeavor was put to the test. The next day, the women pulled the table outside to begin preparations for the dinner meal, *la comida.* Heavy white cloths were spread on the length of the wooden slabs, a make-shift table that would feed many. The bread ingredients were laid out; bowls were gathered and placed nearby.

And then the ground rumbled beneath their feet; rolling dust filled the air. A large man drew up on a splendid white horse, the man's muscular arms heaving on the reins, his face dark with an angry scowl.

The women caught themselves up and placed themselves in front of the table; Manuela hid tightly on the ground beneath it.

"¿Dónde está su hija, Manuela Silván? No ha ido a la escuela." Where is your daughter, Manuela Silván? She is not in school.

The women stared and watched the huge white stallion prance around in front of them with his nostrils flaring and projecting wet snuffles in the air. It was one of the largest horses they had ever seen and they were overawed at the sight.

"Es mi deber llevarla a la escuela ahora." It is my duty to take her to school now. He squinted in the morning sun and glanced around the house and through the open doorway. *"¿Ella está dentro?"* Is she inside?

"No," Rita answered truthfully. Her toe nudged Manuela into silence as she stared at the man steadily.

He was thoughtful a moment before slapping the reins on his horse's flank, turning abruptly to thunder down the road. It would be the first of many trips for that big white horse looking for Manuela[62].

The morning was still dewy and fresh, flowers clinging to the nearby fence post; a fresh breeze bathed the women with coolness. Manuela crawled out from underneath the table and stared after *the man on the big white horse* and would tell the story for years afterward. After several interrogations, he soon tired of his task.

Manuela's father, Juan Francisco, nor Victorino learned of this deception for many weeks. They were not happy. They'd wanted their children educated but she was a just girl and forgiven eventually. Their days were long, tiring and ferocious and it seemed too little to worry about.

---

[62] Source: Manuela Silvan Trascasas

SUGAR CANE - PLANTATION LIFE

Plantation labor involved a wide range of tasks and activities. Laborers were divided into gangs and each gang was given a work assignment: planting, watering, hoeing, plowing, cultivating, ditching, stripping off dead leaves from the cane stalks, cutting the cane, carting the cane, or loading the cane onto small tram cars.

Workers prepared for their long days before the break of day. One by one or two by two, laborers appeared from the shadows, like a brigade of ghosts. From an outlying camp, they came on a train, car after car of silent figures, their cigarettes glowing in the darkness. In front of the mill they lined up, shouldering their hoes. As the sun rose, its rays striking the tall mill stack, quietly the word was passed from somewhere in the dimness.

Suddenly and silently the gang started work by dividing themselves, each heading toward his daily task. They were grouped by the foremen into gangs of twenty to thirty workers and walked or were transported by wagons and trains to the fields. Each gang had a foreman and the ethnicity of the gangs varied[63].

Sometimes women worked in the camps: they washed laundry, cooked, and sewed clothes. "I made custom shirts with hand-bound button holes for 25 cents," recalled a Spanish woman. "My mother and sister-in-law took in laundry. They scrubbed, ironed and mended shirts for a nickel a piece, their knuckles swollen and raw from using the harsh yellow soap."

Sugar plantations stretched as far as the eye could see and had many facets as plantation workers performed a myriad of tasks. Under the foreman's direction, they first cleared grass from tracts of land for cane cultivation and ploughed the soil for planting of cane cuttings.

But by far, the most regimented work was in the fields and one of the most tedious and back breaking tasks was hoeing weeds. Laborers typically hoed for four hours in a straight line. "Hoe… chop… chop… chop, one chop for one small weed, two for all big ones." They had to keep their bodies bent and they ached to stand up to unknot their twisted bodies.

Irrigating the Growing Sugar Cane – HAWI Plantation – Island of HAWAII

Planting sugar cane was done by cutting off the soft leaves, the top six inches of the cane, and thrown away. Then, the workers would

---

[63] Excerpt from Strangers from a Different Shore

cut about one foot of the remaining stalk off, which held about 4 to 5 leaves. This second cutting was placed into a burlap sack and used for planting the next sugar cane crop.

Sugar cane grows to a height of about 8 to 20 feet and has stems 1 to 2 inches thick. Common sugar cane has been cultivated from stem cuttings since ancient times; some varieties do not produce fertile seed. In tropical areas such as Hawaii and Cuba, cane has a growth period of from one year to eighteen months; the growing season is continuous. Much labor is required for the continual replanting and cultivation of the cane to maturity.

Harvesting the cane was dirty and exhausting. When the cane was ripe and ready to be cut, laborers stood and moved forward, swinging machetes and cutting the juicy cane stalks close to the ground. The cutting knife consisted of a large steel blade about 18 inches long and about 5 inches wide, equipped with a small hook on the back and set into a wooden handle. The cane was cut at or near the surface of the ground, stripped of its leaves by the knife hook and trimmed at the top near the last mature joint.

As the workers mechanically swung their machetes, they felt the pain of blistered hands and scratched arms. As they cut the stalks, they sweated from the heat and humidity. The workers prayed for cool breezes. The plant had tough, prickly leaves; their edges like a saw blade, cutting their skin badly. The workers had to wear flour sacks to protect their head, neck, hands, faces and shoulders. The heavy clothing also protected them from the wasps or yellow jackets infesting the cane fields. Their Spanish *chanquillas*, sandals, wore out fast so they fashioned sandals from old rubber and heavy jeans fabric.

Then, to protect their feet and legs from the cane, they wrapped sacks around them tied with rope. While surrounded by clouds of red dust, the workers covered their faces with handkerchiefs.

After collecting the cane stalks, the workers tied them into bundles, piled them in rows along the ground, then picked the huge bundles up, loaded them into carts or sleds and later, loaded onto trucks or railroad cars by crane to be transported to the mill. Sometimes, water-filled flumes were used, built on a slant so the water rushed the cane to the mill, called a sugar factory.

At the factory, the cane was delivered to the grinding mill, where engines, presses, furnaces, boilers, vacuum pans and centrifugal drums crushed the cane and boiled its juices into molasses and sugar. The constant clanking and whirring of the machinery was deafening. The resulting raw sugar was then transported to sugar refineries, which during the time of our families worked were on the mainland Pacific coast.

Male workers were paid $20-$30 a month for this process. To supplement their earnings, young boys were allowed to pick up the left-over sugar cane from the fields and take them to the mill in exchange for $6 per month.

At four-thirty in the afternoon, the plantation whistle shrieked the signal to stop working. Though they were too tired to hoe another row or carry another bundle of stalks, they felt a sudden final burst of energy to go home to their family.

Often, other type of work was required and women worked alongside their husbands doing jobs such as picking potatoes and sacking onions. They wore straw bonnets and two scarves; one to wrap around the face to stop the dust and sun and one to cover the straw hat.

They had two jobs; field work and house work. Earlier that morning, the women fed the chickens, prepared the breakfast, watered the garden, awakened the children, and then all the family sat down at the breakfast table together.

Then, they picked vegetables, cared for the children on the run, just to hurry home to make dinner at the end of the day.

In summary, our families cut sugarcane, bundled it, and piled it in wagons or rail cars so it could be hauled off to the grinders. One can visualize the outbuildings, the houses where they slept, a small garden beside it, and in the distance, the sugarhouse with its long roof and open walls. The smell of cooking cane juice hung in the air and almost coated their tongues.

TWO SATURDAYS A MONTH plantation workers assembled in lines in front of the manager's office where they presented their bango at the payroll desk. They were handed pay envelopes, bango numbers printed on the front. Inside with their pay was also an accounting of deductions for purchases made at the plantation store.

By 1912, the Hawaiian Sugar Plantation Association recommended that plantations act together to raise wages in the form of a bonus, payable at the termination of the worker's contract. Laborers who averaged twenty work days per month annually would be paid a bonus at the end of the year. The bonus system was changed to a so-called "profit sharing" program in which laborers who worked an average of twenty days per month for a year and who received $24 a month or less in wages were paid a share of the plantation's profits. They received a bonus of 1% of their annual earnings for every dollar increase over $70 for the average price of a ton of sugar. Thus if the price of sugar were $80 a ton, workers who qualified for a bonus were paid 10% of their annual earnings on their regular pay day in November or December for the year ending October 31[64]. The whole intention of the bonus was that it should be an annual payment based on an entire year's faithful work with the hope that it would retain the workers as permanent Hawaiian residents.

These pioneer men and women felt a certain boundlessness, driven by their dreams of making the land yield rich harvests and saving their money. And to many immigrants, no bonus was large enough to prevent whispers of a place called California. The American dream was calling and they began to listen, question and dream again.

---

[64] Hawaii Laborer's Association

WANDERING THROUGH HAWAII

Between their arrival in 1911 through the sugar plantations of Ewa on Oahu and later, Kilauea in Kauai, the Silvan family stayed together.

Often during the week, Juan and Victorino would gather in the evening with Felix after the women made their meals and the children quieted for the night. Dinner was served family style most often and their camaraderie lingered among them as in the old way.

In the evenings, they still agreed that regular wages, good

houses and plenty of food, when compared with their mode of living in Spain had been a good decision.   And they tried to recall the old country, the village, the mountains behind it, the nearby river, but their memories were fading.

Sometimes after long days in the sugar cane fields, the Spanish and Portuguese families would share food, stories and their favorite songs.   One notable song was the 1855 Spanish Ballad, *Juanita*[65]. And they sang it often.

The men sang the ballad often by standing shoulder to shoulder with others. It touched their souls, made everyone happy and generated a *simpatico*[66] atmosphere with the other immigrants from different lands sharing their spaces in Hawaii.

The Spanish had *la Jota*; their passionate dance filled with castanets and quick hand movements and the Portuguese had *la Chamarita*, a folk dance they danced at Festas.   They heard often, *"Portugal é o país fantástico!"*   The Chamarita is a combination of tap-dancing and square dancing.

Baseball was promoted with prizes offered to winning teams. Musical activities were supported and encouraged, spawning concerts and dances became a feature of plantation life.   Films and movies were shown regularly at some of the plantations.

Their work days were organized into weeks; week days for working and weekends for tending their gardens[67].   Drawn away from their lands and traditional homes, the workers tried to adapt to their new plantation community while on the weekends, they

---

[65] "Juanita" ("Nita Juanita") is a love song variously subtitled "A Spanish Ballad", "A Song of Spain", etc. "Juanita" was first published in 1855 attributed to Caroline Sheridan Norton, with music arranged by T.G May.

[66] Simpatico =   nice, likeable, sympathetic

[67] Jarvis, quoted in Ethel M. Damon, Koamalu: A Story of Pioneers on Kauai (Honolulu: SB, 1931)

worked their gardens.

Manuela asked neighbors to save their vegetable peelings for their pigs and could often be seen trudging along with her large pail, tossing them over their back fence. The Spanish settlement was near a river and there were several rows of houses lined up as if the plantation was a real city. Several family friends, including the Francisco Ruiz Garcia family from the southern coast of Malaga, lived near the river. Everyone took part in their own gardening; shoving vegetable peelings into ones garden was a natural affair.

Sunday was their spiritual day. Catholic Church bells were a welcome wake-up call and everyone attended mass in flower-filled chapel where music could be heard for miles around. The chapel was quaint, small and reverent. It was a place Manuela, Teodora and Felisa looked forward to because many of their friends attended and it was a day that ended with music and lots of food. And no shoes! Manuela loved the plantation upbringing more every day...

Even though their children, Manuela, Teodora and Felisa chief among them, loved the loose-fitting cotton dresses, the Hawaiians called a Mu-Mu[68], there was still the special parties to mark special occasions and festivals when the girls turned to their crocheted dresses and under slips. They were girls, after all.

But Manuela often shunned the party dresses for the loose and unfettered because she felt like a princess when she skipped along with the other children in her bare feet without the tucks and

---

[68]MuMu, Muu,Muu, Mu'umu'u – When Protestant missionaries arrived in the islands in the 1820s, they determined that Hawaiian women needed to cover their bodies. The Victorian-style Mother Hubbard dress, floor-length and loose fitting with a high neck and long sleeves, was the garment of choice. The Mother Hubbard was called holoku by the Hawaiians. When shorter length garments, minus the sleeves and high neck, were designed, they were called mu'umu'u, the Hawaiian word for cut off or shortened. Source: Spotlight's Kaua'I Gold Magazine.

bows.   She was a fun-loving young girl making friends with the other immigrants.   She loved the weather in all its blue sky and run-for-your-life rain storms that generated the beautiful Hawaiian flowers she learned to recognize by their scent.   Her young life was filled with contentment, although childhood was sometimes heavy with the burden of responsibility.

SOME DAYS WERE BLISSFUL.   Manuela sat near the trunk of a palm tree and accepted the coconut Teodora had picked up.   She'd watched her cousin slam it against the tree.   The coconut broke at her bidding and the girls ate the fresh coconut chunks, while watching and listening to colorful birds caw and fly in the trees above them.   Sharing the coconut milk, Teodora smiled at Manuela's answering grin as the milk sluiced down their chins. They loved the fruits of their new home and never tired of the chance to just reach out for so many globes of wondrous delights that added a blanket of peace to their new lives.

And there was always the music.   The Hawaiian guitar intrigued the girls whenever they heard the plucking strings. Music often wafted through the air.   Interspersing their culture with the Hawaiians added a layer of exotic camaraderie among the Spanish and Portuguese as they intertwined their traditions with others.

The Hawaiian luau was an amazing sight.   At first, they watched from the sidelines but once they smelled the pork, heard the Hawaiian guitars and ukuleles strumming their lyrical sounds across the broad avenues and courtyards, the families were entranced. When the next Luau occurred, they decided to invite themselves and big Hawaiian smiles invited them inside.

Manuela watched in awe early in the day as she stood back just a bit from her father and uncles. Felisa was most interested in the music, but Manuela and Teodora stared as the dark-skinned men dug a very big hole. Wide. They placed large rocks across the bottom of the pit and added pieces of firewood. The men worked steadily, singing and swaying with their traditional songs as they pulled large tea leaves down from the trees. The tea leaves were similar to the hula girl's skirts and she was amazed to see them place them studiously over the rocks at the pit's floor.

Juan watched Manuela's animated face as the traditional Luau began. Gus watched the Hawaiian girls as they walked by with trays filled with enticing bits and pieces of fruit and gray mounds of pudding-like gelatinous food called poi. He liked watching the girls better than the men digging the hole.

Manuela heard the pig squealing for his life long before she saw it. The Hawaiians, whom the Spaniards called *kanakas*, quickly slit its throat. After the pig was dead, the men picked him up by the legs and pulled him over the rocks and laid him out evenly. Then they covered him up with the huge tea leaves and laid a big burlap sack over him. Then dirt covered the sack to hold it all down.

The pig cooked about four hours; the smell of that carcass filled the air until everyone's bellies sang and danced in tune with the guitars. The Hawaiians entertained and danced, playing their music while it finished cooking.

It did not feel like winter. The tropical breezes and balmy weather of Hawaii eased some of the grief and life moved ahead. The women took turns washing one another's hair. Manuela sat on a chair tilted back and propped against the rain barrel while Rita rubbed soap into her scalp and then rinsed it. Water ran in rivulets over her neck and down her chest generating chuckles while lurching for toweling. And then it was Rita's turn.

They had to chase the boys when it was bath time and the parents often gave in and let them clean up in the creek that ran along the edge of the clearing in their ethnic community that joined the path toward the plantation acreage.

STRIFE FOR SILVÁN, RUIZ, SOUZA FAMILIES

Nearly a year after the Silván's arrival in Honolulu, another ship --- the S.S. Harpalion arrived carrying **Bernardo Ruiz Romero** and his family, **Francisco Ruiz Garcia** and **María Rey Garcia Ruiz**, who was his stepmother and his siblings. They moved into the ethnic settlement across the stream from the Silván's cottage and history would begin. One day he would become my grandfather. But that's a story for later.

The Ruiz and Silván families worked together, trading stories, entertaining one another and the surrounding cottages with music from drums, castanets, dancing and musical spoons. The Spanish songs melded from northern and southern Spain and then blended with Hawaiian to intermingle with their cultural beliefs, religion and familial connections.

At this time, the families also cultivated friendships with the Portuguese settlement nearby. The **Souza Bento** family would be a big part of their lives and Teodora Silván would someday become part of theirs.

By the beginning of 1912, Rita was pregnant and Manuela was responsible for José and Gus more and more each day. Rita's pregnancy was a hard one but she continued to cook plantation worker's meals, keeping their laundry clean and raising her children. Heavy with the babe, she often turned to Manuela; her back hurt and her belly strained with a weary pain.

Manuela was expected to be the little-mama. She loved her little brothers, loved playing with them, watching them, teaching them games and songs. Even though she did not learn to read, her intelligence astounded those around her; she heard a song once or twice and she could mimic it word for word along with the tune. The children soon chanted Manuela's pidgin songs as some Hawaiian mixed with her Spanish.

Rita was told of a Spanish woman who practiced midwifery. She'd helped in the birth of many Spanish babies in the plantation camps. Although there was a settlement doctor, she was relieved and chose the skilled Spanish midwife who lived nearby. When summoned, the woman would reach for her apron and supplies and away she went, sometimes a long distance between the plantations.

The rainy seasons with the prickling scent of impending downpour followed by howling winds and pelting showers forced the families to stay indoors and the enveloping dampness aggravated Rita's pregnancy. There was talk of moving to another plantation and she held her belly as it hardened in what would someday be called Braxton-Hicks contractions. Her back ached and the thought of moving out of her house was a nightmare she chose to ignore. The gloomy rain-filled days kept everyone in the small house and when her water broke, Ramona and Crescéncia rushed in, clearly worried.

"*Anda, anda… que el nene ya viene.*" Hurry, hurry… the baby is on its way.

The women were anxious. They sent for the mid-wife but

she was delivering a baby across the island.   They were on their own.

Rita was a tiny woman and the baby was very large.

Juan moved to Victorino's house, taking the small children with him.   Manuela and Teodora remained, running to bring water, towels and pieces of rags saved for the delivery.   Hours dragged by.   Ramona cleansed her sister-in-law's face and whispered soothingly.   Rita whimpered and crushed the blanket against her face trying to blot her tears.   She prayed.

By morning, her final agonizing push brought a stillborn infant into the world.   Rita was devastated.

Manuela stared at the little bundle tightly wrapped in the wet blanket, a crease straining across her young forehead in the waning hours of the night and early hours of the morning. Watching her mother endure such cramping pain was something she never wanted to see again.   She'd dreamed and planned about having and holding the new baby.   Now, her tiny sister lay tightly wound in a blanket and her mother lay crying.   She hated the sadness, wondering if she could ever go through such pain only to have a dead baby afterward.   She became a young adult that morning and she was not yet eleven years old.

Rita burst into tears.   Manuela had never seen her mother sob.   Her face lost all its shape; wide-open eyes, wide-open mouth, eyelids swollen after the first tears, red blotches on her cheeks and neck.   Her mouth was making croaking, throaty sounds like the toneless cry of a child.   Her shoulders trembled and she held the pillow against her face.....

Teodora's face was also wet with tears as Ramona, pulled her out of the room.   Telling a man his infant had died at birth was an emotional burden Ramona abhorred, even though she hoped Rita could birth others. She must concentrate on that for him. For now, she took the sounds of crying and sadness with her as she veered toward her cottage, praying to God for the courage she would need to ease Juan's pain. Depression had stalked her since she lost her own babe; she sniffled and wiped her face again.

Life after that was quiet and remarkably sad. Ramona was Rita's confidante; the wound she carried in the memory's wound of losing her little boy aboard the ship opened again and they cried as one.

Crescéncia gave birth to her first daughter, María Gregoria Gonzales and her birth hailed happy times again as the child smiled, gurgled, laughed and began to totter around. The stilted house and the subsequent porch steps were a source of worry but everyone watched carefully and the toddler gave life to the sadness from before.

Life continued at Ewa Plantation. The cane grew, was cut and processed. The flowers bloomed thick with glorious petals from the daily downpours and tropical breezes. Sugar cane flourished over the hundreds of acres below the azure sky; the Spanish and Portuguese settlements and plantation life thrived.

María was baptized at the church across from the plantation; a party was brewing and the celebration was twofold: Crescéncia was pregnant again.

Eighteen months after Manuela's baby sister died, a traveling photographer arrived at the settlement to photograph family groups. Rita refused. Her arms still felt the emptiness; the painful stillborn birth still clenched in her heart.   But an alternative plan was devised.

Crescéncia and Felix's little girl, María Gregoria Gonzales, was about eighteen months old and often ran to Rita with up stretched arms.   For the photograph, Rita pensively agreed to hold her for the photograph or no portrait would be taken[69].

Many immigrants had family photographs taken to mark their time in Hawaii.   There are various reasons behind their straight-faced gazes; bad teeth, fear of strangers, length of exposure time, uneasiness, long standing periods. The photographer put them into position, returned to the camera and disappeared beneath a black tent of fabric, astonishing the children into stunned faces.

Photo: Manuela, Rita, *María Gonzales*[70], José, Juan Francisco and Agustín (Gus) Silván

Rita's pregnancy progressed normally but for Crescéncia, her

---

[69]   Source: Manuela Silván Ruiz.

[70]   Rita wanted a child in her arms for the photograph after her stillbirth – refusing to sit with empty arms for the photo. After careful sifting through birth information, I believe it is María (Marie) Gonzales (born April 11, 1912).   Manuela was adamant the child was named Mary, but it was not her sister.   The estimated date =January 1914.

pregnancy was another story. Her massive burden soon slowed down her ability to function and problems continued to push her beyond endurance.

The midwife was worried. Felix was worried. Her sisters in law cared for Alejandro, Juanito and little María to allow Crescéncia much-needed bed rest.

The girls watched the midwife push at their aunt's belly every other day and they listened to their mothers talk with her. They learned there were two babies and something was not right.

How many tears can fall? How many times can a heart break? Crescéncia's labor began when her water broke and the midwife was at her side quickly. Soothingly, she spoke to her, massaging her belly, feeling her pulse, wiping her sweat-drenched brow.

A final push and the first child slid into the midwife's hands, a gentle lift and the child lay still. Swallowing the lump in her throat, she handed the babe to Ramona who stood near and reached forward as Crescéncia pushed out its twin.

The sounds of weeping swamped the room as the two quiet infants lay wrapped in swaddling blankets. The women's shoulders shook, their hands covering their eyes. The midwife looked into Crescéncia's eyes and shook her head. But Crescéncia already knew the truth; no infant cries were uttered and her heart squeezed close[71].

Despite the hard work at Ewa Plantation, the lure of sandy beaches and warm ocean water lapping against their ankles created respite that families would recall all their lives. The children could dance through the sand as they ran toward the turquoise water,

---

[71] Family stories and date assumptions used for the loss of these babies

their parents following up the rear. And Crescéncia fought despondency.

The beaches were a dream for the northerners and it was like coming home to the southerners as the Spaniards enjoyed the island and watched their children become healthy and golden under its tropical sun.

As Crescéncia healed both physically and mentally, Juan and Victorino broached the subject of moving to another island. Kauai was hiring workers and they were told it was called the garden island because of the rain and vegetation. The brothers were offered housing and all the same promises they'd received at Ewa and Kauai sounded more like Fuentesaúco.

Talk soon changed to action. The brothers and their families packed up once again. They dared wait no longer as Rita's pregnancy advanced. It meant moving from Honolulu to Kapa'a but relished the promise of rain.

Felix liked working with the horses and donkeys and he knew Crescéncia wasn't ready for a change yet.

She watched her brothers sail from Oahu and Kauai, knowing it was less than a hundred miles and they would see them again.

Kauai was indeed a garden isle. The same palm trees, tropical birds, flowers and turquoise sand pummeling against grains of sand surrounded them as they arrived in Kapa'a.

Victorino and Ramona settled with their three children nearby while Juan agreed they would work in the plantation near Kapaa on the eastern shore of Kauai. Since Victorino had just turned forty-six years old, working in the stables was exactly where he wanted to be. Juan, on the other hand, at thirty nine, used his newly-trained knowledge in the sugar cane fields.

Ramona and Teodora found work in local homes to help cook and clean and the children returned to school. Manuela watched the boys and Rita waited for labor to begin. She swore this baby would live and packing up and moving had been a frightening worry for everyone.

Maria Silván Trascasas was born March 7, 1914 in Kapa'a, a healthy girl. Manuela was thirteen years old and despite the work a new baby entailed, she welcomed this child as if she was her own.

By the next summer, the Silvan family had transferred to the Kilauea Plantation when news of another Gonzales baby reached them. Barceliza Crescéncia Gonzales had been born in March and Crescéncia missed her family. They would soon be together once again.

Kilauea[72] was the most beautiful place Manuela had ever seen. She traced her finger on the map of Kauai to learn they lived on the north shore of the island and the final segment of her life in Hawaii began.

---

[72] Kilauea (defined literally as "much spreading" in Hawaiian) is a small town on the northern shore of Kauai, one of the eight islands that make up the state of Hawaii. The Kilauea Lighthouse was constructed in 1912 and 1913 and the formal lighting ceremony was held on May 6, 1913. From Kilauea Point, one can view humpback whales, monk seals, spinner dolphins, and Hawaiian and migratory birds.

The town receives a great amount of rain because it is situated on the northern coast of the island, and a lot of sunshine due to the proximity to the equator. The two nearest towns to Kilauea are Princeville and Hanalei. The name Hanalei means "lei[72] making," but aside from leis, the village is also popular for its taro. Taro is a tropical plant grown primarily as a root vegetable and as a leaf vegetable.

SPANISH TRADITIONS IN HAWAII

Photo of Hawaii in 1916

Plantation laborers celebrated their traditional festivals in the camps and recreated familiar scenes from their homelands in Hawaii. Although life in Hawaii was a living paradise and our family learned much of the Hawaiian culture, they still retained their traditions from the old world, especially the Matanza, carried on in Hawaii and later in California.

Steeped in tradition, they annually butchered a pig to ensure families had a supply of meat throughout the year. It is called the Matanza, a strong Spanish tradition as well-known as bull fighting and flamenco. The Matanza usually takes place in the cool month of November to ensure the meat is conserved to keep food for months afterward.

Matanza traditionally takes place during the fiestas of saints allowing families to gather together for the occasion. Although the three days of the Matanza involves hard work, families take advantage of their time together and enjoy each other's company while they work. The process took place in the home or on a family plot of land.

Day one of the Matanza started very early in the morning with all the family members gathered together. First, they had to get the pig onto a large wooden table. Usually the strongest male members of the family would hoist the pig up and hold it in place for the slaughter; by stabbing the pig in the neck with a large metal spike to allow the blood to flow from the animal down into a large bowl, or *lebrillo*.

While the blood flows into the bowl, a female family member has the dedicated task of continually stirring the blood with her hands. The blood must be kept moving continuously to ensure it does not clot. Although a tedious task, it must be done by someone with experience because if the blood clots, it will be wasted and the family will have no black pudding.

Eventually, a fine fiber-like mesh forms between her hands, which is then discarded. The remaining blood stays in its liquid form and placed in a large pot to keep cool until time to make the black pudding *(Morcilla)*.

The next task is to move the pig onto a special trough, or *artesa*. Nearby, a large pot of boiling water is poured over the pig. Its skin is removed and the pig is thoroughly cleansed. Once skinned and cleaned, the animal is moved to the coldest part of the house, hung and cut open, lengthwise down the middle. Next, the intestines are removed and soaked for cleaning. This was traditionally done in natural running water such as a spring or a river. The intestines were emptied and the skin wiped down with flour, lemon and vinegar on both sides and cleaned again. Once clean, it is placed in pots with pieces of lemon until it is time to make the morcilla and chorizo.

The offal is also removed at this point and used, along with the fat of the pig to make *migas matanceras,* a typical dish eaten during the Matanza.   It is a simple recipe of flour fried in fat along with the offal and is very filling, but greasy.   It is perfect for cold days.

During the first day, it is customary to prepare the onions. The smell of cooking onions throughout village indicated that the Matanza has begun. For each pig you need four *arrobas*[73] of onions. Several women have the unenviable task of peeling and cutting all those onions, starting early since the onions must be peeled, cut and cooked before the end of the first day. They are cooked several hours in a large pot, usually over a fire, by stirring with an enormous wooden spoon.   A hundred pounds of onions!   The cooked onions are placed in large sacks and hung overnight to allow all the liquid to drain away in preparation for the black pudding which is made on day two.

The first task on day two is to take the pig apart and separate it into different cuts; head, ears, shoulders, front legs (*paletillas*), hind legs (*jamones*), loin, ribs, spine, trotters (pig's feet) and the fat. While the men busily cut up the pig, the women make the *Morcilla* or black pudding using the onions and blood from day one. Black pudding is a welcome dish eaten at the end of the day full of nuts and spices.

The *jamones* and *paletillas* must contain no blood whatsoever. A clean cloth is placed over the leg and strong pressure is applied over the cloth by hand to squeeze out any remaining blood to prepare for curing. Along with the spine and trotters, they are placed in a small trough and covered in salt. After two days, the

---

[73]One arroba is equivalent to 25 pounds

spine and trotters are taken out and shaken off, and then taken to a cellar or cool room to dry out until spring.

The hams remain in salt for a longer period, usually one day for every 2 ½ pounds.   When the salt is removed, they are hung in the bodega to cure for about twelve to fourteen months.   The ribs are sliced up and mixed with cinnamon and lemon and left for a day or two in pots to marinade, then fried in oil and placed in airtight jars for future use.   The pork loins are conserved in a similar way. Cut into large chunks, they are fried and stored in jars with olive oil. This method of conserving the loin was a local dish known as *lomo do orza*.

The third day is reserved for making the *chorizo, salchichon, salchicha, butifarras, lenguados, rellenos* and *sobrasada*.   Sometimes the haunches are smoked into strips of meat and the fat scraped away for rendering into suet and soup.

The well-known phrase, "The only thing you cannot eat from a pig is its squeak," is very true in the case of the Matanza. Nothing is wasted and the products made during this three-day fiesta are either eaten during the course of the day or conserved for use or sold during the coming months.

The children loved the Matanza!   It was not all work and no play; they would clean the pig's bladder and rub it very thin, then blow it up and make big balloons.

Since Manuela's birthday was the third week of June, it coincided with the *Dia de San Juan* (Saint John's Day) June 24, the day before her birthday.

There were many traditions that revolved around the eve of this saint's day, such as if you walk through the dew your skin will be lovely, if you bathe in the sea your skin will be nice, your body healthy and strong.   It was a good omen for a girl look into the future by placing a bowl of water outside the window and break an egg into the water just at midnight.   She could read her destiny in the shape the egg assumed or one could pour melted lead into a bowl at noonday.   If the lead shows a scythe, her future mate will follow the carpenter's trade; a ship indicates that his living would come from the sea.   The saint's day is considered a good time for farmers to sow their fields.   If the sun shines on the 24th nuts will be abundant during the coming year[74].

The *Dia de San Juan* is celebrated in honor of San Juan, saint of the summer solstice.   On that day throughout Spain, the festivities include fireworks, bonfires, and songsters singing old folk songs, regional dancing, processions and cavalcades.

Many cakes were baked J-shaped and decorated with sugar roses and elaborate scrolls.

Many Spanish males such as Manuela's father and Crescéncia's son were named Juan.   On their special day in some instances, the adult Juan sometimes took the day off from work to enjoy the feasting.

That was the way it was celebrated in Spain but our families enjoyed the saint's day in Hawaii a bit differently.   They celebrated it with baking cakes, gathering of friends and family and reminiscing about how it used to be.   Juan, though he did not take the day off from the cane fields, he thought about the J-shaped cake all day; sure it would be waiting for him and Juanito at the end of day.

Three months later, Crescéncia gave birth to her fifth living child, Augustina Gonzales, on September 27, 1916.

---

[74] Source: Festivals of Western Europe – pages 199-200

SPANISH CHILDREN IN TRAINING

Gus watched and learned as his father took him to the company store. It appeared to gather all types of people and he'd never seen people with slanted eyes or yellowish skin before. He was told they were Chinese and Japanese. They were small people and their conversations were stilted in short, staccato sentences. He learned that *gracias* was *arigato* in Japanese, both meaning thank you. He made friends with Kuniko, a Japanese boy his age that always seemed to smell of fish.

The company store was a place where every ethnic group communicated and congregated on Saturdays. Those were the days Gus looked forward to the most because he knew he'd see his friend, Kuniko.

Juan allowed him to visit the Japanese family and watched his son learn to make fishing nets. They learned different types of nets caught different types of fish. And excitement thrummed through the boy when he was taught to fish, where to fish, how to fish, how to clean it and began catching his own.

How proud Rita was when he brought home his first string of fish and how quickly she had him clean up and toss his clothes in a bucket of water. Fish!! But it was worth every minute to have the fish fresh caught from the stream that was fed near their home from the ocean. Rita learned to cook fish like the Hawaiians but the paella dish she made also made the family smile when Gus and Kuniko grabbed their fishing poles. He was groomed for life and would be a forever fisherman.

Manuela learned the art of scrubbing clothes. When she turned thirteen, she was doing her share of the laundry. The large vats were filled with water and a fire kept it very hot. After taking great care to avoid burning, which she often had welts from, she boiled the clothes to remove the red dirt and sweat. After scrubbing the clothes on a washboard, rinsing them in another large bucket filled with water from the outside barrels, she dried them on the clothesline behind their small house. Starching them involved a process of mixing flour with water, dipping them into the brew and then she ironed them with a charcoal-heated iron. Thus Manuela and Teodora contributed directly and indirectly to the process of sugar cane production.

Gus was among several boys who were employed and served as blacksmith apprentices, camp cleaners, and helpers at the medical clinic. Although young, he managed to earn some wages until he reached the age required for sugar cane field workers. His school hours were scheduled around his working hours. To accommodate these jobs, school hours were moved to 7:00 o'clock in the morning until noon to allow children to work in the afternoons and supplement their parent's income. He proudly and responsibly added his wage to the family coffers, moving them that much closer to America.

By the time Manuela turned fifteen, she was hired as a domestic and worked for the friend of the plantation boss. Mrs.

Scott taught school in her home.   With four children of her own, she needed help!   Manuela did all the cleaning, milked the cow, fed the chickens and pigs and picked sacks full of grass to feed the animals.   She also washed the laundry and learned a little about Western cooking.   It was an eye-opening experience to see her employer go off golfing or play croquet.   She felt a world apart but those Hawaiian memories created a bank of stories.

The children kept Manuela busy.   She was a hard worker; she loved earning her own money and learned to be frugal at a very young age.

Mrs. Scott often shared world news with Manuela.   Late October, 1915, Mrs. Scott nearly danced into the house waving a paper wildly in her hands; she forced Manuela to sit down, ignoring the children as she read the article.   Tens of thousands of women marched in New York City, demanding the right to vote.   Manuela stared at the woman, bemused and perplexed, and then raised her hand to her hair....   Vote?   Women?

Another time, she chattered about something called a telephone and a man named Alexander Graham Bell talking in a box between a place called New York and San Francisco.   When Manuela questioned her about it, she said the cities were not next door but some 3000 miles apart.   Manuela kept her own counsel but sometimes secretly thought Mrs. Scott a story teller.

The flu epidemic grew to manic proportions in the summer months of 1917.   Many Spaniards, Portuguese, Japanese, Chinese, Germans, Russians and Filipinos died. The fear mimicked their days on the ship when mumps, measles and scarlet fever raged through their watery voyage.   The doctors couldn't keep up with the mortality as they fought their way through the ethnic communities, trying to heal and clean and save.

Japanese men would drive their wooden carts down the road with a box on the back. It had a black cloth inside and draped over the sides. He was the body man. He would pick up the dead, place them on the black wooden box and drive it to the cemetery to wait for a quick burial. Often the sound of the cart and clomp of the horses hooves made Manuela feel like vomiting.

In the Spanish tradition, when people get sick they eat chicken soup. The Spanish women caught the chickens, cut off their heads, plunked them into boiling water, de-feathered them and boiled their bodies with herbs and spices. Women walked in and out of their neighbor's houses lugging pots of chicken soup, wiping their sweaty brows with their aprons and making the sign of the cross on each door step going in and coming out. And the epidemic wavered and died. The doctors were grateful, the patients were grateful and the remaining chickens were grateful.

WORLD WAR ONE

CHANGES AHEAD

The war ploughed ahead. News was grim. In America, Woodrow Wilson pleaded for an end to war in Europe, calling for "peace without victory." But by April 2, 1917, the United States Congress approved a declaration of war against Germany. America was entrenched in the world war four days later.

However, as our family worked for their living to feed their families, the war seemed far away. And as they listened to neighbors, friends and relatives speak of California, they paused to listen. California had land. California had water. California was on the same meridian as southern Spain, the temperatures similar to what they left behind. America was on the tongues of the workers, their wives and some of their children. America. America.

In the midst of talk of war, several members of the Spanish camp in Kilauea sailed to Honolulu to wait for a boat to California and the Silvan's discussions mounted even though Crescéncia was four months pregnant.

When Bernardo Ruiz, Antonio Rodriquez and Antonio Gaitero left April 25th on the S.S. Ventura from Honolulu, Manuela's thoughts lingered after them for months afterward.

In Pleasanton, California, Bernardo Ruiz completed his military draft registration card on June 5th and by July 3rd, the first wave of the American Expeditionary Force landed in France.

Victorina Gonzales was born in Kilauea on October 3, 1917 as the world war raged across Europe and America tried to stop the flow of death and bring her men home.

By the end of the year, Manuela listened to family conversations change from "if we go" to "when to go."   Maybe she didn't want to go.   But how could she stay?   Her insides quaked at the thought of leaving her home again.   Living in Hawaii had given her a new hunger for the colors and smells of nature.   She'd loved tending her own little garden, a corner just for her and she didn't want to leave it!

Life was changing and Manuela didn't like it.

Kilauea lay on the banks of the river.   She walked up the road and no car or wagon passed her; none came in the opposite direction.   The air was clean and crisp and smelled of gardens. She heard the sound of birds everywhere, the fresh breeze made a slight sighing noise as it passed through the tall trees and the occasional murmur of the stream.   In a quarter of an hour she reached the spot where she could wade in the little pool and day dream ---- about America and more.

She ached to stay.   She raised a hand to her hair and swirled her fingers through the water.   She couldn't leave the paradise she had learned to love over the years but couldn't fight the realism of being a single Spanish girl; she had no choice but to follow her family.   And there was Bernardo...She placed her hands on each side of her face and looked into the water, staring at the wavering image and smiled at the flower's reflection in her hair.   She vowed to remember this place always, just as the little girl leaving

Fuentesaúco had seven years earlier. For just a moment, she visualized her old home and village in the breath of a heartbeat. She sadly admitted time had taken away some of her memories.

Now she had to leave home again. A breeze blew strands of hair across her face, and she found a ribbon in her pocket and tied it back. She inhaled the familiar scents around her. And she wasn't happy because of the shoes. She threw a stone into the water and smashed her image. She hated shoes.

Preparing for the ship journey to San Francisco, boxes were being packed and filled with pots, pans, utensils, bedding, clothing and mementos. Legal papers were stowed in bags and the families prickled with excitement. A ship voyage reminded each of them of the horrific trip seven years earlier and the filth, pestilence and disease they lived through.

The ship bound for San Francisco was a military ship and since it was war time, soldiers had priority over civilians. Juan and Felix applied for papers, releasing them from the Selective Draft in the Territory of Hawaii and paid the $4.00 tax the United States required for aliens, as an act to regulate the immigrations of aliens into the United States that went into effect on July 1, 1907.

Manuela was sixteen and a half years old. She had run with wild abandon for several years; loose-fitting dresses, bare feet, flowers in her hair and around her neck. She and her cousins were free spirits.

Manuela pouted. She argued. She wanted to run away. But more than that, she vowed to return to Hawaii one day. One of the reasons she fought the trappings of womanhood was the idea of those shoes. Imagining the binding leather after the freedom of bare feet, she grimaced with disgust.

But when Rita and her aunts mentioned a new white dimity dress for her trip, she decided the shoes might not be so bad. Ramona had hand sewn a dress for her; a duplicate of Teodora's. When Manuela saw it, she was overwhelmed; it had tucks in places children's clothing lacked and tiny brightly-colored embroidered flowers dotted the bodice and lacy collar. A new dress definitely added a different slant to the situation and its memory would later dance in her heart.

She and her mother went shoe shopping. The store in Honolulu had shoe barrels along the sidewalk for customers to touch and smell the lingering scent of leather. Even though Manuela fought the idea of wearing shoes, she was sure her new dress would probably cover them and they were pretty...

"What can I help you with today, Señorita?" Did the man see *Spanish* written on her forehead? She and Rita Silván stroked the leather shoes he offered for sale.

"*Deseo estos zapatos negros brillantes.*" I want these shiny black shoes. She lifted a short boot.

"*Un momento.*" One moment. He quickly returned with a brown paper package wrapped with string and held out his hand, palm up, for payment.

Rita paid him directly and pointed to a straw bonnet with ivory silk roses and pale yellow buttercups clustered on the brim. Nodding to the man, he promptly whisked it off the shelf and gave it to Manuela with a bow. She grinned and promptly placed it over her nutmeg brown hair.

"*Muchas gracias, Mama.*"

Rita nodded and guided her daughter out of the door. It was rare to share mother-daughter time without work or children in between. Gripping the shoes with one hand and holding onto her hat with the other, Manuela decided being a grown up might not be so bad after all, even with shoes. Maybe she could delay squeezing her feet into them until she actually arrived in America. She smiled at the idea and followed her mother back home, anxious to ask Teodora what she thought about it.

Suddenly, her steps faltered. Teodora wouldn't be going to America with them. Her family was remaining in Hawaii, at least for the time being. Tio Victorino wasn't well and they were still undecided whether to stay in Hawaii or go to California. Manuela disliked leaving behind again. She still missed her cousin, Manuela Marzo, as if it was yesterday.

As she pondered the leaving, she knew there were more changes to come. Tio Victorino and señor Souza Bento were discussing a marriage between her cousin, Teodora and their son, Juan. She sighed heavily; she would lose another cousin across another ocean. She chuckled as she remembered when Teodora told her of the meetings and the match.

Love. It must be a wondrous thing. The Souza Bento family had become good friends even though they were Portuguese. Some people only wanted to keep Spanish with Spanish and Portuguese with Portuguese. She shook her head. Why couldn't people just be people without labels? She liked Manuel and José Souza Bento and their little babies. Everyone seemed the same to her.   The brother, Juan, was quieter and not as friendly. He was always so serious! How could Teodora be so smitten?!

There was much discussion about when Ramona, tio Victorino and their children would follow them to California.   But the Gonzales family was ready now.

So many Gonzales cousins!   Alejendro and Juan had sailed from Spain; now in Hawaii, their sisters kept arriving. She counted on her fingers, the six Gonzales children born in Hawaii; María Gregoria and Crescéncia Barceliza at the Ewa Plantation, Augustina, named for her grandmother Agustína Hernández of *Fuentesaúco,* and Victorina, who was godchild to their tio Victorino Silván. They were both born in Kilauea on Kauai and then the twins who died. She thought there was one more baby who died but her aunt never mentioned the child.   Manuela loved them, especially the tiny baby, Victorina, just three months old[75].

Mildred…   Mildred…She grimaced a second over the Americanized name they called her. Mildred. She wasn't sure she liked it. She'd always been Manuela and wondered why she must change her name along with so many other things in her life?

---

[75] The ship manifest for the SS Governor sailing from Hawaii to California lists Koloa and Honolulu as birth villages for Maria G. and Barceliza Gonzales – The villages are near EWA Plantation so it is unknown whether the villages were their true birth cities or whether they were born on the plantation but the birth documents certified Honolulu.

MELANCHOLY IN HAWAII

Despite the little changes, Manuela hugged her smiling memories as they played through her mind. She'd miss the tiny *Wal'oll Hul'la Church* in Hanalei, a quaint, green shingled sanctuary and the tiny choir singing traditional hymns backed by ukuleles and a washtub. That was where she learned the hymn, *"We shall dwell in the city of God where our tears shall be turned into dancing….."* She'd miss making the fresh leis to present to guests on Sunday mornings accompanied with a customary kiss on the cheek. Saint Sylvester was the mother church but the small one was fine enough for her. The bright blue and green stained glass windows took her breath away. She would always remember!

She'd miss the magic of the lush mountains, jewel-toned waters, small seaside villages and friendly people. She'd been told Hawaii was the only place chocolate trees grew and smiled, knowing she'd been privileged to see a chocolate farm. Even though the farm also grew sugar cane, star fruit, Tahitian lime and sapodilla, the chocolate trees were the best, grown in the foothills above Kapa'a, (Kah-PAH-ah) where her sister, María, was born.

And the whales! Every year, like clockwork, the mighty humpback migrated from its summer feeding grounds in Alaska to the warm waters of Hawaii.   It stayed from Thanksgiving to Easter to mate and give birth, which made humpback whale watching one of the highlights of her life.   The massive creatures, measuring up to 62 feet long and weighing as much as 40 tons, mesmerized. They swam.   They fed.   They breached – oh, how they breached!

She told herself when sad memories cascaded through her mind, she would think of Tia Crescéncia's words, "Brighten the corner where you are."   Manuela sighed softly, studied the Plumeria petals she held gently in the palm of her hand and let them flutter to the ground with a sly smile.   She would miss Hawaii but she would take part of it with her.

She'd learned how to let the soil run through her fingers, push in tiny shoots, and watch them grow in the garden she'd claimed as her own.

The tropical flowers grew amid vegetables and her special flower had become a tree in the corner, marking the spot where she'd placed the cigar-like stalk into the ground years earlier.

.

A *Frangipani* was the name the islanders called it and they made beautiful flower necklaces from its petals.   Others called it a *Plumeria* and each spring it would pop tiny buds out on the end of what she called its fingers.   The little stumpy stalk had grown each year, sprouted leaves and bloomed with glorious petals. She carried a piece with her in the bag without telling her mother.

She'd been told that fruits and plants should remain on the island but just one couldn't hurt, could it? She'd cut the top ten inches off one arm and nearly cried, praying it wouldn't kill the tree as she'd wrapped it carefully in a wet rag. She would keep it moist all the way to America, her own little piece of Hawaii!

She'd miss the cool flowery dresses. And she'd miss running bare foot. All the children ran bare footed and yes, she'd probably miss that most. Maybe she would just do it in California!

Inside her bag lay the beautiful dress Tia Ramona gave her plus two other white dresses. She liked more colors, especially lavender but young ladies wore white, she was told. One special dress was made of a silky fabric that felt slippery and cool to her skin. It was hand stitched around the hem and the round neckline. The long sleeves fell loosely and sort of kissed her skin. The skirt had more fabric at the bottom and swished when she walked. And Ben Ruiz Romero liked it.

Ben. She missed the Ruiz family, especially Ben. It wasn't as if he was her *novio*[76] since the culture for a young Spanish girl did not encourage, nor allow, dating. She'd miss his laughter, his funny way of talking that made her stomach dance and his large family the Silváns had made their own. She'd also miss his stories about the Spanish village he left behind when he and his family sailed from Gibraltar in February of 1912 on the Harpalion. It always made her smile when he told her about the sun, the soil, the olives and ocean beaches not far away…

She had memorized their last moments together before he left the plantation camp. She'd stared into his dark eyes and felt

---

[76] Novio = boyfriend / Novia = girlfriend

giddy. Ben's look was penetrating. Mystified, Manuela felt a tangle of reactions like a secret thicker than fog.

She blushed at the memories. She enjoyed the excitement, stimulating and crazy even though they were never alone. Would she ever see him again? She'd already lost two special cousins to distance, but Ben was different. She remembered it had been May, last year, when all the news was about America joining the war. She'd been almost sixteen and he, twenty-one. He said he might see her when they arrived in California but America was a big place, not like their camp at the sugar plantation with a little creek, a little road and.... He would turn twenty-two next month and probably had a *novia* already, one closer to his age. She wouldn't think about it, she decided.

Instead, she thought of her friends; the ones she was also leaving behind. She closed her eyes and remembered their trips to church in bare feet, wearing their long colorful Mu'u Mu'u dresses adorned with the beautiful Hawaiian flower leis wrapped around their necks. The flowers caught her attention again. She wore flowers all the time, a fresh bloom in her hair. She bit her lip; she'd wear flowers in America too.

She glanced down at her dress. It looked like spun gold with a round neckline and fluffy sleeves, pleated from neck to hem near the floor. It was really too small and the sash tied at the dropped waist made her look like a child. Maybe she'd leave it for Felisa.

She would also miss being nanny to the four Scott children in Kilauea. She'd worked for the woman for nearly a year and earned some money; for that she was grateful. She wouldn't miss milking the cow or feeding the chickens and pigs all that funny grass but she would miss the people, the place... all of it.

Her father had allowed her to keep some of the coins, although he expected to receive the bulk of her earnings. That was the way it was and she did not question it. She was, however, happy to feel the heaviness of the coins in her drawstring purse hanging from her arm. She felt rich for a moment, thinking she might come apart like a cloud of dust.

The last day in Kilauea, Teodora stood before her. Manuela watched her cousin struggle with a landslide of emotions: sadness, anger, regret, hope. Finally she managed a smile.

"You will be all right. I have no idea what I would have done here without you. But I will have Juan now and you will see California before we do. I wish you could be here for my wedding. Papa and Madre have not decided if they will go to America yet. He is not well... but you and I? We will find each other in California. I just do not know when..." She stomped her foot a bit before offering a trembling smile and squeezed her younger cousin's hand.

"I know," Manuela offered with great seriousness. "You will have Felisa and Celestino and the Souza family and of course, John. But I will miss you, cousin." Manuela sighed and hoped her eyes didn't leak. She hated the leaving part.

BUT LEAVE THEY MUST. They arrived in Honolulu the next day after a short boat ride and then they faced more waiting. The soldiers would sail first and they'd wait for their turn. It was war time after all.

Preparing for a lengthy wait for their ship to sail to San Francisco, the Juan Silván and Felix Gonzales families shared a community-type house in Honolulu close to the depot with two other families. They were told the trip would last about seven days, a mere speck of time compared to the Orteric's trip in

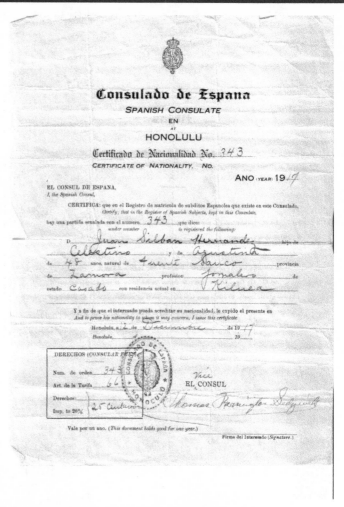

1911, which lasted forty-eight days and seemed like a year.

Since soldiers had priority on ships leaving Honolulu at that time, several ships left without them. They were relieved when the S.S. Herman Governor arrived and it was finally their turn.

SS GOVERNOR – SAILING TO AMERICA
January 12, 1918

That January morning, she was most interested in the blue sky, the birds swooping around the pier, and the flower petals littering the wooden quay from leis. The birds made a squealing sound as they dipped and swooped above her. It was as if time stood still. She raised her face and felt the sun warm her eye lids a moment before she gripped her bag and shoes. Someone was yelling her name telling her to get moving and to keep hold of her sister Mary's hand.

Gus and his father carried the heaviest load in front of the women. The Silván men were small in stature but strong and capable. Gus and little Joe led the way. Everyone was staring around them, ogling the ship, the flag that flew high above them and the ocean that drummed against the side of the quay where a sea of travelers stood waiting their turn.

Once again they were leaving their home with a bracing journey before them. Once again they were perilously close to tears. 1917 had just ended. And they felt the promise of a new beginning that January in 1918 as the sun streaked across the Hawaiian horizon. They were freer than they'd ever been, with social and industrial justice more secure but the shadow of World War I and the frightening aspects the war might generate worried them.

Since Congress had approved a declaration of war against Germany and joined the war nine months earlier, there would be ten more months of fighting, death and fear. Not until November 11 would World War I end with the signing of an armistice between the allies and Germany.

The huge military boat's arrival at the depot was met with crowds of people, large boxes and loud music. It seemed like a big party as Manuela's family gathered in line waiting to board.

During their month waiting for the ship, they'd heard stories about the ships arriving but anchored from shore because of massive ocean wakes. Life boats had been lowered and rowed to the pier by longshoremen and when the wakes rose up to the pier, they would grab a trunk or a traveler to board the ship. The short trip was rocky, wet and worrisome. And the stories didn't cheer the family, wondering if their embarkation would tell the same story.

LIST OF UNITED STATES CITIZENS
(FOR THE IMMIGRATION AUTHORITIES)

Record on this blank United States citizens and citizens of insular possessions of the United States arriving at a port of continental United States from a foreign port or a port of the insular possessions of the United States, and such citizens arriving at a port of said insular possessions from a foreign port, a port of continental United States, or a port of another insular possession.

S.S. GOVERNOR — sailing from HONOLULU — January 14 19 18, Arriving at Port of San Francisco — January 19 18

Family Name	Given Name	Age (Yrs. Mos.)	Sex	Native birthplace / date	Address in United States
de Dos	Juan	1	M	Ewa, Hawaii — November 9, 1916	California
Casado	Maria C. Diaz	2 6	F	Ewa, Hawaii — June 16, 1915	"
Gonsalves	Maria G	5 9	F	Koloa, Hawaii — May 18, 1912	"
Gonsalves	Barcelisa	2 9	F	Honolulu, Haw — April 1916	"
Gonsalves	Augustina	1 4	F	Kealia, Hawaii — September 1916	"
Gonsalves	Victoria	4	F	Kealia, Hawaii — October 1917	"
Moreno	Atancio	5 6	M	Ewa, Hawaii — May 21, 1912	San Francisco
Moreno	Juliano	3 9	M	Ewa, Hawaii — February 16, 1914	"
Moreno	Eduardo	1 8	M	Ewa, Hawaii — May 21, 1916	"
Villela	Deolinia	2 8	F	Zapte, Hawaii — April 1917	"
Rios	Gregorio	5	M	Puhala, Hawaii — November 1912	"
Del Rio	Antonio	1 6	M	Puhala, Hawaii — December 1916	"
Aponte	Edward	33	M	Ponce, P.R. — December 1884	"
Aponte	Rosie	18	F	Ponce, P.R. — May 1899	"
Aponte	Elena	4	F	Peanilo — August 1913	"
Rosales	Jose	3 6	F	Wailuku, Hawaii — May 21, 1914	"
Bilbao	Maria	3 9	F	Kealia, Hawaii — March 29, 1914	"
Salvan	Antonio R	3	M	Hilo, Hawaii — March 1914	"
de Mello	John	23	M	Honolulu, Hawaii — September 3, 1917	"
de Mello	Saturina	22	F	Spain	"
Garcia	Rafael	4	M	Ewa, Hawaii — March 1914	"
Garcia	Cecelio	1 10	M	Ewa, Hawaii — February 1916	"
de Mello	John	6		Honolulu, Hawaii — June 1917	"
Contreras	Marcelo	3 5	F	Wailuku, Hawaii — August 20, 1914	"
Souza	Lydia	4	F	Puunene, Hawaii — September 9, 1913	"
Fernandez	Manuel	2 6	M	Wailuku, Hawaii — June 20, 1915	"
Fernandez	Phillipe	4 4	M	Wailuku, Hawaii — July 26, 1913	"
Fernandez	Vincentus	10	M	Lahaina, Hawaii — March 22, 1917	"
Pena	Geronina	1 6	M	Honolulu, Hawaii — 1916	"
Sobriza	Madaline	6	F	Honolulu, Hawaii — 1916	"

Admitted Jan. 19/5

IMPORTANT NOTICE.— 1. Great care should be taken *not* to place on this list the name of any passenger who was not born in the United States or who has not taken out final naturalization papers.
2. Where one or more members of a family are aliens, the names of *all* such members should be recorded upon the *alien* manifest. Suitable notation may be made upon such manifest opposite the names of those members who claim citizenship.
3. Failure to observe the terms of this notice may result in delay to passengers at the port of arrival.
4. List on this form only U. S. citizens or citizens of an insular possession of the United States.

That January morning, good news waited, their fears eased! The lumbering gray S.S. Herman Governor was solidly anchored to the pier as they slowly made their way toward it, straining to keep everyone together. She could already see this trip would be much better than her chaotic voyage from Spain. It didn't stink and they had a room, not the bottom of the boat to lose each other in all the filth and disorganization.

Juan Francisco Silvan Hernandez and Felix Gonzales Hernandez families. The Gonzales family names are shown as Feliso G. Hernández and the children's names are spelled Gonsalves. The children were listed on a separate page of the Governor's manifest titled, "List of United States Citizens" because they were born in Hawaii.

261

Rita Silván and Crescéncia Gonzales walked behind their enormously pregnant friend, who was due any day. They'd tried to sway the family of Dioniseo Legoines Herrero[77] into waiting until after the babe was born but they'd waited long enough. Manuela touched Dominguez Perez's back as they walked. Her belly was swollen and heavy beneath her coat and she looked uncomfortable. She patted Manuela's cheek with a nod of thanks.

Dominguez's discomfort soon turned to birthing pain after the ship left Honolulu and the ladies worked with the ship's nurse acting as mid wives. Manuela was part of the commotion just as she had been for her little sister Maria's (Mary) birth nearly four years earlier. A little boy this time and Manuela's heart swayed with the beauty of the baby's birth. She stared at his tiny hands and feet, the little tuft of hair, the squirming body and the love in his mother's eyes.

The newborn boy was named Geronimo. He was called Herman Governor Legoines Perez, in honor of the ship that carried them to America. And Manuela would be Godmother. She couldn't stop smiling and became his nanny for the remainder of the trip, hugging him close to give his mama time to heal.

And her mother, Rita, was pregnant again, due in six weeks. Manuela loved babies and was anxious for a new brother or sister. She prayed the child would live. The memory of the other time stayed with her still, even little Mary's healthy birth in 1914 hadn't cured those deep-seated fears.

---

[77] This family is shown on Page 7 of the S. S. Governor's manifest pages

PART THREE

SAN FRANCISCO, CALIFORNIA, U.S.A.

The S.S. Herman Governor sped across the Pacific Ocean within the week and the ship bleated its horn while maneuvering into San Francisco Bay on a wintry day in January. The fog and cold was a shock to their system after leaving the balmy breezes of Hawaii.

Manuela's straw hat was beside her and her brand new dress covered her slim body. Flushed with excitement, she pressed her hand to her throat when she saw the fabled city looming ahead. San Francisco, California was now more than just a name.

She stared at the shoe bundle and knew it was time to slip her feet into the confining leather, so she hauled it up, broke the string and unwrapped it. Her heart beat fast. They would soon be at the dock. Finding a bench away from the railing, she looked at them closely and frowned. She thought they looked bigger than she remembered. She slipped her foot into the shoe and her foot kept going, going, going. What?

She took a deep breath and shook her head, clearly startled. She would just carry them! No, she had to wear them, that was all... they'd be hidden beneath her long dress anyway. She grabbed the second shoe after buttoning the first one and slid her foot into it. This time, she was prepared for the oversized shoe....but she wasn't prepared to find the **same** shoe... Both shoes for the left foot![78] *Madre de Dios.* Mother of God. She laughed suddenly, buttoned it and stepped forward as her right toe nudged uncomfortably against the short edge of the second left-foot shoe. Too large was one thing, but...

"California," Felix whispered.

---

[78]There is some discrepancy with this 'shoe' story between Rose Ruiz Gobert and Tony Silván Ruiz. Either way, I also heard she wore those crazy shoes until she could replace them with her first paycheck!

"America. We made it brother." Juan responded.

Manuela stared at the men briefly and sighed. Their brief conversation played itself over in Manuela's head as she walked carefully, her skirts gathered tightly in one fist so she could watch her feet.

Juan Francisco Silván stared at America's coastline and felt strangely warm. They'd traveled the oceans. They'd struggled, worked tirelessly and sacrificed to remake their dream. It hadn't been easy but he knew a bubbling brook would have lost its song without the rocks. He'd harnessed his apprehension again with a bold move and the ground shifted beneath him. Seeking a future with peace and dignity would be worth it; his past heritage was strength, not weakness. With humble gratitude, faith and determination, he **would** make this work, feed his family and nourish their freedom.

The S.S. Herman Governor sailed into the bay and turned toward a wooded bluff to swing alongside the wharf at Pier 7 in the San Francisco Bay. Connected to the wharf by a broad wooden walk was the main building devoted to the United States Immigration Service. The cry of the sea gulls was in the air, bells or whistles sounded from different vessels nearby.

Walking the length of the wooden platform, Manuela's ill-shod feet pumped up and down as her hold-your-breath attitude soon replaced her anxiety. California stretched before her.

SPECIAL NOTE: In 1775, a Spanish expedition led by Juan Manuel de Ayala anchored on the nearby island and named it *Isla de Los Ángeles*, Ángel Island.[79]

As Erika Lee and Judy Yung state in their book, Ángel Island, Immigrant Gateway to America, "*Ángel Island* shows how the United States has simultaneously welcomed and restricted immigrants. Certainly, Ángel Island did become the gateway into America for thousands of immigrants who went on to strive for the opportunity, freedom, and fortune that the American Dream represented---if not for themselves, then for the children and grandchildren.   Several nationalities found refuge from political persecution and revolutionary chaos in their homelands and some eventually owned their own farms or businesses.   For them, Ángel Island was a stepping-stone to better lives in America, and their journey was made easier by the social workers, immigrant aid societies and religious organizations that assisted them on and off the island.   These Ángel Island immigrants went on to help build this nation of immigrants."

They further conclude that Ángel Island's history complicates our understandings of America as a "nation of immigrants."   It forces us to ask these essential questions: Is the United States a "nation of immigrants" that welcomes newcomers and helps them to achieve their dreams?   Or is it a "gate-keeping nation" that builds fences and detention centers to keep out certain groups of immigrants who are perceived as undesirable and dangerous aliens?   Many immigrants were taken to Ángel Island for inspection; our Spanish families were not among them.[80]

---

[79] Angel Island was first opened as an immigrant station in October, 1909.   When a vessel bearing immigrants to California sails into San Francisco Bay through the Golden Gate, anchorage is made at Meiggs' wharf, the vessel signals by whistling and the immigration officials go aboard.   The vessel proceeds to its dock in San Francisco, where first-cabin passengers land but most others are sent on to Ángel Island, which corresponds with Ellis Island on the eastern coast.

[80] Our family did not stop at Ángel Island because they had already gone through inspection at Honolulu in 1911. They landed off the ship when they arrived in San Francisco. There were only three individuals detained by the Board of Special Inquiry from those who arrived on the Governor in January 1918. They were all of Japanese descent -- none of them matched our family members. Our family likely did not spend any time on Ángel Island and were admitted directly from the ship to the wharf in San Francisco.   Sources: Judy Yung, Erika Lee and especially Marisa Louie at the Archives for Ángel Island.

During and after World War I, new passport controls were instituted by the U.S. government. As the campaign to restrict immigration intensified, new laws also followed. A numerical quota was put into law for each immigrant group based on national origins. Luckily, many Spanish immigrants arriving from Hawaii had already been approved by the U.S. Immigration Board when they arrived from Spain. Despite the ethnicity segregation generating a dark time in our history, being Spanish instead of Asian, they were favored from Northern and Western Europe. But the door was closing...

The *Ángel Island Ferry* came alongside to receive the immigrants who did not pass the doctor's standard inspection on the S.S. Herman Governor. The Silván and Gonzales families watched and wondered why people were being led to the ferry. The water was choppier, arms tightened around children and belongings were moved. They watched it make a short trip toward a long covered shed.

They would learn from fellow immigrants much later to thank God they were not hustled toward that ferry. The story was stark and unbelievable.

An excerpt and introduction to Ángel Island and the indignities many immigrants lived through and tried to forget.

When the ferry docked at Ángel Island arrivals deposited their bags in the arrival shed at the end of the wharf and then walked toward a two-story wood framed structure. The narrow passageway ran around the building and felt fresh salt wind smite their faces as they looked toward the Golden Gate Bridge. Between them and the bridge rose Alcatraz, the island whose cannon guarded the entrance to the bay. The buildings on Alcatraz gave the island somewhat the shape of a man-of-war. For many years it had been used as a military prison.

Inside the Administration Building, they showed their documents to the old doorkeeper, who later led them from the main room of the building into a long curving passageway, made secure by wire netting on the side opening outdoors, and ushered them past four separate waiting areas.   They realized these areas were each designated for a different class or group of individuals with rows of wooden benches.

Something didn't feel right.

And their gut feeling wasn't wrong.   As the families moved forward, they were met with a long table strewn with papers and register books where a group of official inspectors waited; the registry division room and processing desk.

These immigration officials were charged with protecting the nation from undesirable and dangerous aliens.   How both sides interpreted the intent and application of immigration laws often resulted in conflict.   For all immigrants, race, class and gender-based laws worked together to either open the gate to America or keep it closed.[81]

The men were startled and the women felt their anxiety.   There were large groups of Chinese and people from other countries sitting on benches; some sat alone, others in groups.   And they all appeared agitated. There were frightened voices raised in anger and scuffling erupted as families were led out of the farthest door.

With bellies in knots and eyes round with exasperation, they handed their documents to the official behind the table who seemed unaware of the ruckus; as if it was an everyday occurrence.

Once the documents were examined and the intake inspection began, the arrivals were lined up and shepherded up a curved path to the two-story hospital located on the hillside northeast of the administration building for the medical examination.

The astonished immigrants were presented a numbered wash basin.   A nurse told them by voice and gesture to squat down behind a protective barrier near the bed and produce something in its immaculate bottom of the basin.   If the immigrant tried and would not be allowed to leave until they produced something no matter how little.[82]

The hospital on Ángel Island had a state-of-the-art bacteriological laboratory, and bacterial examinations of blood and feces samples from applicants became a vital technique in the health screenings of immigrants.

---

[81] Source: San Francisco Chronicle, August 18, 1908

[82] Source: Gontard, "Second Class on Ángel Island" 8-9

Once that grueling indignity was behind them, the men were stripped naked and checked for abnormalities; their teeth, ears and nose was inspected as well as their eyes. The women were not required to disrobe unless they showed specific signs of disease. Children stayed with their mothers under the age of twelve.

Many immigrants were deported back to their country or kept inside the facility for weeks or months and interrogated before being "admitted" to the United States. The reasons were varied and among them, not only disease and exclusionary practices based on race, class and connections but World War I still raged; there was fear of espionage and sabotage. Many immigrants were asked about their financial situations, *occupational backgrounds and contacts in America.*

For our Silván and Gonzales families, several questions were answered through a translator and the official stamped an ink blotch on their papers. They were admitted to America the day they arrived as noted on the manifest.

Excitement and relief burrowed into them and they wasted no time in gathering their belongings, eyeing the fog and gulping San Francisco air.

THEIR AMERICAN DREAM

CALIFORNIA. The name rolled off our ancestor's lips; musical, magical and foreignly progressive. The scope and depth of their new world shook them to the core. They wanted to be Americans and yet much of the older generation that arrived in California could not read or write. The news surrounding their entrance into America was beyond their comprehension, so to give you an idea of some of the news worthy articles, this chapter will focus on that before jumping into the life they encountered.

As arranged, the Legoines family met them at the pier in San Francisco on January 18, 1918. A beehive of Spanish conversation ricocheted around them as they stared, wide-eyed, at their first view of America and moved to sit inside the automobile and old truck that waited for them. Bags, boxes and luggage were stuffed inside the trunk and the Legoines' family truck bed housed the chests retrieved from the piles of baggage deposited at the quay.

They arrived in San Lorenzo, (formerly called Squattersville) Alameda County, California where they would remain for some months.

Juan, a very pregnant Rita, Manuela, Agustín (Gus), José, and María (Mary) joined two other families the next day in the rented downstairs of a small house. They had separate living spaces, but shared a community kitchen.

The families were Crescéncia, Felix, Alejandro, Juan, María

271

Gregoria, Barceliza (Sally), Augustina and Victorina Gonzales and their friends, Dioniseo Leigones Herrero, his wife Dominquez Perez and their children, Rosa, Manuel, Francisco and baby Geronimo also known as Herman.   There were nineteen in the household and Rita would soon to give birth to total twenty.

Another new beginning.   They would find more strangers. Ethnic slurs.   Different food.   But they would slip their old culture into California where a new culture and generation would begin.

The families began to settle in various cities in the Sacramento valley of central California; Sunnyvale, Mountain View, Santa Clara Valley, San Francisco, Hayward, San Leandro, San Lorenzo, Winters, Vacaville, Fairfield, Sacramento and Rocklin among many.

It wasn't only money that pulled them from Hawaii to California.   Many of their friends sent word to the Silván, Gonzales, Souza and Martin families through shared letters from California to Hawaii.   The land in California promised harvests from the same sun that shone over Malaga.   The soil was fertile, rich and cried for farmers.   One didn't have to have a pocket full of money to be a success in America.

As Ms. Jastrow states in her book, *Looking Back*, "the circumstances may explain the special traits of the American personality.   The typical American is less bound by tradition, more impatient of constraints, more independent-minded of almost anyone else."   She continues, "Perhaps it is because they are nearly all immigrants or descendants of immigrants.   There are few among us who did not have to struggle to reach these shores."

It's been documented that dreadful conditions and despair

thrust these immigrants forward. They'd been promised an American dream and they were crusty and strong-minded enough to pursue it. They were mostly farmers. They knew the soil. They proved this with hard work by earning enough money to bring them to California, struggling through the sugar plantation's rigorous conditions.

They had seeds, grapevines, muscles, stamina and pride. Their families felt the freedom they promised when they arrived in California despite the economy and life and times from 1907 and afterward. They were often treated like second or third-class citizens. Many faced ethnic slurs due to their language barrier, their traditions, the food they enjoyed and the many children their religion encouraged.

Many of the first generation Spaniards were so strongly focused on becoming an American in America they forbid their children to speak Spanish and sadly the generations that followed paid the price. The irony of these phenomena was the generations after... who learned and spoke English helped those same first generation Spaniards do their business, understand contracts and make financial decisions.

Living the American dream for many of them was following the fruit harvests, putting their children to work beside them during the long summers. It was putting cardboard inside their shoes when the soles wore thin. It was eating beans, corn, asparagus and all the vegetables they grew in their gardens to feed their families. Pigs, cows, lambs, chickens and the farm animals they nurtured were killed and shared with family members or the eggs, milk, butter and cheese they could either eat or barter with.

Nothing of the American dream came easy but for some,

after the crops they found success from either being in the right place at the right time or meeting people who gave them the connections to become self-employed.   These immigrants led the subsequent generations to have a toehold in their own American dreams.

Employment ranged from canneries, a cigarette factory, the mines, the seaports, trucking, shop keeping and farming.   There were grocers, butchers, shoe repairmen, maids, cooks and piece work.   There was the Chinese Dry Yard in Loomis, picking hops in Rancho Cordoba, the Loomis fruit house.   And there was farming.

Since the families arrived in California before WWI ended in 1918, they would later contend with returning soldiers who joined the workforce to add to the dilemmas of employment availability.

Back to the soil, many followed the crops by working on farms doing what they did best: farming.   Many farmers' wives offered mid-day dinner to the laborers for ten cents a meal.   The days were long, dirty, sweaty and painful.

Their never-ending focus on the dream that pushed them away from Spain to eventually land in America gave the gift to the generations of us who take America for granted.

THE GIRL IMMIGRANT IN CALIFORNIA

The words raced through Manuela's brain like a whizzing windmill. *I have a job.* Within a short time, she was busily making thread in the cotton mill in San Lorenzo. Connections counted to get a job but her tenacity and hard work kept her on their payroll. The days were long, tedious; her concerns were earning money and helping her family so she gave her paychecks to her father just like all Spanish children of her time. It was the way they were raised and it was the way it would be. Keeping a few dollars of her own was a bonus and she always used them wisely. She would be a saver all her life.

However, her first payday took her to the shoe store. She couldn't work barefooted and those mismatched, too-large shoes had to go!

Juliana Martin Sesmilo and Felisa (Alice) Silván Martin also worked at the factory. The cousins had lost touch after arriving in California, so they delighted in renewing their connection.

The California Cotton Mills Co. Factory was located at 1091 Calcot Place in Oakland, just outside San Lorenzo. The factory started in 1883 and at its height employed over 1,500 people. The factory produced thread, upholstery and mops.

With the construction of the highway in the mid 1900s, the factory was later cut into two

Two months after their arrival in California, Rita's first American-born daughter, Juanita, was born March, 7, 1918. Her four-year old sister María (now called Mary) was ecstatic – a new sister born on her birthday!

The War was over!

People danced in the street, jumped and clapped on street corners and the celebration welcoming soldiers home was a sight to see. And with it, came the Americans who had left their jobs behind and wanted them back again.

The Silvan family moved to the Santa Clara Valley near San José area for some time and worked in Suisun, California in the pear harvests. Suisun City is in Solano County, California. It takes its name from the adjacent Suisun Bay which in turn is named for the *Suisunes*, Native American tribe of the area.

Despite working long hours during the day, Manuela helped her mother after work with all the children; she was a busy girl since she cared for Agustín, José, María and then baby Juanita.

Eight months after arriving in San Francisco, Rita was pregnant again and World War One was nearly over. Rita's health was failing, her belly damaged; too many pregnancies had caused major harm but regardless, she gave birth to Celestino Fernandez Silván in June of 1919. By then, with her body ravaged the older children were caring for the younger ones.

The families often gathered with friends from Hawaii with music and food and dancing. It was during this time that Juan Silván heard of abundant jobs in the asparagus fields. So, gathering everyone up, off they headed to follow the crop. They moved closer to farms, pleased to learn the farm work was easier than the sugar canes of Hawaii.

Although he'd become a wood worker, Juan said he would work anywhere to earn money. Settling around Rocklin, the family worked in the pears and plums before eventually moving to the small farming community of Winters, California about forty-five miles southwest.

Following the crops was an event Manuela would always remember for she met Bernardo Ruiz Romero once again.

Yes, Manuela keenly remembered Ben, his easy smile.

His father, Francisco Ruiz Garcia and his wife, María Carmen Rey Garcia arrived in Hawaii on the S.S. Harpalion in 1912 with their family and they'd become good friends while in Kilauea in Kauai. Of course she remembered…

Ben. She smiled when she thought of him and his gray eyes, heard his name, remembered where they met and…she wanted to see him again. In those days, of course, they were never allowed alone even in America; they still held true Spanish traditions. He was a chink over five years older than Manuela. Their lives mirrored one another following the crops like many other immigrant Spaniards.

Later as she lay in bed at night staring at the ceiling, she wondered if he thought of her too.

It felt strange and wonderful all mixed together as he insinuated himself within the Silván family. Friendships were re-ignited along with the Martins, Alvas, Boizas, Corrals; who'd shared their long-ago voyage from Spain on the Orteric.

Ben asked permission to court Manuela and he did come, his jacket flapping behind him as he strode up the path from the truck, his posture erect and his head swiveling back and forth as he looked for her.   Behind him followed half a dozen children.

And the courtship began.

After her parents allowed Ben to treat Manuela to the cinema… they went several times…surrounded by several of her siblings. One such date, her sister Mary sat on Ben's lap in the movie theater, so Manuela shrewdly suggested other venues.

One day Ben asked Manuela if she wanted to see a Vaudeville show. Juan Silván agreed and the threesome enjoyed the show very much... That was the way courting continued for the young couple; a parent or a gaggle of children always accompanied their outings.

Their courtship became more serious as the days passed, in and out of the fruit orchards, during family gatherings filled with music and laughter.

By August, when Celestino Silván was two months old, Manuela paused as an emotion sprung full-blown in her breast. She was in love.

Ben continued to court her entire family and marriage became a serious consideration. In the weeks that followed as she worked in the cotton factory and wrapped bandages for the Red Cross, her romantic life stood in limbo until a wedding could be planned… but with little money, their prospects were limited.

By the end of September when the fruit harvests slowed down, Ben planned a marriage ceremony and a celebratory train trip to Esparto.

Juan and Rita approved the match although they wished they would wait another year. Ben was twenty three. Manuela was only nineteen. But they didn't want to wait.

Early in the morning on Wednesday, October 15, 1919, excitement tickled Manuela's thoughts. It was her wedding day. She had washed and changed and put her hair up in a neat roll on the back of her head. A few damp strands lay against her nape and touched the lace collar. It was a morning dress, of a light fabric the color of rich, but gentle turquoise, with lace along the layered hems of the skirt and sleeves. There was embroidery across the bodice, gleaming white, a pattern of small birds and flowers. Against the dress her coloring seemed fresh, from the rich brown of her hair to her cheekbones and earlobes.

There wasn't enough money for a church wedding but it would be a wedding nevertheless. She shakily circled her throat with a string of creamy white pearls, threaded small pearl pierced earrings into the lobes of her ears and carefully placed a pearl-studded comb in the crux of the roll she'd created on her head. She smiled at herself in the mirror. She was a bride and felt like one, bubbling with nerves inside.

Ben arrived shortly afterward in his brown three-piece suit and a borrowed twenty-dollar bill in his pocket to pay the Justice of the Peace. In his vest pocket, their round-trip train tickets. His knees shook as he pressed his hair in order and knocked on the front door of the Silván's home.

Just after lunchtime, the couple entered the chamber at City Hall and nodded toward the witnesses provided. They would not have family witnesses and she was sorry for it.

Her smile was anxious but there was courage there too. Throughout the ceremony her hand trembled in his though her voice was calm and strong when she spoke. His own caught a little and she glanced up at him. And then she squeezed his hand and that made him smile. They were both grinning when the final words were spoken.

The Justice of the Peace turned to Ben and at the right moment he produced a simple gold band and put it onto Manuela's finger. "You are now husband and wife. You may kiss your bride."

Ben's eyebrows flew upwards at the suggestion. "Not here!" he answered quickly and they were gone from the chambers, a blur of blue and brown.

The luxury of a honeymoon was impossible, but a train ride from Alameda to Esparto on the Vaca Valley Railroad[83] wasn't. As she gathered her skirt and stepped onto the train, she was transported back to Spain to the little girl staring at the wonders there. She laughed like a child and Ben lifted her hand to his heart. It was the first time the rare but fleeting freedom touched them.

---

[83] Traces of the abandoned grade can be found. From the Vacaville/Allendale area, the line crossed Midway Road on the west side of I-505 and ran north to Winters on the east side of Hartley Road. At Udell Road the line ran northbound on the east side of Winters Road. The trestle where the line crossed Putah Creek is on the east side of Winters Road. Present-day Railroad Ave in Winters was the old grade through town and continued north along the east side of Yolo County Road 89. At a small town near Highway 16 the railroad crossed 89 and ran on the east side of Railroad Street where it then turned west along Highway 16 towards Esparto. Source: Wikipedia

In 1919, Esparto was a busy town and there was talk of it becoming the county seat.   Vaca Valley Railroad officials gave the name Esperanza, which means "hope" in Spanish, to their new town site in 1888, but when the post office was established in 1890 the name had to be changed because there was already an Esperanza in Tulare County. First Escalante, then Esparto was chosen as the new name and it means "feather grass" in Spanish

The elegant Esparto Hotel stood near the depot three stories high featuring glass lights, a pressurized water system and electric bells.   A wrap-around porch welcomed guests and chairs littered the spaces.   It was there the newly married couple began to create new memories.   They talked about everything.   They shared their stories and learned about one another; Manuela, finally alone with Ben, began to learn about love far beyond the cinema.

He told her family stories, sad and funny and outrageous, about his grandfather Juan Ruiz Vallejo, his long-dead mother Rosa from Álora and his grandfather whose name was Miguel Romero Fernandez, his own adventures in *Arroyo de los Olivas* as a boy.

She talked of grandmothers left in Spain, the poor times she survived, a pet pig that trotted up to her when she called, the long walk to Gibraltar, her mother's stillbirth, her cousins deaths on the ship. She laughingly told him about her button-up shoes in San Francisco and her fiery determination to make this land her own.

They would always remember the day, the train, the graceful hotel and their own vulnerability.

AND THEIR LIFE BEGAN. She returned to her job at the cotton mill, he to the shipyard at Mare island. And they moved in with Francisco Ruiz and Ben's family on their ranch.

Married life had its pleasures woven among many demands as she was pulled in several directions. Instead of becoming a wife to Bernardo, she became a maid to the Ruiz family. She helped cook and washed all the laundry for the family who she'd just become a part of. It was a large family; John, Miguel, Manuel, Diego and Antonio and the girls were Josefa, Dee and Connie. All the laundry was scrubbed by hand and it was soon apparent to Manuela she'd traded nannyhood for a life as a family maid. And she didn't like it one bit. .

Her new marriage and continuing-maid status was fluid as they followed the crops to earn their living and feed their families. During the summer harvesting season, they saw more of California than they liked. They moved toward the Santa Clara Valley where Manuela cut fruit and Ben picked and later pruned fruit from the trees or vines.   Many agricultural areas scattered throughout California called immigrants to work.

The Silván and Ruiz families worked near San José and as far north as the harvested crops dictated.   Many of their friends settled near Newcastle, Rocklin, RoSevilla and Sacramento.   But when the harvesting was over, they moved back to wherever their home base brought them.

Winter months slowed down their frenetic lives while winter celebrations lit up homes. Spanish tradition has it that the Magi Kings, *los Reyes Magos*, are the ones who on the morning of January 6th, el *Día de Reyes*, bear presents for all the children, repeating the ritual they performed after baby Jesús was born.   Often los *regalos*, the gifts, were fruit, nuts, a hand-made toy.

And the special treats during the season were often created together, a festive occasion. Christmas sweets such as *el turrón*, a nougat, is almond-based and often made in two versions, duro (hard) with whole almonds in a paste of sugar, honey and egg whites or *blando* (soft) where the ingredients are ground together. Another expected and very special holiday treat is the *rosquette*[84], wine-soaked, anise cookies dipped in sugar, rolled up like a coiled snake and dipped in wine and more sugar.

The kitchens were filled with flour, sugar, cinnamon, anise, wine, laughter, conversation, children sneaking samples off the cookie lined table.   And aromas that announced the holidays more than any other time of the year.

Celebrations stretched from December 22nd to January 6th. Then, between Christmas Eve and New Year's Eve, another celebration the equivalent of April's Fools Day took place on

---

[84] Rosquettes recipe at end of book

December 28th, *el día de los Santos Inocentes* (Holy Innocents' day). Nativity scenes with figurines are laid out on a table at home and candles beckoned in the homes and churches.

Family celebrations kept everyone busy with cooking, cleaning, singing Spanish carols and enjoying spiritual traditions.

And by this time, Manuela knew she was pregnant. She wanted a place to call her own. The summer crops would call them away from home in a few months and it would be rigorous; long hours, back-breaking and hot. She wanted to be a wife and mother with a sliver of time for herself.

And Ben listened.

In early January, Ben did the best that he could; they moved into an apartment at 292 Foothill Blvd., in the Hayward Park area of Alameda County with his brother, Miguel Ruiz Romero.

The brothers both had jobs in the shipyard; they made a pact to share expenses and though Manuela also worked outside the home, she was thrilled to be away from the big family.

Making it their home was appealing to Manuela and added a new confidence she enjoyed; and cooking for both men was an achievement she could be proud of.   They ate everything put in front of them.   She cooked Ben stewed tomatoes and garbanzo soup and Tortilla Española with peas.

But stray thoughts about her pregnancy plagued her and shot ahead to the summer and how it would impact their lives. Aunt Crescéncia Gonzales had birthed her cousin, Alfredo Gonzales, five months earlier and the heat had been very hard on her.

Manuela wondered how she would react to her own pregnancy; and for this reason, she was not looking forward to summertime.   By mid-May her fears were realized; the heat scorched, the fruit grew thick and some of the grapes burned on the vine.   Work was plentiful and it seemed there were never enough laborers to meet the needs so Manuela joined the work crews.   It would soon be prune season, money was scarce and her income was needed.   Then, there were peaches, cutting sheds and the drying of the fruit.   It wasn't an easy life; she could pick fast and removed seeds from stone fruit even faster.   By then, she was six months pregnant.   She could not and did not slow down.

Crescéncia was pregnant again and the summer's heat of 1920 took their breaths away.   It would be her eighth living child. They lived in Oakland in a two-story wood frame house.   The outside stairway led into the house and a shaded arbor was covered with grapevines.   Crescéncia did not follow the crops by then; Felix found work in the Oakland area in several places; a Chevrolet plant, a sugar beet factory and later a bologna factory.   He yearned for country just like the Silván and Ruiz families and he hoped to buy land near Winters, California at Putah Creek, close enough to retain their family gatherings.

Victorino Silván and his family lived in San Leandro near San José. He did not have an automobile but the train brought him, Ramona, Felisa (who was now called Alice), and Celestino to enjoy the family parties. Dora and her husband, John Souza, sometimes joined them but their family grew fast and the money did not allow the family visits long into the 1920s.

The Silváns often reminisced about Spain and Hawaii and the shadow of conversations trailed behind them. Wine flowed, music boundless. They spoke of the strange and sad ship journey, the forced military expectations in Spain, yesterday's harvest, the gardens. Children danced with adults and each other. Music, food and loud chatter accompanied the dancing with children running underfoot.

Juan thumped on his drum. Ramona danced with her daughter, Felisa, who always jumped as music thrummed. Manuela made music with spoons bouncing off pot lids and the younger children mimicked her.

The children loved the long summer days, when twilight stretched itself out and they were allowed out to play until it was full dark. They only had to stay within shouting distance. They played hide and seek, hopscotch, dominoes and rolled tires, teased each other and laughed.

At day's end, bellies full of good food, they were tucked in next to wiggling brothers and sisters and cousins to fall asleep by the sound of a guitar or drum music and whispered laughter.

When August arrived, dancing was left to others as Manuela's enormous belly slowed her down, bumped against tables and the stove as she stirred the pots. Despite her condition, she still liked being barefoot, wearing flowers in her hair and singing. She could still dance her feet in rhythm from a chair when music shook the walls. And always.... a crochet needle clicked in her hands as she created baby booties, sweaters and little blankets.

During these times in the hot summer as the sun scorched down upon them in northern California, harvesting time meant sleeping in tents or small trailers. The children often chose to sleep beneath the stars, the adults vying for trailers but they couldn't always have their way. Sometimes, instead, the families slept under the fruit wagons in a crush of bed linens to count stars and tell stories.

The days seemed endless as the families picked and packed fruit, storing them in small cubicle sheds filled with sulphur. Then they had the tedious task of crating them to dry in the sun for two weeks, night and day.

Everyone had their jobs. The women bent over washboards and large wash buckets to scrub their laundry just outside the tents. They instructed their children to pull and tie ropes between the tents and the clothing would be hung to dry in the summer heat. Often, the older daughters had the chore of scrubbing, twisting out the soapy water, rinsing, twisting again and then hanging them on the make-shift clothes line.

Manuela's father grew his own grapes, produced red wine, filled several barrels each fall and stowed them in his cool cellar. Several types of grapes were grown by the farmers such as Tokay and Merlot. Sometimes the grapes burned on the vine forcing some farmers to travel to Woodbridge to buy more durable vines such as Zinfandel.

Making the wine was a family event as the children crushed the grapes with bare feet in a massive wooden tank to 'walk them juicy'. Then it sat for a time to ferment before the crushed grapes were placed in a presser, stems and seeds intact.

The summer heat sometimes turned the wine sour before they could drink it. But that almost-sour wine became vinegar to clean and cook with.

Their wine was made during a time before prohibition laws; when the law passed in 1920; "bootlegging" did not stop them from growing, fermenting and drinking it. Most often, the men would keep a bottle at their feet beneath the dinner table. They poured glasses of wine for everyone, including children, as it was well known in Spain that wine was good for the blood and the soul.... Those grapes were also eaten as finger fruits, grown among fruit trees and their massive vegetable gardens.

Others made wine also, including Felix Gonzales. But Felix made more than wine, something many of the neighbors called *White Mule*. Some of the sour wine was poured into a pot with copper coils on a hot wood-burning stove in the cellar's summer kitchens. The distilled liquor flowed very slowly into a cloth-topped funnel over a large jar. As the liquid filtered through the white cloth, it turned beautifully turquoise. At Christmastime, he added fresh cherries to the jar and they had Cherry Vodka.[85]

Our family's thrifty souls allowed nothing to go to waste. All food counted for something and their children learned to do the same.

They canned vegetables and fruits and turned fruit into jams and jellies. They dried grapes, figs, peaches and pears. They

---

[85] Source: Theresa Gonzales Sackett, from Winter Tales, 2000

baked bread by the dozen in the beehive oven and fried *tortas* (fried bread) on bread-making day, sometimes called *sopaipilla*.

Sopaipilla is traditionally made from leavened wheat dough to which shortening or butter is added. After being allowed to rise, the dough is rolled onto a sheet and then cut into various shapes. The dough is deep-fried in oil, causing the shapes to puff up, forming a hollow pocket in the center.

Some families preserved grapes in sawdust to enjoy at Thanksgiving and Christmas.

There was raw honey from beehives.

There were chickens giving them eggs, cows and goats giving them milk, butter and cheese. There were almonds for eating, cooking, sharing, bartering and selling. Plums, peaches, apricots were eaten and often bartered for bananas at the fruit market from Sacramento.

They planted, harvested and cooked with herbs. They picked wild flowers along the creek beds, rivers and fields. And they transplanted wild flowers into their own gardens and grafted trees in the winter, hoping for green buds and flowers in the spring.

Pruning was an important event. If one didn't prune, the trees would not flourish. Ben became so adept at pruning that several farm owners hired him for their orchards, the brush piled high for later bonfires.

Hanging chorizo and blood sausage over the wood stove on bamboo sticks had to be watched carefully. However, the braided onions, garlic and home cured hams could be left unattended in the cool cellars with the barrels of home-made wine.

Manuela's pregnancy slowed her down. But it did not stop her. The cutting and drying of fruit in the stifling orchards, however, was a trial she found very difficult as summer lumbered through staggering heat. Moving sometimes like molasses, she wondered how she would survive the next few sweltering weeks.

There was a box filled with tiny crocheted blankets, soft cloth diapers, undershirts and dresses. She lovingly created them by hand while imagining the infant she would hold to her breast. She had compiled baby clothes from her mother's cache of shirts and blankets as well but her favorite? A dress and matching lace bonnet with matching booties. A gift from her tia Crescéncia that she was wearing thin from constantly fingering its cloth.

She was ready for her child. Each time her baby stretched or bumped inside her body she smoothed a hand softly over her belly, amazed at the miracle within.

Midwives prepared for her baby this time. She wouldn't be a bystander for others; cleaning, bringing cloths, boiling water, heating scissors, holding hands, wiping brows and learning midwifery by example. Now it was her turn.

Despite the enormity of her belly, the ache in her back, her swollen feet and her long experience with other children, this was different. She imagined holding this child in her arms; a smile split her face and her feet wanted to dance.

She didn't, however, ignore the memories from Hawaii. Her mother and aunt birthed babies after loving them through nine long months only to lay with empty arms afterward.

She shook the recollections away. Her mind moved forward as other thoughts ran rampant. Could she endure the birthing pain? And how would it feel to hold her own child to her breast? A child she and Ben would love and nurture. Watching her aunt and mother breastfeed had always touched her deeply.

She watched their tiny lips suckle, gurgle and often grin as milk dripped from the sides of their mouths. The newborn smell, the crying in the night, the wet diapers and ones filled with poop the color of *Toro's* mountain bluffs. She laughed. Yes, she was ready for it all.

The names were chosen: Francisco for a boy; Rosa for a girl. It had been decided months earlier. The Spanish naming rules were different in America. Instead of Rosa Ruiz Silvan, she would be Rosa Ruiz. Instead of Francisco Ruiz Silvan, he would be Francisco Silvan Ruiz. No longer would there be first surname and second surname. Maybe a second name but only one surname, the name of the child's father. It would no doubt bring much confusion in Spanish communities but in America, it would be correct. The child with Spanish blood running through its veins would have the naming rules of America through its life.

The muddle of thoughts wove through her head with the speed of her crochet needles. It was a rich and steady time as she waited and waited. Sighing anxiously, she reached for thread in a basket at her feet and the sounds of her needles urgently clicked through the room. A bucket sat nearby, her Plumeria pushing two tiny blooms through its growing stalk and shiny green leaves.

By late August, Ben Ruiz knew summer and his wife's pregnancy were both nearly over. Orchard work in San José kept him busy as he pruned, picked and harvested the fruit until dark. They came in from the fields, ate their meals and then played cards late into the night. As he nervously waited for Manuela to make him a father, the lure of the card games became less important for a time.

And then everything happened at once.

Manuela woke up at about midnight on a dark August morning with the disquieting sense that her waters were beginning to break. She wandered about the house for an hour or so, feeling some relief that the waiting might be over, which was dwarfed by alarm at the immediate prospect of her impending labor.

A sharp spasm down low and she knew it was real. She woke Ben, who jumped up and rushed around blindly for pants. He knew his job was to get the mid wife and Rita. The door slammed behind him.

Manuela started to shake, grabbed towels to wedge between her and the bed and lay down to wait. Another spasm and the room suddenly lit up with voices and the chatter of Spanish women. Ben was evicted from the room and her labor began in earnest.

Finally, she stopped shaking and gripped her mother's hand. It helped enormously to have something actually to do. Finally, she thought the end was in sight, but everything about birth had taken longer than she expected, and she pushed at the baby for an hour and a half. Just when the midwife was making unpleasant noises about cutting so her child could put in an appearance, she felt like she was trying to pass a rocking chair.

In great excitement the midwife said, "Give me your hand." And she took Manuela's hand and placed it on the top of her baby's head as it was emerging. Manuela had never known such a magnificent moment. She could feel beneath her fingertips a soft, pulsing skin, the top of a tender head, the sense of wondrous, unknowable, new life. In two pushes her baby was born and she heard the cries. And then she shed tears of triumphant relief as the midwife cut the cord and weighed and washed her son.

That day, Manuela changed from nanny to mother.

Francisco Silván RUIZ was born August 18, 1920 in San José, Santa Clara County, California. His father was twenty four, his mother just nineteen.

Infant clothes waited, diapers were piled near the baby cot and the lacy dress and cap hung near the window for the babe's baptism. Her breasts were heavy with milk and motherhood began.

Their child, Francisco, was their first of fifteen children.

PHOTO: Ben Ruiz is standing on the far right in back. Manuela is sitting in front of him with baby Francisco in her lap, named after both of their fathers[86]. John and Rita Silván are seated and their children from left (front): María, Juanita on John's lap, Celestino on Rita's lap and from the left (back) is Agustín (Gus) and center back is Joe Silván .

---

[86] Juan Francisco Silván Hernandez and Francisco Ruiz García

As I sigh my way through the memories and end this tribute to abuelita just after her first child is born, I come back full circle to her flowers once again.   Flowers were in her blood and I am instantly transported back to her garden many years afterward with just the whiff of strong-scented roses.   She was laughter, twinkling eyes, softness, love, flowers and anemone shells to me. I hear her voice and honor her history. She was the beginning link to our green thumbs, our love of music and storytelling; just a few of the legacies that follow us still.   Now I have my own yellow Plumeria in my courtyard and enjoy every tiny change as it grows and blooms, reminding me of the many scents of Hawaii and the flowering memories it brought to abuelita.

The rest, as they say, is history.
Book 2: SILVÁN LEAVES[87]
Book 3: RUIZ LEGACIES. [88]

---

[87] Silván   Leaves, a detailed exploration of the Silván family projected: 2013
[88] Ruiz Legacies, a detailed exploration of the Ruiz family projected: 2014

SPANISH DOCUMENTS

Crinkly, pink, pale with age, an extract certification of Manuela's birth certificate

Manuela's Certified Birth Certificate - June 25, 1901

Serie C   Nº 196669

MINISTERIO DE JUSTICIA

REGISTROS CIVILES

Folio 34   Certificación Gratuita
(Ley 25/1986 de 24-12)

ACTA DE NACIMIENTO.

NÚMERO 93.
Manuela
(sin tachas)

En la villa de *[illegible]*
á la *[illegible]* del día *veinte y siete*
de *Junio* de mil *[illegible] uno* ante
D. *Luis Gómez [illegible]* Juez municipal
[illegible]
y D. *[illegible]*
Secretario. *[illegible]*
compareció *Vidal [illegible] Baena*
natural de *esta villa* término
municipal de *la misma* provincia
de *Zamora de treinta y cuatro años* de edad,
de estado *casado*, profesión *[illegible]*
domiciliado en *la misma villa* calle
de *la Torre* núm. *[illegible]* con cédula personal
que exhibe talón núm. *688* expedida por *el agente de
la villa* en *[illegible]* de *Mayo*
de mil *[illegible]*, presentado con objeto de que
se inscriba en este Registro civil una niña y al efecto como *[illegible]*
[illegible] de *[illegible]* misma declaro.
Que dicha niña nació en *esta villa, calle del Ma-
[illegible]* a las *veinte y tres y media*
del día *veinte y seis del corriente*
Que es hija *legítima* de *[illegible]
Hernández [illegible]* natural de *esta villa*
término municipal de *[illegible]*
provincia de *Zamora de veintiséis años de*
[illegible] de [illegible]
[illegible] veinte años, natural de [illegible],
domiciliados en esta villa
Que es nieta por la línea paterna. *de Celestino [illegible]*
[illegible] de esta villa,

término municipal de *la misma* provincia

Back of Manuela's certified birth certificate

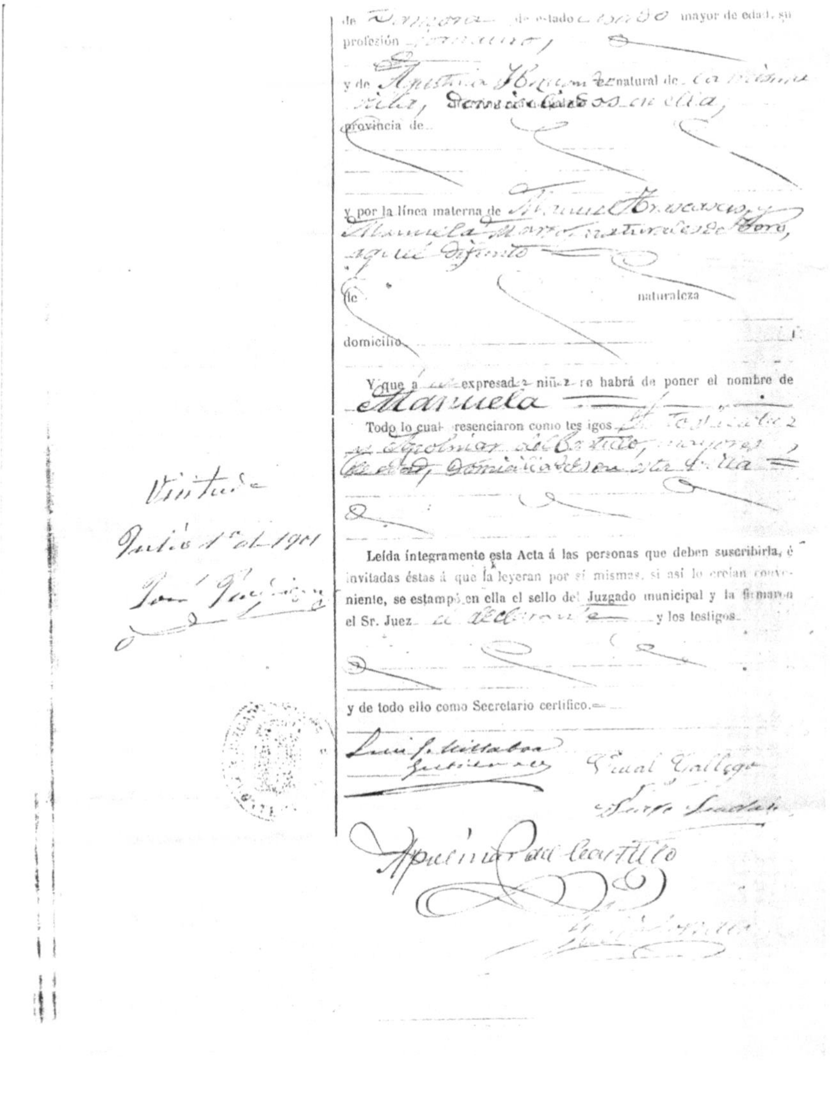

de Zamora de estado casado mayor de edad, su profesión jornalero

y de Agustina Herrero natural de la misma villa, domiciliados en ella,

provincia de

y por la línea materna de Manuel Herrero y Manuela Marcos naturales de Toro, aquel difunto

de naturaleza

domicilio

Y que a la expresada niña se habrá de poner el nombre de Manuela

Todo lo cual presenciaron como testigos

Leída íntegramente esta Acta á las personas que deben suscribirla, é invitadas éstas á que la leyeran por sí mismas, si así lo creían conveniente, se estampó en ella el sello del Juzgado municipal y la firmaron el Sr. Juez y los testigos.

y de todo ello como Secretario certifico.

1907 Character Letter, Juan Silvan Hernandez

Document stating Manuela Silván Trascasas is their legitimate daughter for immigration

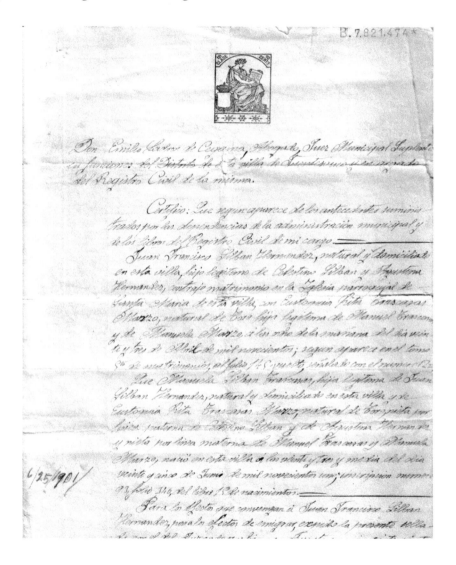

Extract of Baptismal Certificate: Manuela Silván Trascasas – Baptized 2 July 1901

Manuela's Godfather: Uncle Victorino L. Silván Hernández

3600 BAKER ST
SAN FRANCISCO, CALIF. 94123

Sra. Manuela Silvan Vda. de Ruiz
125 Laurel St.,
Vacaville, California, 95688

CONSULADO GENERAL DE ESPAÑA
EN San Francisco, California

Certificado de Nacionalidad N.° 950 ....-XII-19.. 73

EL CONSUL GENERAL DE ESPAÑA

CERTIFICA: Que en el Registro de Matrícula de Españoles que existe en este
Consulado General hay una partida que dice así:

Número 10.058
Don MANUELA SILVAN TRASCASAS Vda de RUIZ
nacido en Fuentesauco .... provincia de Zamora
el 25 de Junio de 1901 profesión Su Hogar
estado Viuda .... residente en 125 Laurel St. Vacaville, Cal.
titular del Pas# .... expedido en San Francisco
con fecha 27 Marzo 1973 .... por Consulado General

Y a fin de que el interesado pueda acreditar su nacionalidad, expido el presente en San Francisco , a 27 de Marzo de 19.73

del Arancel.
El Cónsul General,
...
Amparo C. Murchie
Canciller

....
(Firma del interesado)

Certified Copy of Death Certificate, April 2001

Manuella 'Silvan' Ruiz

Manuella (Silvan) Ruiz died in Alderson Convalescent Hospital, Woodland Saturday, April 21, at age 100.

Born June 24, 1900, in Fuento Sauko, Spain, Mr. Ruiz had been a Yolo County resident for 82 years. She was the daughter of Juan F. and Estoquia Rita (Trascasas) Silvan. She had come to California as a young woman of 18 with the family settling in Yolo County. After years of home schooling while working on the family ranch, she married Bernardo Romero Ruiz of Malaga, Spain, and together they moved to the Winters area. As a young wife of a farmer, she took on the day to day chores of the farm and began her family, which was soon to number 15 children. According to her family members, "she was a devoted mother, grandmother, who loved her family, gardening and crocheting. She was especially fond of John Wayne movies, cowboys and horses." She had been a member of St. Anthony's Church in Winters since moving to Yolo County and had made sure every one of her children went to school and church there.

Mrs. Ruiz is survived by her daughters, Rose Gobert of Capitola, Mary Sanderson and husband Hans of Tucson, Ariz., Millie Cortopassi and husband Fred of Woodland, Rita Frost and husband Palmer of Battle Creek, Mich., Antoinette Alves and husband Barney of Woodland, Josie Ruiz of Reno, Nev., and Carnie Potter and husband Jerry of Homer, Alaska.; sons, Frank Ruiz and wife Norma of Grass Valley, John Ruiz and wife Mary of Winnemucca, Nev., Michael Ruiz and wife Grace of Sacramento, Joe Ruiz and wife Barbara of McKinleyville, and Antonio Ruiz and wife Mary Helen of Santa Clara.

She is also survived by her 50 grandchildren; and numerous great-grandchildren and great-great-grandchildren.

Mrs. Ruiz was preceded in death by her husband, Bernardo Ruiz; daughters, Deloris and Bernalda Ruiz; and son, Benny Ruiz.

A funeral Mass is scheduled to be said at 10 a.m., Thursday, April 26, in St. Anthony's Catholic Church, 511 W. Main St., Winters, with Father Luciano Valenzuela officiating. Burial will follow immediately at Winters Cemetery. No visitation is scheduled.

Kraft Bros. Funeral Directors of Woodland is assisting the family with arrangements. Inquiries may be made by calling 662-4658, or by contacting www.legacy.com.

305

Documents reveal inconsistencies.

Manuela's name is misspelled with an extra 'L' and her year of birth is incorrect, but it is a beautiful stone and sits next to her husband, Bernardo Ruiz. She often spelled her name this way instead of the legal account found on her birth and baptismal documents. That is why her daughter, Manuela (Millie) had the stone the way her mother would have wanted it shown.

Ben's name is also misspelled with an 'L' instead of an 'R', undoubtedly because the rolling Spanish 'R' sounds like an 'L'; mistakenly pronounced *Ben-al-do* instead of *Bernardo*.

FOTOGRAFIAS - PHOTOGRAPHS

Fuentesaúco, Province of Zamora, Spain
Iglesia de Santa María del Castillo

Photo: Patricia Steele - Santa María Church / September 2012

Fuentesaúco Cemetery and family gravestones

The
Fue
nte
saú
co
crest was painted on a large old building that had once been a cinema near the church beside the Plaza Mayor

The signs entering the villages are well marked.   And then when you leave the edge of the villages, you see the same sign with a line through it so you know you've left~

Photo below: Eusebio "Sab" Gonzales (shared by his daughters, Patte and Linda Gonzales): Fuentesaúco, Zamora, Spain

Manuela with her Spanish fan, her pearls, her 5-diamond
ring[89]and her embracing warm smile

---

[89] This ring was a gift from her daughter, Millie Ruiz Cortopassi

SPANISH FOOD and RECIPES

Why do Spaniards place such importance on food? Perhaps because eating is an ongoing social affair and a tremendous source of pride. In Spain, the workday grinds to a halt for a traditional three-hour lunch. Presently, tea and pastries or tapas are served early evening and dinner is around 10:00 p.m.

Spain's road to *la buena mesa* has been a bumpy one. The Romans brought good eating to Spain, introducing wheat, wine, and olive oil, and the Moors embellished the foods with Eastern flavors. However, five centuries ago, when Spain expelled the Moors, food lost a lot of its diversity and excitement when the nation tried to eradicate all traces of foreign foods that had dominated the country nearly 800 years in the spirit of reunification. As a result food became somewhat plain and unimaginative. Many wonderful dishes disappeared, although fortunately Moorish influence had already been incorporated into Spanish cooking. For example, rice on the eastern coast, lemon and orange trees thrived; Saffron, anise, sesame seed, nutmeg, and black pepper were essential to Spanish cooking, and convent nuns became the makers of wonderful Moorish sweets.

From the Americas, tomatoes, peppers and potatoes were introduced and soon considered among the most important ingredients in Spanish cooking.

The mountains that crisscross Spain isolate one region from another. Without sufficient contact and with differing climates and terrains, styles of cooking and ingredients vary significantly. That is why we speak of Spanish cuisines in the plural. Food retains local character, hence food prepared in *Fuentesaúco* and *Toro* differed immensely from the south in Malaga, and Almogia.

MANTECADOS (Rita Silván to Juanita Silván and then to Linda Hyatt).

1 pound lard or ½ cup oil + ½ cup Crisco sticks
1 cup sugar
2 eggs
2 Tablespoons Baking powder
3 -5 cups flour (more as needed to make a soft dough)
¼ cup red wine or white-cooking sherry
2 teaspoons Anise seed (slightly crushed)
      Mix oil and Crisco sticks and add anise seed.   Melt together and cool

      In a bowl mix the wine, sugar, anise and eggs. Then add the flour and place in the refrigerator to chill awhile. Knead dough slightly and pat or roll to a ¼ inch to a ½ inch thickness. Cut dough into desired shapes. Place on un-oiled cookie sheet and bake at 325 F. for 15 min. Take off the sheet and dip in a bowl of wine and then into a bowl of very fine sugar._

SPANISH POTATO OMELET   Serves 6

3 Tablespoons olive oil
1 cloves garlic, peeled
3-4 potatoes
4 eggs
½ yellow onion, diced
      Preheat non-stick fry pan over medium heat.   Add olive oil, garlic and onion. Fry until the onion is transparent.   Remove from pan and set aside.
      Add potato slices and fry until bottom is crispy brown.   Turn potatoes over and add onion, salt and mashed garlic.   Cover and continue cooking about 15-20 minutes until potatoes are tender, turning as needed.   Reduce heat to low, remove lid and pour beaten eggs over potatoes.   Shape edges and continue cooking until egg is set.
      Cover top of pan with a plate and carefully flip the omelet onto plate and carefully slip omelet back into the pan --- uncooked side down and continue cooking until egg is fluffy and tender, not browned. For variation, add ¼ cup diced green or red onion or celery with onions before you fry them in top paragraph.

      Excerpt from Josephine Ruiz Martin's family recipe book

ICY LEMON WATER

Agua Limón
8 large lemons (makes 4-6 glasses)
1 cup superfine sugar, plus extra to taste
3 cups boiling water

• Finely grate the rind and squeeze the juice of 7 of the lemons into a large heatproof bowl; remove all the seeds. Finely slice the remaining lemon and set aside 4-6 slices to use for serving; stir the remainder into the juice.

• Stir the superfine sugar into a bowl. Add the boiling water and let cool to room temperature. Chill until required.

• To serve, strain into a serving pitcher and dilute the cold water to taste. Stir in extra sugar, if desired. Serve in chilled glasses, garnishing each one with a slice of lemon.

CHUNKY SPANISH GAZPACHO.   Serves 6

2 large tomatoes
1 large cucumber, peeled & de-seeded
1 large onion
1 cup green bell pepper
1 Jar Pimientos (4 oz.) diced & drained
2 cans   V-8 Juice (12 oz.)
1/3 cup red wine vinegar
¼ teaspoon hot pepper sauce
1 ½ teaspoon sea salt
1/8 teaspoon black pepper/freshly ground
2 cloves garlic/minced
¼ cup chives, fresh/chopped

Chop tomato, cucumber, onion, bell pepper, pimento and fresh chives into tiny chunks. I do not use a blender because I like to eat the chunks instead of all juice.

Mix vegetables with the V-8 juice, ¼ cup olive oil, vinegar, hot pepper sauce, salt and ground black pepper. Cover mixture and refrigerate until it is well chilled, about 2 hours. This soup can be stored in the refrigerator up to a week.

GARBANZO BEAN SOUP #1

Aunt Millie Cortopassi tells us: Do not add salt until serving.

1 package Dry garbanzo (chick peas) beans
2-3 Ham hocks or smoked ham slices
1 Onion, medium/chopped
3 Mint leaves, fresh/chopped
1 clove Garlic/minced
1 Tablespoon Parsley
4-5 White potatoes/peeled/chopped
3 Carrots/peeled/chopped
1 Cup Celery/sliced
1 Cup Mushrooms/sliced (optional)
1 can stewed tomatoes (15 oz.) /chopped in small pieces

- Place garbanzo beans in HOT water and boil with garlic and parsley the day before.

- The next day, drain beans & wash them well.

- Re-fill pot to cover beans and add the all ingredients EXCEPT the potatoes.

- Bring the beans, bacon, mint, onions and garlic to boil.

Cook slowly on medium/low heat until nearly done, about 2 or 3 hours.

The beans will not be completely soft, so testing is required. Add potatoes and cook about 20-30 minutes longer, until done.

GARBANZO BEAN SOUP #2

From Linda Hyatt – She thinks this is from Rita Silván's Kitchen

Boil a whole chicken. Add celery slices (1 stalk), crushed garlic, parsley and ¼" white salt pork. After chicken cooks, drain and strain – cool and debone the chicken. Rinse 2 cans garbanzo beans and add 4-5 potatoes, peeled and chopped and 2 cups green beans. Place all in one pot and season if needed. Cook until potatoes are soft. Add a little saffron (optional).

BEEF SOPA

Fry ½ pound hamburger with 1 onion, chopped fine and a fresh minced garlic clove.

Mix in Swiss chard, chopped small and stir.

Add one potato, peeled & chopped fine.

Add 2 cups (or more) of beef broth.

Cook everything.   Then add garbanzo beans.

Aunt Millie (Ruiz) Cortopassi's CANNELLINI

Boil baby white beans a couple of hours in water.

Turn off heat and cover.

Add a handful of sausage and finely chopped onions, fresh Swiss chard (washed and chopped) and garlic.

Fry in black skillet.   When it is done, add to pot of garbanzo beans.   Add a little paprika, salt and pepper.

For more soup, add potatoes.

ROASTED GARLIC

Cut the pointed top off whole garlic.

Add olive oil into the garlic.

Wrap tightly in foil and twist the top.

Bake at 350 degrees until done (soft).   Squeeze out onto a plate and smash.

Add a little more olive oil and serve like butter on French bread etc.

PINTO BEAN SOPA

Cook pinto beans with ham hock all day.

Add a couple potatoes (chopped and peeled) with small chunks of peeled carrots.

Add one chopped onion and cook until vegetables are done.   Add dry spices such as paprika, Italian seasonings, a little cinnamon.

Manuela's recipe to my mother, Neyda (Hubbard-Ruiz) Bettencourt

<u>ROSQUETTES</u> (SPANISH CHRISTMAS COOKIES)

Makes about 4 dozen

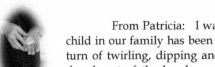

From Patricia: I watched abuelita make these cookies and every child in our family has been a part of our holiday tradition by taking our turn of twirling, dipping and especially eating. This entails pulling the dough out of the bowl, working it between our hands to shape a rope about 8" long, then swirling it into a "snail" shape in the palm of our hand. THEN the fun begins.

Heat in a small pot & cool: (Cool in the freezer to hurry the process for 30 minutes): 1 Cup canola oil and 1 Tablespoon Anise seeds

When cool to touch, **Mix oil** in very large mixing bowl with:

1 Cup Muscatel wine (or Moscato)

    2 eggs

½ Cup granulated sugar

1 teaspoon Pure Vanilla Extract

1 Tablespoon baking powder

¾ teaspoon Salt

Add enough flour to make dough workable

Pull dough out of the large mixing bowl to fill palm of your hand.

Rub between palms until it resembles a thin rope, about 8" long and ½ "wide. If it is too thick, it will not bake properly so uniformity is best. Think small! Then, **curl it into your palm** like coiling a snake and tuck the end underneath

Place cookies on a Pam-sprayed cookie sheet.

BAKE about 20 minutes in a 350-degree oven

AFTER BAKING:

Warm a mixture of ¾ C Muscatel wine and ¼ cup water.

Dip hot, freshly baked cookies in the warmed wine mixture. THEN, dip each warm cookie in granulated sugar. **If the sugar starts to 'clump' replace with fresh sugar for dipping immediately.** Place on waxed paper to cool. Store in airtight containers... *Best eaten the same day or 2ⁿᵈ day but our family makes about 8 dozen, puts them in Tupperware between waxed paper.*

Manuela's recipe to Aunt Millie Ruiz Cortopassi
(Transcribed by Jeff Cortopassi) Christmas 2012
GRANDMA'S SPANISH WINE COOKIES ROSQUETTES

INGREDIENTS NEEDED:

- Crisco oil – 1 cup
- Anise seed – 2 tablespoons
- Eggs – 4
- Sugar – 3 cups (in separate steps)
- Anisette liqueur – ½ cup
- Moscato wine – 2 cups
- All-purpose flour – 5 to 7 cups
- Baking powder – 2 tablespoons

STEP ONE: OIL PREPARATION:

In small pot, pour one (1) cup of Crisco oil, and two (2) tablespoons of anise seed. Heat on medium heat until oil starts "popping "seeds. Remove from heat to let cool and set aside.

STEP TWO: WINE, OIL, & ANISETTE MIXTURE

In a large mixing bowl crack four (4) eggs and whisk them vigorously. Add one (1) cup sugar, one half (½) cup Anisette liqueur, and one (1) cup Moscato wine, and whisk together. Add the cooled down oil with anise seeds, and again whisk entire mixture together. Set aside.

STEP THREE: DOUGH PREPARATION

Sift five (5) cups of flour and two (2) tablespoons of baking powder into another mixing bowl. (This can be done ahead of time).

Starting with a cup at a time, slowly add the flour and baking powder into the step two liquid mixing bowl, and whisk until it begins to thicken. Then start to use a spatula and continue adding all the sifted flour mixture. Continue adding more flour sprinkled on top of the dough until it stops sticking to the edges of the bowl when folding the dough with the spatula. Begin to use your hand and fingers to fold the dough, adding a big pinch of flour at a time, working the dough until it stops sticking to your fingers. Let the dough sit for at least 30 minutes. (It is a good time to clean up and get out baking sheets and cooling wire racks for next step.)

STEP FOUR: ROLLING AND SHAPING ROSQUETTES FOR BAKING

Pre-heat oven to 350 degrees F. Place one-fourth (1/4) cup of flour on a flat plate and place near dough mixture bowl. Grab "small meatball" sized globs of dough and drop onto flour plate. Dust a glob and make "snake" shaped "ropes" by rolling back and forth in the palm of your hand letting gravity hang the rope shaped dough downward until it is at least 6 to 8 inches long. Place a finger in the middle area of the rope and make a loop and twist the ends. Place them on an ungreased cookie sheet, keeping them separated until sheet is full. Place full sheet into oven for 15 to 18 minutes. Cook until the tops are light brown and the bottoms are a toasted brown color. Remove sheet from oven and remove cookies from sheet placing them on the wire cooling rack. Repeat step four until all dough is done.

STEP FIVE: DIPPING IN WINE AND SUGAR COATING

Place a cup of wine into a soup bowl, ½ cup of sugar in a flat bottom pie plate, and ½ cup of sugar and a teaspoon in a small bowl. Having two people doing this step works best. Dip a cookie in the wine and place on sugar in flat bottom pie plate, pushing down to coat the bottom. Using the teaspoon, sprinkle the tops of the cookie. Gently grabbing the loop sides of the sugar coated cookie, place on serving plate or cookie container. It is best to NOT stack these initially. Repeat until all cookies are dipped and coated. Save remaining sugar for coffee. Drink remaining wine with a fresh Rosquette!!!!

MANUELA SILVÁN TRASCASAS RUIZ
with her third grandchild, Patricia Ruiz Steele
1948 and 1986

Frank, Audrie and Christina (1977)

Children of Patricia Ruiz Steele

HISTORIC NEWSPAPERS IN HAWAII
The Hawaiian Star, Honolulu --- April 1, 1911 shows the sugar plantations Castle & Cooke, Ltd. Supported

Castle & Cooke, Ltd
Honolulu, T. H.

**SHIPPING AND COMMISSION MER-
CHANTS, SUGAR FACTORS**
and
GENERAL INSURANCE AGENTS
Representing

Ewa Plantation Co.
Waialua Agricultural Co., Ltd.
Kohala Sugar Co.
Waimea Sugar Mill Co.
Apokaa Sugar Co. Ltd.

Fulton Iron Works of St. Louis.
Babcock & Wilson Pumps.
Green's Fuel Economizers.
Matson Navigation Co.

IMMIGRANTS OFF TO PLANTATIONS

Only Fifty Left Out of Fifteen Hundred That Came On S. S. Orteric.

Fourteen hundred immigrants out of the number that arrived on the Orteric have been sent out to island plantations, and the Territorial Board of Immigration has probably established a record in handling laborers coming to the islands to work.

Between April 19 and May 2 the entire shipload, with the exception of two families that are held because there were sick children in them on arrival, has been handled and scattered among four islands—Oahu, Maui, Hawaii and Molokai.

Had it not been for the quarantining of the ship here on account of alleged scarlet fever epidemic among the children, the immigrants would have been handled in half the time, for instead of getting them from quarantine in squads, the Board of Immigration could have taken the whole shipload ashore and sent them out to the other islands as fast as the smaller steamers could carry them.

About fifty people are left in Honolulu now, all of the others having been sent away, a number going Tuesday on the Mauna Kea to Hawaii Ewa and Waialua plantations on this island took about one hundred each, many of them being Spaniards. The outside islands got about twelve hundred.

The members of the Board of Immigration think that the immigrants brought by the Orteric will be very valuable laborers. Nearly all are from the mountainous and agricultural districts of Spain and Portugal, used to outdoor life, simple fare and hard work. They were remarkably easy to handle and almost without exception were anxious to get to work at once. They didn't want to stop and see Honolulu, but asked for tickets to the plantations, gathered up their baggage and were taken to the steamer.

Orteric arrives with many laborers
April 14, 1911

Fifty Seven Children Died on Orteric (disputed number: 47 died)
April 13, 1911

Conditions of Departure of the Orteric
April 22, 1911

Orteric Dispute For Courts of England
May 1, 1911

More Emigrants in Few Months
May 17, 1911

1918 NEWS HEADLINES IN AMERICA

The United States House of Representatives consisted of Democrats, Republicans and Prohibition parties.

Daylight Saving Time started Sunday, March 31, 1918 and ended Sunday, October 27, 1918. It was first adopted to replace artificial lighting so they could save fuel for the war effort in Germany during World War I

The Twin Peaks Tunnel is a 2.27-mile long street car tunnel in San Francisco, California running under Twin Peaks. It opened February 4, 1918 and considered the longest United States railway tunnel west of New York City at that time. It was designed to enhance the western part of San Francisco after the big earthquake of 1906. The original eastern entrance to the tunnel was in the middle of Market Street at Castro.

DMV Created

The first Department of Motor Vehicles was created in 1915 with enactment "Vehicle Act of 1915." Vehicle registrations that year had climbed to 191,000.

From 1916 through 1919, California issued a basic plate, in white with blue characters, without year designation. Metal symbols affixed to the upper left corner of the license plates validated registration. In 1916, the symbol was a bear; in 1917, a poppy; in 1918, a liberty bell; and in 1919, a star.

In 1921, the powers and duties of the Department of Motor Vehicles were transferred to the Division of Motor Vehicles, part of the newly created Department of Finance. The move reflected recognition of the division's revenue producing status.

The Northern California tsunami struck the coastline August 15, 1918, with an estimate wave height of 4.6 meters.

The 1918 California earthquake that occurred on

April 21 had a magnitude of 6.8 caused $0.2 million dollars in damage in Jacinto, California

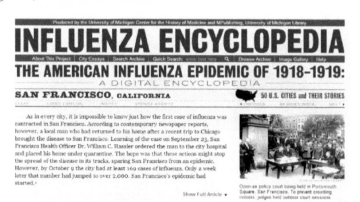

1918: After the Russian Revolution and the end of WWI, many Americans became suspicious of the "new" immigrants and the dangers they posed to American society.

As late as 1921, Gertrude H. Folks, writing in the American Child Magazine, asks, **"When is child labor not child labor?"** and answers her own question by saying, "Every state in the Union answers, `When it takes place on a farm'." She continues: "In seventeen states agriculture is specifically exempt from the provisions of the child labor laws regulating both the age at which children may work, and the number of hours during which they may work. In the other states, a definite exemption is not stated, but agriculture is omitted from the list of occupations affected by the child labor law.

farmerettes of the Woman's Land Army of America took over farm work when the men were called to wartime service in WWI.

1917 to 1919, the **Woman's Land Army of America** brought more than 20,000 city and town women to rural America to take over farm work after men were called to war. Most of these women had never before worked on a farm, but they were soon plowing fields, driving tractors, planting and harvesting. The Land Army's "farmerettes" were paid wages equal to male farm laborers and were protected by an eight-hour workday. For many, the farmerettes were shocking at first--wearing pants!--but farmers began to rely upon the women workers.

Sugar Plantations in Hawaii

Honomu Sugar Co. (Big Island of Hawaii)
Koloa Sugar Co. (Kauai)
Lihue Plantation & Sugar Mill (Kauai)
Kilauea Sugar Plantation (Kauai)
Hanalei Sugar Mill (Kauai)
Grove Farm (Kauai)
Eleele Plantation (Kauai)
Paukaa Plantation (Big Island of Hawaii)
Kawaihau Plantation in Kapa'a (Kauai)
Ewa Plantation (Oahu)
Hakalau Plantation (Big Island of Hawaii)
Kukuehaela Plantation (Big Island of Hawaii)
Waiakea Plantation (Big Island of Hawaii)
Papaikou Plantation (Big Island of Hawaii)
Harvey Plantation (Moloka'i)
Puunene Plantation (Maui)
Kilauea Plantation (Kauai)
Onomea Sugar Company

Newspapers in Hawaii
Pacific Commercial Advertiser
Hawaiian Gazette
Star Bulletin
Garden Island Newspaper - Kauai

Mileage assumptions

12-day walk from Sanlúcar

Day #1-5: Sanlúcar to Chipiona, Rota, El Puerto de Santa María, Puerto Real, San Fernando and Chiclana de la Frontera = 44 miles

Day #6-10: Barrio Nuevo, Vejer de la Frontera, Facinas and through the mountains toward Los Barrios = 53 miles

Day # 11-12: San Roque to La Línea = 15 miles

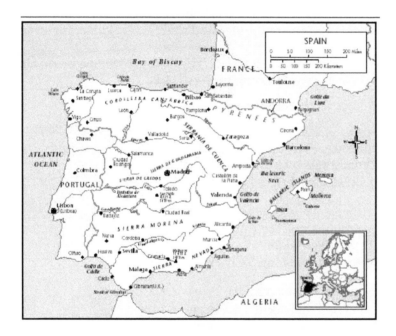

BIBLIOGRAPHY

Ancestry.com - Spain Database Search
www.mundia.com

http://www.maritime-database.com/country.php?cid=105
http://www.bne.es/es/Inicio/index.html-Spanish-National-Library
http://www.genealogytoday.com/family/researcher.html
www.archives.gov – National Archives
www.loc.gov – Library of Congress
http://www.hawaii-guide.com/kauai
http://es.wikipedia.org/wiki/Emigraci%C4n_espa%C3%B1ola
http://poipuwebdesigns.tripod.com/id3.html
http://en.db-city.com/Spain--Castile-and-Le%C3%B3n--Zamora--Fuentesa%C3%BAco
http://www.genealogyforum.com/files/HI/PortugueseImmigration.htm
http://members.virtualtourist.com/m/7cbc2/4c0/

http://www.yourislandroutes.com/ships/orteric.shtml -

http://www.worldportsource.com/ports/ESP_Port_of_Sevilla_1206.php -
http://en.wikipedia.org/wiki/Immigration_to_Argentina   -
http://konglungkauai.com/kilauea-history.html
http://www.portalcultura.mde.es/cultural/archivos/castillaLeon/archivo150.html
http://chroniclingamerica.loc.gov/lccn/sn82015415/1911-12-22/ed-1/seq-1/
http://Silvánsfromfuentesauco.wordpress.com/
Hawaii's Laborers Association
http://www.everyculture.com/Sa-Th/Spain.html

While in Spain ~ Research:
Genealogist interview and documents received
Juzgado (court house) clerks and documents received
Cemetery visits, photos of family gravestones
Interviewing family members living in Spain
Ayuntamiento (city halls) in the ancestral villages in Spain
Oficina de Turismo – (tourist offices): *Toro* and *Álora*, Spain

Books ~ Research

Williams, Mark R. *The Story of Spain, 1990, 2004*

Blasco Ibanez, Vicente, *Alfonso XIII Unmasked*

Shubert, Adrian & Alvarez Junco, Jose *Spanish History Since 1808*

Eyewitness Travel, *Andalucía & Costa del Sol*

Gobert, Rose Ruiz, *Mama & Dad and their Fifteen Kids*

Gordon, Jan and Cora, *Poor Folk in Spain by*

Aguilar Santucci, Anne, *Memories of Spain*

Ryskamp, George R., *Finding your Hispanic Roots*

Takaki,Ronald, *PauHana, Plantation Life Labor in   Hawaii*

Ma, Eve A.& Cader, Jaime, *Weaving with Spanish Threads*

Everton Publishers , *The Handbook for Genealogists*

Lopez, Gloria, *An American Paella*

Lee, Erika-Yung, Judy, *Ángel Island: Immigrant Gateway to America*

Casas, Penelope, *Delicioso!*

De Molina , José Manuel - *La Emigracion a Andaluzia a América*

Crow, J.A., *The Root and the Flower*

Hemingway, Ernest, *For Whom the Bell Tolls*

 Patricia Steele researched, interviewed, and processed documents letting the emerging mosaic tell its story, whether the picture was pleasing or not. The human tendency to twist facts into pretzels in order to produce a desired result was avoided.

"Any journey not only takes you places you never expected to go," she says, "but it also leads you all the way back to your own front door." It is a story inspired by her Spanish ancestors between a small village in northern Spain, *Fuentesaúco*, to the villages of southern Spain and Hawaii before leading them to America in the early twentieth century.

Desperate, courageous and hopeful, they left homes, families, graves of their ancestors and familiar landmarks. Many of them had never stepped beyond the boundaries of their own villages; little in their experience had prepared them for the passage to Hawaii in the steerage area of immigrant ships or for the sugar plantations that waited. Despite being recruited by agencies to fill orders placed by the planters, they all came for their own reasons. As they traveled across seemingly endless watery prairies toward the islands, each carried visions of the land and their future.

A self-described *accidental memoirist*, Steele sprinkles her book with tales of her ancestral families and dreams that dominated their spirit and character. Amazed at her grandmother's story heard through the family tree, she believes that everything starts with the past.

"Some people think where they are now is the beginning, but it's far from the beginning," said an Ellis Island immigrant. This is her family's story of migration, of people moving and adds color and richness to the telling.

And of course, she knows that every good story deserves embellishment.

CPSIA information can be obtained
at www.ICGtesting.com
Printed in the USA
BVHW07s1458070818
523804BV00001B/139/P